Make It Easy in Your Kitchen

Also by Laurie Burrows Grad
Dining In—Los Angeles

MAKE IT EASY IN YOUR KITCHEN

LAURIE BURROWS GRAD

J. P. TARCHER, INC.
Los Angeles
A Houghton Mifflin Company/Boston

Library of Congress Cataloging in Publication Data
Grad, Laurie Burrows.
Make it easy in your kitchen.
Includes index.
1. Cookery. I. Title.
TX715.G744 641.5 81-85208
ISBN 0-87477-213-3 AACR2
ISBN 0-87477-349-0 (pbk.)

Library of Congress Catalog Card No.: 81-85208

Manufactured in the United States of America

P 17 16 15 14 13 12 11 10 9 8 7

Design by John Brogna
Illustrated by Lynn Lieppman

Portions of this book have appeared in *Los Angeles Magazine*.

A Houghton Mifflin Company paperback, 1985

To my wonderfully supportive husband, Peter,
and my incredibly understanding son, Nicholas,
who gained more than just knowledge from this book.

CONTENTS

ACKNOWLEDGMENTS

The author wishes to thank the following people for their advice, counsel, support, and discerning taste buds:

—Mary Carey, a truly special friend, who fought to decipher my hieroglyphics and transpose them into the real thing, copy after copy after copy. . . .

—Millie Loeb, my wonderfully helpful editor, who, without undue pressure, helped me find the right direction.

—My publisher, Jeremy Tarcher, who tried to please, and did.

—My agent, Dominick Abel, the big-deal maker in New York.

—My official testers, for their show of friendship and support: Bob Broder, Catherine Bergstrom, Michelle Naumberg, Fred Roberts, and Barbara Tenenbaum.

—And my unofficial testers, for their aid and abettance.

—Gary, Steve, Marty, Bob and all the people at *Hour Magazine* for their continued support.

—All my friends at *Los Angeles Magazine.*

—Judi Kaufman, who provided valuable wisdom.

—Dan and Leora Garner, for the gracious loan of their kitchen.

—Linda Burrows, who waded steadfastly through the manuscript, in her ninth month of pregnancy.

—Carolyn Spencer, who made an extra effort to help.

—Joan Leemhorst, who thoroughly copy edited.

—All my supportive friends, for encouragement and for just being there: Sandy, Betsy, Diane, Barbara G., Barbara T., et al.

—My mom, Ruth Burrows, the gourmet, for introducing me to bouillabaisse, my dad, Abe Burrows, the writer, for introducing me to a short sentence, and my brother, Jim Burrows, the director, who told me I should never be an actress or listen to my parents!

—My super-patient family, for their indulgence and support in my kitchen experiments.

INTRODUCTION

I love to cook. I also love to eat and serve food that looks as delicious as it tastes. However, as a working woman with a family, I have neither the hours nor the energy to spend in the kitchen making believe I am another Julia Child. Don't misunderstand me, I love Julia Child—her style, her wit, and especially her cooking. But there just isn't the time. I assume that my life isn't particularly unusual and that, like me, you too are busy with a schedule full of commitments. But that doesn't mean our desire for good food goes away. In fact, it can increase, since there is something very pleasing about a well-prepared, beautifully presented meal after a long day jammed with activities. But again, the issue is time. How are we to find it? The Make-It-Easy style of cooking described in this book is an answer to this dilemma.

For the past two years I have been demonstrating Make-It-Easy cooking on the nationally syndicated television show, *Hour Magazine.* In doing so, I have become expert at just about every trick in the cook's repertoire for making life easier in the kitchen. The response to the television segment, in the form of thousands of letters asking for recipes or suggesting even newer and better ideas, indicates the incredible interest in this approach to food preparation.

What has been most appealing to viewers is that Make-It-Easy Cooking emphasizes quality. It doesn't mean visits to the Colonel or the deli or a retreat to canned or frozen dinners. Instead, I will show you how to create meals that look complicated, taste fantastic, and can be prepared with the greatest of ease in the least amount of time—using fresh ingredients.

The assembled recipes—a combination of tried-and-true favorites and many that are more unusual and exotic—emphasize a balance between high- and low-calorie foods, expensive and inexpensive ingredients, and a variety of international flavors. In these pages you will find everything from *Scandinavian Gravlax* and almost-instant pâtés to an *Ice Cream Cookie Freakout* and *Zabaglione*.

What makes the new wave of easy cooking possible are the food processor and the blender. The processor, especially, is a magical and wondrous invention that, once mastered, will save you hours. In fact, if you make only one new investment for your kitchen, I would strongly advise that you consider this piece of equipment, especially since the price of good processors has been greatly reduced during the past few years. However, a good blender is a suitable substitute. It may not be able to julienne or finely chop, but it can purée a pâté, process a cold soup, and whip up a chocolate mousse, acting as a tremendous time-saver.

Obviously, the key to Make-It-Easy cooking is cutting the preparation time. Most recipes take less than 20 minutes to prepare, some ten or 15, and a few, miraculously, can be whipped up in only five. The cooking times vary in length from 5 minutes to 2–3 hours, although most dishes are done in under 60 minutes. I save the recipes with longer cooking times, the soups and the stews, for weekends, when I can wait for a pot to boil. No matter how long the simmering, the preparation time is always short.

In order to get the most out of *Make-It-Easy in Your Kitchen,* I suggest reading the chapter introductions before proceeding with the recipes. I've tried to include in them a wealth of general information, along with specific tips on purchasing and storing ingredients. For instance, if you read these sections you will discover how to select and perfectly season a wok and how to prepare just about every conceivable kind of crumb pie-crust for a spur-of-the-moment dessert. You will also find other recipes, such as *Perfect White Rice the Chinese Way* and *Raspberry Vinegar,* which can be used in an array of dishes.

All of this is aimed at inspiring you, since there is something so satisfying about preparing fabulous dishes—especially ones that are put together quickly—that previously seemed too difficult or time-consuming. In fact, the entire book has been designed to ease your experimentation.

ABOUT THE RECIPES

Each recipe includes both its preparation time and its cooking time, followed by a list of ingredients, and step-by-step instructions given in an understandable and concise manner. To simplify menu planning, entrées and main-dish salads are followed by *Accompaniments.* If these suggested accompaniments are italicized (for example, *Perfect Baked Potatoes*), the recipes can be found in the book. Most recipes include a section called *Variations.* Some of these are specific ideas for lowering the price of the dish or its calorie count; others illustrate how changing one or two ingredients leads to the creation of an entirely different dish, but one that is just as appealing.

At the close of most recipes you will find *Make-It-Easy Tips.* These are those marvelous pieces of wisdom—concerning how to use your equipment most efficiently, the secrets of culinary chemistry, reheating and freezing—that can make any cooking experience more satisfying and successful. I know that each time I learned one of these tricks—how I could chop onions by hand without crying, prevent the blueberries from sinking to the bottom of the batter, and tenderize meat without using preparations full of strange chemicals, it was a revelation. I will pass on this information and much more, in the hope that you, too, will be happily surprised. Many of the tips are repeated over and over again as they apply to specific recipes, since I assume no one wants to read a cookbook as if it were a novel.

So thumb through and then select one dish that is especially appealing but that you never considered trying before. Once you learn that you can Make-It-Easy in Your Kitchen, you will see that great food can be made from scratch in less time than you ever imagined. The result will be a sense of achievement, and the discovery of a way of cooking that reflects the way we live now and would like to eat.

A NOTE ON INGREDIENTS

Some ingredients appear over and over again in recipes throughout the book, so Make-It-Easy general information about them and tips regarding them belong here at the beginning. What you will find below is the accumulated knowledge of experienced cooks.

Herbs

Fresh herbs can make all the difference—a point I will stress repeatedly throughout the book. Keeping them on hand is really rather simple. The food processor can chop large bunches at once, and they can be frozen in small containers or plastic bags. Frozen herbs may not look as bright and green as fresh, but they taste much better than the dried variety. If you are using dried herbs, crumble them between your fingers just before adding them to recipes to release their optimum flavor. In general, 1 *tablespoon* freshly chopped herbs is equivalent to 1 *teaspoon* dried herbs.

Seasoning

In all the recipes in this book, with the exception of the baking chapter, I have limited the amount of salt to ½ teaspoon. Even this is optional. I have adopted this approach because the medical evidence seems to suggest that salt isn't very good for us, and it is easy to substitute other spices or herbs or even lemon juice to heighten the flavor of food. In contrast to the substitutes for sugar, there is no controversy about chives or dill or onions and garlic. They taste good and are good for us. If you are concerned about the deleterious effects of salt, remember that soy sauce, mustard, canned chicken or beef broth, smoked meats, and many other ingredients contain high levels of sodium.

Adding ground pepper is another easy way to heighten flavor. It is just as easy to turn a peppermill a few times to get freshly ground pepper as it is to give a few shakes of the flat, flavorless, ready-ground pepper in the can. White pepper is simply black pepper with the outer husks removed. The white is less pungent and spicy than the black and is aesthetically more pleasing in an all-white sauce.

Butter, Margarine, and Oil

I recommend unsalted butter (also called sweet butter). It has a more delicate taste. I also suggest it because the addition of salt can often camouflage a poor or rancid taste in the butter. It allows you, once again, to keep the sodium content down.

Unsalted margarine can be used in place of unsalted butter if you wish to avoid saturated fats. Read the labels carefully and select one that lists liquid corn, safflower, sunflower, or soy bean oil (all polyunsaturated fats) as the first ingredient.

There is a wide variety of oils on the market. A good Italian olive oil should be reserved for light salads, whereas the chartreuse-colored, heavier, thicker, and more pungent olive oil can be used in limited amounts for some of the new and unusual salads or in sautéing, where a stronger flavor is required. The liquid vegetable oils such as corn, cottonseed, soy bean, safflower, and sunflower, which are higher in polyunsaturated fats, are more healthful to use and lighter in taste. Oil is a great help when added to butter for sautéing. The higher smoking point of the oil prevents the butter from burning. In Chinese cooking, I recommend peanut oil for stir-frying, and oriental sesame oil, which adds a nutty flavor to cooked dishes and salads.

Eggs, Cheese, and Dairy

Large or extra-large eggs should be used for the recipes in this book. Jumbo eggs will add too much liquid. Since I find no taste difference between brown and white eggs, I purchase the brown ones one week and the white ones the next. By alternating colors, I can remember to use the older eggs up before starting on the new ones.

Stale, dried-out, and over-aged packaged, grated Parmesan cheese in the can bears no resemblance to freshly grated. It takes only a few seconds for the food processor to grate a block of cheese, which can then be kept in a covered container for at least a week. A hand grater works almost as easily. Although it may not be as Make-It-Easy, it definitely qualifies for "make it better."

Swiss cheese, Monterey Jack cheese, Muenster cheese, brick cheese, even mozzarella cheese can be used interchangeably in recipes in this book. Cheddar can also be substituted, but its stronger taste keeps it from being interchangeable. Grate the cheese in large batches in the food processor or by hand. It will keep in sealed plastic bags for several weeks. Garlic-herb cheeses such as Boursin, or the delicious, less expensive copies, Rondele and Alouette, are useful as instant appetizers, stuffing for mushrooms, or unusual fillings for rolls. The new soft version of cream cheese or whipped cream cheese makes preparing a dip or spread easy. If unavailable, soften the cream cheese in the food processor or blender.

Light cream is a thing of the past and has been replaced by half-and-half. Heavy cream and whipping cream are one and the same. Whenever possible, stay away from the ultra-pasteurized cream, which lasts longer but does not whip well or taste as good. The nondairy cream substitutes are a dreadful conglomeration of chemicals, preservatives, and saturated fats that are to be avoided.

Flour and Bread Crumbs

I recommend an all-purpose unbleached flour, which is a blend of hard and soft wheat flours and is high in gluten. Either pre-sifted or not, the unbleached variety is preferable to the bleached. Self-rising flour is plain flour mixed with baking powder and salt. Use self-rising flour within 2–3 months of purchase since it tends to lose its effectiveness after this time.

Packaged bread crumbs may seem Make-It-Easy but this is another case where you should not sacrifice quality. If a food processor or blender is available, make dry crumbs from toasted bread, either white or whole wheat, or soft bread crumbs from slices of fresh bread. It should take about 1 minute. Avoid stale bread. Stale bread produces stale-tasting crumbs. One slice of bread produces about ½ cup fresh crumbs. Cracker crumbs can be used in place of bread crumbs. Use unsweetened, unsalted soda crackers and pulsate in food processor or blender until they become crumbs, but are not pulverized. Store bread crumbs in sealed containers or plastic bags for short-term storage or place in sealed containers in freezer for long-term storage.

Broth, Stock, and Soup

Since Make-It-Easy cooking does not allow time for preparing fresh stock, I find canned chicken or beef broth (without gelatin) an adequate substitute. I learned this tip from chefs and cooking authorities who found the taste difference negligible. If the recipe calls for strong broth, I use the undiluted variety. When using canned broth, always salt to taste after adding broth, since the broth contains large quantities of salt. I find that powdered stock or bouillon cubes are mostly chemicals, and I prefer not to use them. I also abstain from using any canned, creamed, gookey soups laden with preservatives. As a substitute for fish broth, I favor bottled clam juice, especially when cooking *Quick and Easy Cioppino* or similar fish and shellfish stews. If there is extra time to whip up some homemade stock, place the finished product in an ice-cube tray and use the frozen cubes as flavor enhancers.

Wines

I find the best and most readily available white wine to use in cooking is dry vermouth. Vermouth in itself is not a variety of wine. It is actually a wine that has been treated in a certain way, usually with the addition of distilled alcohol, and herbs and spices. Vermouth can be kept for a longer period of time once opened and is often less expensive to use in cooking than most white wines.

As a substitute for red wine, particularly when I want a sweeter taste for a stew or pot roast, I often use Marsala, Madeira, port, or sweet vermouth, which have longer shelf-life than an opened bottle of wine.

ON STORING AND FREEZING

In the introduction to most chapters, and in the *Make-It-Easy Tips* following the recipes, you will find specific information about storing ingredients once you have them home. For example, taking the chicken out of the supermarket package and wrapping it properly will keep it fresh for an extra day. In Appendix B, you will find a freezer chart listing every major ingredient and type of dish along with their freezer life spans. Since I advise cooking many recipes in double batches or, if you have a small family, freezing one-half of what you have prepared, this freezer chart can be very helpful.

CHAPTER ONE

APPETIZERS AND HORS D'OEUVRES

Crudités

Vegetable Basket

Guacamole

Caper Dip

Yogurt Vegetable Dip (Indian Style)

Hot Crab Dip

Hummus Bi Tahini (Chick Pea Spread)

Liverwurst Pâté

French Chicken Liver Pâté

Mushrooms Stuffed with Garlic-Herb Cheese

Drumettes

Carpaccio

Celery Root Rémoulade

Hot Baked Sausages

Baked Artichoke Hearts

Double Salmon Mousse

Gravlax (Scandinavian Salmon Marinated in Dill)

The preparation of appetizers can be made incredibly easy if you just remember that they were originally designed to be appetite stimulators. They are meant to whet the appetite in anticipation of taste thrills to come. *Hors d'oeuvre,* the French words for appetizer, means "outside the meal," or little tidbits to start the juices flowing.

Appetizers should be uncomplicated little samples. All your guests, not only the ones on diets, will thank you for not pre-stuffing them with extra calories, and you'll have extra time to put into the preparation of the main meal.

If you are planning a very special occasion or the boss is coming to dinner unexpectedly, you can transform most of the following appetizer recipes into first courses. The cocktail hour can be limited, and a lovely, easy, more formal dinner can proceed. (On most occasions, however, first courses require too much work, time, energy, and extra dishes to qualify for a Make-It-Easy dinner.)

Appetizers and hors d'oeuvres come in a variety of sizes, shapes, and temperatures. The cold dip may appear to be the easiest to prepare, but cutting up the multitude of colorful vegetables to accompany that dip makes it a more difficult procedure. Hot canapés often involve working with complicated pastry, and hours of time-consuming activities and are, therefore, almost eliminated from a Make-It-Easy schedule.

Your goal is to find the easiest dishes to prepare that fit into your menu plan and the time of year. Obviously, hot appetizers are more appealing on a cold winter night, and cold appetizers can be prepared beforehand, giving you more time to spend with your guests.

For a large cocktail party, finger foods are easy to serve without using too many plates or too much cutlery. In addition to *crudités* (raw vegetables), chicken wing *Drumettes, Carpaccio* (raw steak slices), and prosciutto ham wrapped around a variety of fruits and vegetables make excellent nibbles at a large party, or delicious small bites before a dinner.

Keep in mind that, even though appetizers may be kept simple, the garnish surrounding them is all important. The addition of a few sprigs of parsley, some tiny sour pickles, and assorted crackers to a plain piece of pâté makes this an appealing and special treat. Baskets make especially attractive serving containers for appetizers such as raw vegetables, crackers, or cheeses.

The simplest appetizer, of course, is cheese and crackers served on a board, in a basket, or on a platter. The appetizers that follow are designed for those who want to serve something special but still want to keep it easy.

Crudités and a Vegetable Basket

Crudités are crisp fresh raw vegetables served as an appetizer, often with a dip. If eaten alone, they are perfect for the dieter, and with a dip they will satisfy those who want something a bit richer. The Make-It-Easy trick to cutting up raw vegetables is to choose those vegetables that need as little work as possible. The list below provides a basis for making the easiest crudité basket possible. The use of a large serrated slicer or smaller decorating knife can make the vegetables even more attractive and takes no more time than regular slicing. The vegetables can be cut up in advance and chilled in ice water to crisp them and keep them crunchy.

When really in a hurry, stick to cherry tomatoes, with the stems on (your guests can easily manage to remove them).

VEGETABLE BASKET

Line a small basket (with or without a handle) with several soft lettuce leaves or a colorful napkin. Boston and curly leaf lettuce are easy and attractive choices. A few sprigs of parsley take up enough room to make the vegetables stand up. Pick from the following assortment of

vegetables, depending on seasonal availability and color preference, and arrange in a decorative fashion in the basket.

If the basket is still full enough after the cocktail hour, use it as a centerpiece, bolstered with a few more sprigs of parsley.

1. *Cherry Tomatoes:* Wash, but leave stems on. They look prettier and guests do not mind removing them.
2. *Unpeeled Zucchini, Cucumber, or Crookneck Squash:* Slice into spears or circles with serrated slicer if available. They are colorful and particularly attractive when alternated, green and yellow.
3. *Snow Peas:* Wash and, if possible, remove strings by pulling from the top down the sides.
4. *Broccoli Florets* (or Cauliflower Florets): Wash the broccoli and cut off the florets (the stems can be peeled and sliced and used as a vegetable at another time).
5. *Turnip Slices:* Peel and slice.
6. *Medium-Size Mushrooms:* The easiest way to clean them is to dip a mushroom brush or paper towel into lemon juice and brush or wipe away the dirt, leaving the mushrooms clean and impervious to discoloration. Serve them whole.
7. *Red Radishes:* Wash and remove ends. They are colorful and easy to clean. A radish flowering tool can be used for an even prettier arrangement.
8. *Daikon* (*Japanese Radish*): Peel only a thin layer and slice with a serrated knife into strips and slices.
9. *Green and Red Peppers:* Wash and cut into wedges, removing seeds.

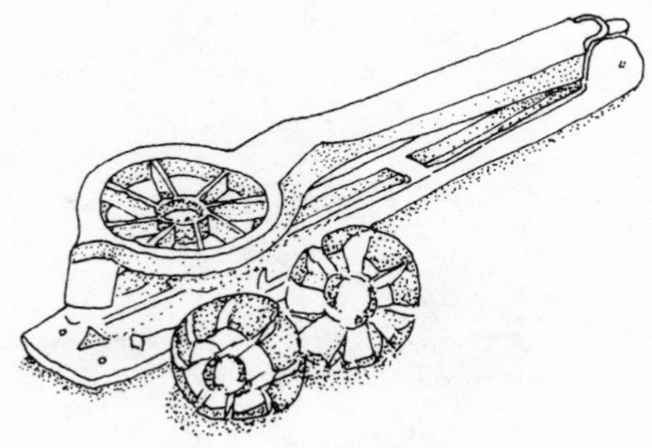

Radish decorator

10. *Scallions:* Cut off root ends and leave greens on. They look beautiful as part of the basket arrangement.
11. *Celery:* If you have a little extra time, use celery or, if available, fennel (finocchio, fenucchi) for an interesting taste addition.
12. *Thin Asparagus:* Very thin asparagus can be eaten raw as a crudité. Just wash, break off the tough fibrous stem ends, and arrange in a basket.
13. *String Beans:* Wash, and break off tips if desired.
14. *Jicama:* A crunchy Mexican vegetable with a sweet taste, similar to a water chestnut; peel, and slice with a serrated knife to resemble french fries, or cut into thin pieces.

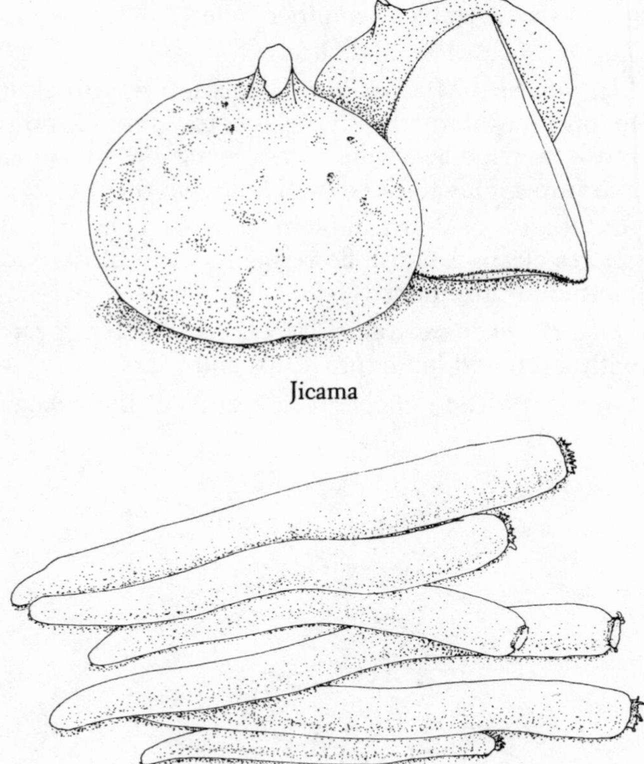

Jicama

Daikon

Guacamole

SERVES: 4
Preparation time: 10 minutes

The Ingredients:

1 ripe avocado, peeled
1 tablespoon fresh lemon juice
⅓ cup finely chopped red onion
⅓ cup finely chopped green pepper
¼ teaspoon chili powder, or to taste
¼ teaspoon salt, or to taste
1 ripe tomato, sliced in half, squeezed of seeds, and finely chopped
Garnish: Chopped scallion stalks or corn or taco chips

The Steps:

1. Mash avocado with lemon juice to prevent discoloration.
2. Fold in onions, green pepper, chili powder, and salt, and stir until smooth.
3. Add chopped tomatoes, and serve immediately. Garnish with chopped scallion greens and surround with corn or taco chips.

Variation:

Lime juice can be substituted for lemon juice.

Make-It-Easy Tips:

√ Use a pastry blender to chop guacamole ingredients.
√ Serve guacamole with avocado pit in center; it will help prevent discoloration.
√ To remove seeds from tomato easily, slice tomato in half and gently squeeze it until the seeds fall out.
√ Ripen avocados quickly by storing in a brown paper bag. Check daily.
√ The guacamole can be chilled for 2 hours before serving but for not much longer or it may discolor.

Caper Dip

SERVES: 6–8
Preparation time: 10 minutes
Chilling time: 1–2 hours

For the smoothest consistency, use a food processor or blender.

The Ingredients:

3 scallions, white part only, finely chopped
1 4-ounce jar small capers, drained and chopped
½ cup dairy sour cream
½ cup mayonnaise
Salt and freshly ground pepper to taste

The Steps:

1. In food processor, blender, or by hand, chop scallions and capers together until just minced.
2. Transfer to a bowl, stir in sour cream and mayonnaise, and chill for 1–2 hours.
3. Season to taste with salt and freshly ground pepper, and serve chilled with vegetable crudités.

Variations:

Any leftover dip can be used as a sauce for cold poached fish or poultry.

For an extra special dip, try using homemade *Basic Blender Mayonnaise, see* page 247.

Make-It-Easy Tip:

√ Chop and reserve scallion greens as garnish or flavoring. Store in refrigerator or freezer.

Yogurt Vegetable Dip (Indian Style)

SERVES: 4
Preparation time: 10–15 minutes
Chilling time: 1–2 hours

In most Indian *raitas* (relishes), the cucumber is salted to extract the moisture. Since there is only a small cucumber used in this recipe, I bypassed the salting step. This is a fantastic low-calorie dip to serve with vegetable crudités.

The Ingredients:

1 small cucumber, peeled, seeded, and finely chopped
2 radishes, finely chopped
3 tablespoons finely chopped scallions (green and white included)
1 teaspoon fresh lemon juice
¼ teaspoon ground cumin, or to taste
Pinch of cayenne pepper
Pinch of salt
1 cup plain low-fat yogurt
Salt and freshly ground pepper to taste

The Steps:

1. Chop vegetables in food processor, blender, or by hand.
2. Pour vegetables into a bowl and add remaining ingredients. Mix well.
3. Chill 1–2 hours
4. Taste, and adjust seasoning if necessary. Serve chilled with vegetable crudités.

Variations:

Yogurt vegetable dip can also be served as a *raita,* an Indian relish that accompanies spicy dishes such as curry.

Any leftovers can be added to a basic vinaigrette salad dressing, which will make it creamy, but still not high in calories.

For thicker variation, add ⅓ cup sour cream.

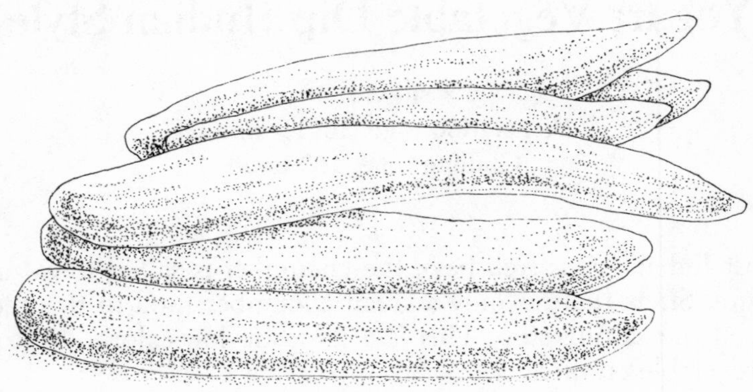

Hothouse cucumbers

Make-It-Easy Tip:

√ Substitute ⅓ of a European hothouse hydroponic cucumber for the small cucumber. It needs no peeling and has fewer seeds.

Hot Crab Dip

SERVES: 6–8
Preparation time: 10 minutes
Cooking time: 15 minutes

Frozen crab is used in this recipe since it is to be cooked. If fresh crab is reasonably priced, by all means use it.

The Ingredients:

12 ounces cream cheese
1 6-ounce package frozen snow crab or king crab, thawed, drained, and flaked
½ small onion, minced (2–3 tablespoons)
1 tablespoon lemon juice
2 teaspoons white horseradish
½ teaspoon Worcestershire sauce
½ teaspoon salt, or to taste

½ teaspoon freshly ground white pepper, or to taste
¼ cup slivered almonds
Garnish: Crudités, sesame crackers, or corn chips

The Steps:

1. Using a food processor, blender, mixer, or by hand, combine cream cheese, crabmeat, onion, lemon juice, horseradish, Worcestershire sauce, salt, and pepper.
2. When well mixed, place in an oven-proof dish and refrigerate.
3. When ready to serve, preheat oven to 375°, top crab dip with almonds, and heat until bubbly, 10–15 minutes.
4. Serve hot, garnished with crudités, sesame crackers, or large-size corn chips.

Variation:

The crab dip can be reheated or served cold the next day.

Make-It-Easy Tips:

√ Whipped cream cheese, which is easier to blend, can be substituted for solid bars of cream cheese, eliminating the need for a food processor or blender.

√ To thaw crabmeat quickly, place sealed package of frozen crabmeat in warm water for half an hour.

Hummus Bi Tahini (Chick Pea Spread)

SERVES: 8
Preparation time: 10 minutes

This easy to prepare Middle-Eastern specialty is an exotic and interesting taste addition to an hors d'oeuvres table.

The Ingredients:

1 15½-ounce can garbanzo beans (chick peas), drained, washed, and drained again
¼ cup *tahini*, also called sesame paste (available in some supermarkets, Middle Eastern groceries, or by mail order—*see* Appendix A)
Juice of 1 lemon

1 large garlic clove, peeled
2–3 tablespoons olive oil
Salt to taste
Garnish: Fresh coriander or parsley, and Pita toast or crackers

The Steps:

1. Combine drained beans, *tahini*, lemon juice, garlic, and olive oil in food processor or blender, and process until smooth. If gummy and too thick, add a little water to thin. Taste, and add salt if necessary.
2. Mound on a flat plate and serve at room temperature; garnish with fresh coriander or parsley and Pita toasts or crackers.

Make-It-Easy Tip:

√ Squeeze lemons at room temperature to release the most amount of juice.

EASY PÂTÉS

The preparation of a true French *pâté de campagne* (Country Pâté) can be a whole-day affair. In order to Make-It-Easy, pâtés should consist of liver spreads, fish spreads, vegetables, or even leftover meat dishes processed until smooth with the aid of a food processor, blender, or even a Foley food mill or ricer. Keep in mind that pâtés are usually rich enough so that a little goes a long way.

Liverwurst Pâté

SERVES: 8
Preparation time: 10 minutes
Chilling time: 1 hour

This decorative and delicious hors d'oeuvre can be garnished to suit your holiday or festive mood.

The Ingredients:

½ pound liverwurst, at room temperature
1 teaspoon grated onion
¼ cup mayonnaise

Liverwurst pâté

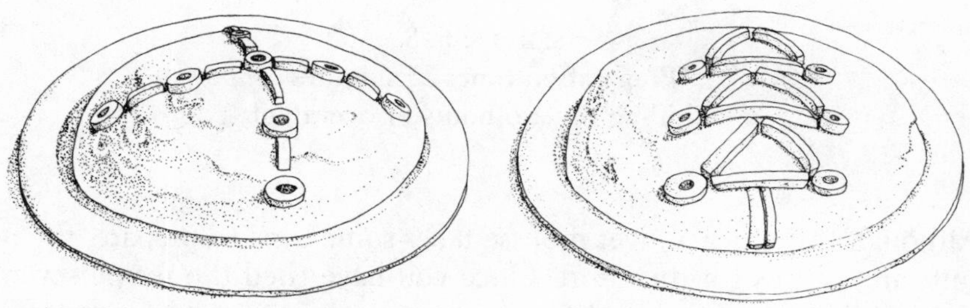

Regular version Christmas version

Frosting:

3 ounces cream cheese, softened
1 tablespoon mayonnaise
Garnish: Sliced stuffed olives and strips of pimiento

The Steps:

1. In a food processor, blender, or with a wooden spoon, mash liverwurst. Blend in onion and ¼ cup mayonnaise, and shape into a smooth round. Chill until firm.
2. To prepare frosting, use food processor, blender, or combine by hand. Mix cream cheese with 1 tablespoon mayonnaise until smooth.
3. Frost chilled pâté as if you were frosting a cake, covering the mound entirely. Then decorate with sliced stuffed olives and strips of pimiento in whatever design desired.

Variations:

Decorate pâté for Christmas using strips of pimiento as tree branches and stuffed olive slices as ornaments.

Crisp bacon bits can be added to liverwurst mixture.

Make-It-Easy Tip:

√ To ready the pâté quickly for frosting, place in freezer for 10–15 minutes.

French Chicken Liver Pâté

SERVES: 6–8
Preparation time: 25 minutes
Chilling time: 6 hours or overnight

Although this chicken liver mousse takes some time to prepare, the results are well worth the effort. Once you have tried the recipe several times (which is guaranteed to happen once you've tasted it), you'll find it easier to make. It is extra rich, so a little will serve a large group.

The Ingredients:

½ pound chicken livers
¼ pound (1 stick) unsalted butter, softened
3 tablespoons grated onion
½ teaspoon salt, or to taste
¼ teaspoon dry mustard
⅛ teaspoon ground cloves
Fat pinch of nutmeg
Pinch cayenne pepper
1 teaspoon dry sherry
2 teaspoons Bourbon
Garnish: 1 loaf of thin baguette-size French bread, sliced into rounds, or crackers

The Steps:

1. Lightly oil a small loaf pan (about 7″ x 4″ x 2″) or similar shallow mold.
2. Fill a medium saucepan ⅔ full with water. Bring to boil. Add chicken livers. When the water returns to the boil, cook livers for 12–15 minutes over medium heat; drain and set aside.
3. While livers are cooking, place butter, onion, salt, mustard, cloves, nutmeg, and cayenne in a food processor or blender and process until combined.
4. Add the warm livers to butter mixture and continue to process until smooth; add sherry and Bourbon and process another few seconds.
5. Pour the liver paste into the oiled pan, cover, and chill 6 hours or overnight.

6. When ready to unmold, place pan in sink filled with 2–3 inches of warm water and count slowly to five; run a knife around edges. Turn upside down on platter and shake to unmold.
7. Serve garnished with sliced French bread rounds, or crackers.

Make-It-Easy Tips:

√ This French liver pâté keeps well for at least 5 days in the refrigerator, so it can be made several days ahead.

√ If leftover liver pâté is frozen, make sure to stir around well by hand or in the food processor or blender to restore texture after defrosting.

√ Mold can be sprayed with non-aerosol vegetable shortening instead of oil.

Mushrooms Stuffed with Garlic-Herb Cheese

SERVES: 4–6

Preparation time: 5–10 minutes

The Ingredients:

12 large mushroom caps, stems removed
Lemon juice
2 4-ounce packages garlic-herb cheese (Alouette, Rondele, or Boursin)
Garnish: Parsley sprigs

The Steps:

1. Clean mushrooms with paper towel or mushroom brush dipped in lemon juice to prevent discoloration.
2. Fill the caps generously with cheese and serve garnished with little parsley sprigs on top, if desired.

Make-It-Easy Tip:

√ Use an egg carton to transport stuffed mushrooms to office or picnic luncheon.

Drumettes

SERVES: 6
Preparation time: 15 minutes
Cooking time: 25–30 minutes

Drumettes are the meaty portion of chicken wings with the tips severed so that they look like mini-drumsticks. They are available in most supermarkets today and make great hors d'oeuvres for adults and great snacks for kids.

The Ingredients:

¼ pound (1 stick) unsalted butter, melted
14 chicken drumettes
1 cup buttermilk
1½ cups cereal crumbs

The Steps:

1. Preheat oven to 400°.
2. Melt butter in 9″ x 13″ baking dish.
3. Dip drumettes in buttermilk and then in crumbs, pressing crumbs onto chicken. Place in pan in a single layer.
4. Bake for 25–30 minutes or until golden all over.
5. Serve hot, at room temperature, or chilled.

Variations:

Substitute 6–8 chicken thighs for the drumettes. Cook for 40–45 minutes and serve as a main course, picnic dish, or put in lunch bags the next day.

Make-It-Easy Tips:

√ Use packaged cornflake crumbs for cereal or substitute any of the unsweetened cereals and crush for 2–3 seconds in a food processor or blender.

√ If you have the time, place breaded chicken in refrigerator for 10–15 minutes before baking since this helps crumbs to adhere.

√ You can substitute the following for buttermilk: Add 1 tablespoon vinegar or lemon juice to 1 cup fresh milk and allow to stand 5 minutes. You can also purchase dried buttermilk in many supermarkets. Or you can freeze a quart divided into one-cup portions to defrost and use as needed if no one in your family drinks buttermilk.

Carpaccio

SERVES: 6–8
Preparation time: 15 minutes
Chilling time: 2–3 hours

The name for this dish of sliced raw beef is somehow attributed to the Venetian Renaissance painter, Carpaccio. The sauce-topped slices of meat should be eaten as finger food.

The Ingredients:

12 slices boneless shell steak (1½ pounds), cut into ¼-inch-thick slices (some meat markets may call shell steaks New York Strip, Kansas City Strip, or plain strip steak)

Mustard Mayonnaise Sauce:

1 cup mayonnaise
2 tablespoons minced *cornichons* (sour pickles)
2 tablespoons freshly minced parsley
4 teaspoons Dijon mustard
1 teaspoon lemon juice
½ teaspoon salt, or to taste
¼ teaspoon freshly ground white pepper
Garnish: Parsley sprigs, lemon wedges, freshly cracked pepper

The Steps:

1. Place steak slices between 2 sheets of waxed paper and pound with a flat mallet until wafer thin; transfer the beef slices to a platter and chill until ready to serve.
2. Prepare the sauce by combining all ingredients in a small bowl. Mix until smooth and chill for 2–3 hours.
3. To serve attractively, arrange chilled meat slices on a platter and spread about 1 tablespoon of sauce over each slice; garnish platter with parsley sprigs, lemon wedges, and freshly cracked pepper.

Variation:

Serve the beef with *Spinach Mayonnaise* (*see* Chapter 8).

Make-It-Easy Tip:

√ If food processor is available, use it to slice the beef very thin. Place meat in freezer until just semi-frozen (or, if frozen, defrost to this state), and then slice with thin blade of the processor.

Celery Root Rémoulade

SERVES: 6
Preparation time: 15–20 minutes
Chilling time: 1–2 hours

Celery Root Rémoulade is a traditional French dish. Celery root, or celeriac as it is sometimes called, has an interesting taste, especially when mixed with this mayonnaise dressing. Prepare during the fall and winter months when it is more readily available.

The Ingredients:

1 pound celery root (celeriac or celery knob), peeled

Rémoulade:

1 cup mayonnaise
1 hard-cooked egg, chopped
2 tablespoons finely minced parsley
1 tablespoon finely minced sour pickles (called *cornichons* in France)
1 tablespoon finely chopped capers
1 tablespoon finely minced chives or scallion stalks
1 teaspoon Dijon mustard
1 teaspoon finely minced fresh tarragon or ½ teaspoon dried tarragon crumbled
2 teaspoons lemon juice
½ teaspoon salt, or to taste
¼ teaspoon anchovy paste
¼ teaspoon freshly ground white pepper, or to taste
Garnish: Parsley sprigs and crisp sesame wafers

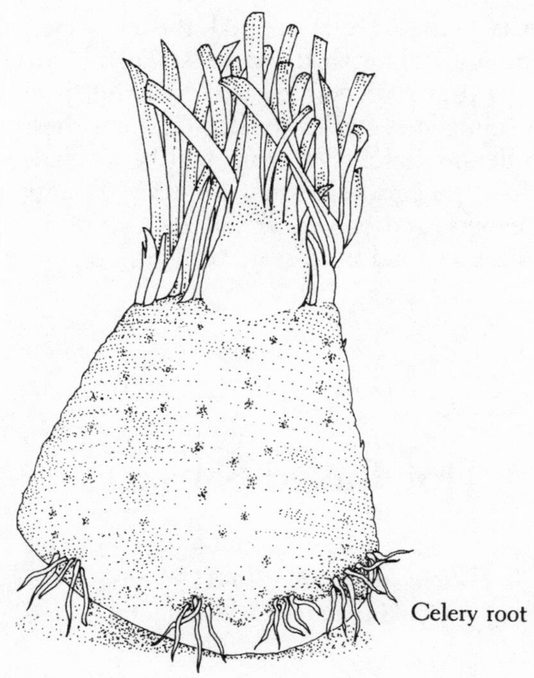

Celery root

The Steps:

1. Prepare the rémoulade in a food processor, blender, or by hand by combining all rémoulade ingredients and blending until smooth.
2. Cut celery root into julienne strips (matchstick shapes) by hand, in food processor, or with hand food-grinder.
3. Toss the celery root strips with the rémoulade until coated, and chill for 1–2 hours.
4. Taste, and adjust seasoning if necessary. Serve on a lettuce-lined platter garnished with parsley sprigs. Spread on crisp sesame wafers.

Variation:

Serve Celeriac Rémoulade as a salad course for lunch or dinner.

Make-It-Easy Tips:

√ Any leftover sauce can be refrigerated for several weeks. Use it on eggs for a quick Eggs à la Russe, with shrimp or crabmeat for a spread, or as a dip with vegetable crudités.

√ The sauce is prepared first so that the cut celery root can be tossed immediately with the sauce to keep it from discoloring.
√ To julienne a round vegetable easily by hand, peel, slice in half, cut into thin slices, stack the slices and cut the stack into thin strips. Julienne matchstick strips will be formed.
√ If using a food processor, it is not necessary to chop egg, parsley, pickles, capers, and chives separately. Cut up roughly in large pieces, place in food processor, and chop together.

Hot Baked Sausages

SERVES: 10–14
Preparation time: 10–15 minutes
Cooking time: 35–45 minutes

Any variety or combination of sausages can be used, so select your favorites.

The Ingredients:

12 Italian sausages (6 hot and 6 sweet), or 3–4 Polish *kielbasa,* or 6 Spanish *chorizos,* or 6 Portuguese *linguiças*
8 long, thin, pale green peppers or 6 dark green bell peppers, cut into eighths
3 medium onions, peeled and cut into eighths

The Steps:

1. Preheat oven to 375°. Lightly oil a large foil-lined roasting pan with vegetable oil.
2. Cut sausages into ½-inch slices and place in pan.
3. Add peppers and onions to pan.
4. Place in preheated oven and bake uncovered for 35–45 minutes, stirring occasionally.
5. Slip under the broiler and brown for a few minutes, if necessary.

6. Serve the sausages hot, on little plates with forks or large toothpicks.

Variations:

The cooked sausages can be frozen or reheated. Use leftovers for fantastic hero sandwiches.

Serve baked sausages as a main course for 6–8 people with lots of Italian bread and an Italian salad.

Make-It-Easy Tip:

√ Line the pan with aluminum foil to save on clean-up chores.

Baked Artichoke Hearts

SERVES: 6–8
Preparation time: 10 minutes
Cooking time: 15 minutes

The Ingredients:

1 14-ounce can artichoke hearts (8 per can), drained and cut in half horizontally
16 round melba sesame crackers
¼ pound (1 stick) unsalted butter, melted
½ teaspoon salt, or to taste
¼ teaspoon freshly ground pepper
⅛ teaspoon freshly crushed garlic
2–3 teaspoons sesame seeds

The Steps:

1. Preheat oven to 350°. Very lightly butter an attractive oven-proof dish that can accommodate 16 rounds and can be used for serving.
2. Place one artichoke half, cut side up, on each sesame round and arrange in the prepared dish.
3. Add salt, pepper, and garlic to the melted butter and generously spoon the seasoned butter into the artichoke crevices, allowing some to run on the rounds.
4. Sprinkle with sesame seeds and bake for 10 minutes.

5. Just before serving, run under broiler for 2–3 minutes to brown. Serve hot.

Make-It-Easy Tips:

√ Use only the canned artichokes packed in water. Avoid the marinated variety.

√ Garlic can be crushed with a food processor or in a garlic press a few cloves at a time, and stored for several weeks in the refrigerator in a small, tightly-capped jar with a few tablespoons of oil.

Double Salmon Mousse

SERVES: 6–8
Preparation time: 15 minutes
Chilling time: 6–8 hours or overnight

The addition of smoked salmon gives this Salmon Mousse a strong, smoky taste. A fish mold is not necessary for the recipe but provides a very attractive result. If using a ring mold, serve with the *Cucumber Dill Sauce* in a bowl in the center.

The Ingredients:

4 thin slices smoked salmon, cut into small pieces
½ cup boiling water
2 tablespoons lemon juice
1 thick slice onion, cut in half
1 envelope plain gelatin
1 15½-ounce can salmon, drained and flaked
½ cup mayonnaise
1 tablespoon freshly snipped dill or 1 teaspoon dried dill
¼ teaspoon paprika
Pinch of cayenne
1 cup heavy cream
¼ teaspoon salt, or to taste
¼ teaspoon freshly ground pepper
Garnish: Pitted black olives, sliced capers, watercress, dill sprigs, cherry tomatoes, *Cucumber Dill Sauce* (*see* Chapter 2)

Salmon mousse

The Steps:

1. Lightly oil a 4-cup fish mold or ring mold.
2. In food processor or blender, place smoked salmon, boiling water, lemon juice, onion, and gelatin and process until smooth.
3. Add salmon, mayonnaise, dill, paprika, and cayenne; continue to process until smooth.
4. While machine is running, add cream, blending until smooth.
5. Taste for seasonings, adjust with salt and pepper, pour into prepared mold and chill for 6–8 hours or overnight.
6. Unmold and serve garnished with olives, capers, watercress, dill sprigs, cherry tomatoes and *Cucumber Dill Sauce*.

Accompaniments:

Dark pumpernickel bread with sweet butter and/or sesame seed crackers.

Variations:

On a warm summer night, this dish will serve as a main course with a tossed green salad, black pumpernickel bread, chilled white wine, and a bowl of summer fruits.

Double Salmon Mousse makes a great luncheon or brunch dish with baked eggs and French bread.

A more traditional Salmon Mousse can be prepared without the smoked salmon.

Make-It-Easy Tips:

√ A blender or food processor is essential for this recipe.

√ When adding liquid to blender while it is running, remember to keep a towel near the opening to catch splatters.

√ To unmold easily, dip mold in a sink filled with 3″ of warm water for a few seconds.

Gravlax (Scandinavian Salmon Marinated in Dill)

SERVES: 8–10
Preparation time: 10 minutes
Marinating time: 3–4 days

Although the marinating time is long for this dish, the preparation time is short and the result is sensational and very low in calories. It's the Scandinavian version of Japanese *sushi.* The raw fish is "cured" with salt, sugar, and lots of fresh dill. You can't substitute dried dill weed in this recipe; the fresh is essential.

The Ingredients:

2–2½ pounds salmon, filleted
3 tablespoons sugar
1½ tablespoons coarse salt (also called Kosher salt)
1 teaspoon whole white peppercorns
½ teaspoon freshly ground white pepper
4 large bunches fresh dill
Garnish: Lemon wedges, dill sprigs, capers, *Mustard Dill Sauce* (see page 47), dark pumpernickel bread

The Steps:

1. Lay salmon on sheet of waxed paper. Sprinkle with half the sugar, salt, peppercorns, and pepper; turn, and sprinkle the other side. Press down firmly on salmon to make sure seasonings permeate fish.
2. In shallow, nonmetallic pan, spread out 2 bunches of fresh dill. Place salmon on top. Then arrange remaining 2 bunches of dill over salmon creating a sandwich effect.
3. Cover well with foil or plastic wrap; place a weight on top (use a heavy pot lid, brick, canned foods or a combination of these) and refrigerate.
4. Turn salmon twice a day (in the morning and at dinner time) for 3–4 days.
5. When ready to serve, remove all dill and peppercorns. Lightly pat dry with paper towels. Thinly slice on the bias and serve garnished with lemon wedges, dill sprigs, capers, *Mustard Dill Sauce,* and dark pumpernickel bread.

Accompaniments:

Gravlax can be served as part of a smorgasbord of Scandinavian hors d'oeuvres or as part of an international array.

Variation:

Leftover gravlax makes a wonderful sandwich on dark pumpernickel or rye with *Mustard Dill Sauce.* (Gravlax will keep for 3–4 days after "curing".)

Make-It-Easy Tip:

√ The easiest weight to use on the gravlax is a cast-iron pot or pot lid filled with canned goods. My alternate method is to use an iron bacon press, which also works efficiently.

CHAPTER TWO

BASICS AND SAUCES

Crème Fraîche
Double Cream
Reduced-Calorie Sour Cream
Mustard Dill Sauce (Gravlaxas)
Hollandaise with Ease
Marinara Sauce
Pesto
Creamy Horseradish Sauce
Dill Watercress Sauce
Cucumber Dill Sauce
Low-Calorie Yogurt Dill Sauce
Cucumber Raita
Homemade Vanilla Extract

In this section you will find a group of basics, those sauces and flavorings that accompany many of the other recipes in the book. For example, the Pesto sauce is called for three or four times, and the Marinara can become a basic part of your cooking repertoire for a wide variety of dishes.

Crème Fraîche

YIELD: 2 cups
Preparation time: 5 minutes
Marinating time: 12–24 hours

Crème Fraîche is a French sour cream prepared here from buttermilk and cream. Because of its high butterfat content, it can be used in cooking since it will not curdle like sour cream. Its tartness makes it a wonderful topping for fruit desserts, cakes, or mousses.

The Ingredients:

1 pint heavy cream
2 tablespoons buttermilk

The Steps:

1. Place cream in glass container or jar. Add buttermilk, stir lightly, and cover.
2. Allow jar to stand at room temperature until thickened to the consistency of sour cream. (This can take anywhere from 12 to 24 hours, depending on the temperature of the room. The warmer the room, the faster it will turn to Crème Fraîche.)
3. Crème Fraîche will continue to thicken as it chills. It will keep for about 10 days under refrigeration.

Double Cream

YIELD: 4 cups
Preparation time: 5 minutes
Marinating time: 12–24 hours

Double Cream is a thicker version of Crème Fraîche, similar to the clotted English Devonshire cream. It needs only 5 minutes of preparation and the same 12–24 hours to thicken at room temperature as Crème Fraîche. Chill it and use it in place of whipped cream as a topping for fresh fruit or as an unusual and fabulous accompaniment to chocolate cake.

The Ingredients:

3 cups heavy cream
1 cup buttermilk

The Steps:

1. Combine cream and buttermilk in a glass jar. Stir, cover, and allow to sit at room temperature for 12–24 hours or until thickened to the consistency of sour cream. (The timing depends on the temperature of the room.)
2. The Double Cream will continue to thicken as it chills. It will keep for about 10 days under refrigeration.

Reduced-Calorie Sour Cream

YIELD: 2¼ cups
Preparation time: 10 minutes

This puree can be used as a dip, flavored with chives, freshly chopped vegetables, curry, garlic, or whatever special flavors you like. Add a dollop to a cold, low-calorie soup, thicken a sauce with it, add it to a salad dressing, or use it in place of mayonnaise in egg, tuna, or chicken salad.

The Ingredients:

1 pint cottage cheese or pot cheese
½ cup buttermilk

The Steps:

1. Place cottage cheese in food processor or blender and puree until smooth.
2. Add buttermilk gradually through the feed tube or top of the blender and process until thick. Desired thickness is obtained by varying the amount of buttermilk.
3. Remove, and refrigerate in a covered container.

Mustard Dill Sauce (Gravlaxas)

YIELD: 1 cup
Preparation time: 10 minutes
Chilling time: 2–3 hours

Mustard Dill Sauce is the perfect accompaniment to *Gravlax* (*Salmon Marinated in Dill*) and can also be used with cold poached fish, smoked salmon, or even roast lamb. If possible, use fresh dill for a better flavor.

The Ingredients:

¼ cup dark mustard (spicy mustard, Dijon mustard, or dark-style mustard)
3 tablespoons dark brown sugar
2 tablespoons white vinegar
1 teaspoon dry mustard
⅓ cup vegetable oil
2–3 tablespoons freshly snipped dill (or 2–3 teaspoons dried dill)

The Steps:

1. In food processor or blender, mix the dark mustard, brown sugar, vinegar, and dry mustard and process for a few seconds.
2. While machine is running, pour oil into container jar in steady stream until sauce is thick and smooth.
3. Pour sauce into small bowl. Add dill, and chill for 2–3 hours or until ready to use.

Make-It-Easy Tips:

√ The sauce will keep for several weeks under refrigeration, so make double the amount and keep for use with fish or lamb dishes.

√ Chop large bunches of fresh dill when it's most plentiful in the spring and summer months and freeze it in small containers for use year 'round.

√ The sauce can be prepared by hand with a wire whisk, but the food processor or blender makes the preparation Make-It-Easy style.

Hollandaise with Ease

SERVES: 3–4
Preparation time: 10 minutes

The easiest way to prepare Hollandaise Sauce is in a blender or food processor. It takes just a few minutes to process and, once prepared, can be reheated in a double boiler or kept warm in a Thermos jar that has just been rinsed with hot water.

The Ingredients:

- 4 ounces (1 stick) unsalted butter
- 3 large egg yolks
- 2 tablespoons fresh lemon juice
- ½ teaspoon salt
- ¼ teaspoon freshly ground white pepper or pinch of cayenne pepper

The Steps:

1. Melt butter in small saucepan until bubbling hot.
2. Place egg yolks, lemon juice, salt, and pepper in blender jar or food processor bowl. Cover and mix for a few seconds until just combined.
3. Remove top and, with machine running, pour hot butter into machine in slow, steady stream.
4. When butter is incorporated, serve the sauce immediately or keep warm in double boiler. Do not let sauce boil or it will curdle and separate.

Variations:

Hollandaise Sauce can be served with asparagus, broccoli, cauliflower, leeks, or with artichokes as a dipping sauce.

Add 2 tablespoons Dijon mustard with the egg yolks for a *Sauce Moutarde,* or add 1 tablespoon freshly snipped dill or other herbs for heightened flavor.

Make-It-Easy Tips:

√ Eggs separate more easily when cold.

√ It is best to cook with eggs (whole or separated) when they are at room temperature.

Leftover egg whites can be frozen in small containers. Be sure to mark number of eggs and date they were put in container and frozen.

Although blender or food processor hollandaise is almost foolproof, occasionally you may end up with a thin, watery liquid instead of thick hollandaise. This can happen if the container or bowl was not properly dried, or the butter was poured in too rapidly. To rectify this disaster, pour the liquid into a dry bowl. Then wash and thoroughly dry the processor bowl or blender container. Place an additional egg yolk in the container and, while the machine is running, pour the hollandaise mixture into the container in a slow, steady stream. Process until thickened.

Marinara Sauce

YIELD: 3–4 cups
Preparation time: 20–25 minutes
Cooking time: 40 minutes

Use Marinara Sauce over cooked pasta, adding sausages, meatballs, mushrooms, green peppers, or whatever desired. It can also be used as the base for *Quick and Easy Cioppino,* an Italian shellfish stew (*see* Chapter 5). Prepare the sauce in large batches and freeze in small containers for future use.

The Ingredients:

¼ cup olive oil
2 cups finely chopped onion
2 cloves garlic, finely chopped
1 large carrot, grated or chopped
4 cups canned Italian plum tomatoes, coarsely chopped
1 tablespoon freshly chopped parsley
1 teaspoon dried oregano, crumbled
1 teaspoon dried basil, crumbled
½ teaspoon salt, or to taste
½ teaspoon freshly ground pepper, or to taste

The Steps:

1. Heat oil in a large skillet and sauté the onion, garlic, and carrot over medium heat until soft and golden brown.
2. Add tomatoes, parsley, oregano, basil, salt, and pepper. Partially cover, reduce heat, and simmer 10 minutes.
3. Adjust seasoning with salt and pepper to taste, and continue to cook, partially covered, for 30 minutes.

Make-It-Easy Tip:

√ It is best to freeze the Marinara Sauce in small (8-ounce), durable plastic containers so that you can defrost what you need without having to thaw the whole recipe.

Pesto

YIELD: 1 cup
Preparation time: 15–20 minutes

Pesto is a great Make-It-Easy aid. Once made, it can be frozen and later defrosted and used in a variety of dishes. Pesto is very rich so only 2–3 tablespoons are necessary for each recipe. It makes a wonderful pasta topping, a tangy addition to soups, a flavor booster for sautéed mushrooms, or a sauce for seafood. Once you've tasted Pesto, you'll want to try it on everything!

The Ingredients:

1 cup tightly packed fresh basil leaves (stems removed), washed and dried on paper towels. (Only *fresh* basil will do.)
½ cup olive oil
3 tablespoons freshly grated Parmesan cheese (or use a combination of Parmesan and Romano or use Pecorino cheese)
2 tablespoons pine nuts (*pignoli*) or chopped walnuts
3 small cloves garlic, peeled
1 tablespoon freshly chopped parsley
½ teaspoon salt, or to taste
¼ teaspoon freshly ground white pepper

The Steps:

1. In the bowl of food processor or in blender container, place all ingredients; process in a pulsating motion, turning machine on and off until well blended and smooth.
2. Place in container with a ¼″ layer of olive oil covering the Pesto, cover, and refrigerate or freeze until ready to use.
3. When ready to use, discard the layer of oil, measure out the Pesto, and proceed with the recipe. (Put another ¼″ layer of oil on the remaining Pesto before storing.)

Make-It-Easy Tips:

√ Grate the cheese and parsley in the food processor or blender before proceeding, and have all the ingredients ready to use.

√ Prepare Pesto in large batches in summer months when fresh basil is plentiful; double or triple the recipe, and freeze for use year 'round.

√ Remember to keep a ¼″ layer of oil on top of stored Pesto at all times. Pesto can be stored for several months in the refrigerator or in the freezer indefinitely. (If freezing, omit the cheese and add later, which will extend the freezer life of the Pesto.)

Creamy Horseradish Sauce

YIELD: 2 cups
Preparation time: 5–10 minutes
Chilling time: 2 hours

Creamy Horseradish Sauce accompanies roast beef, pot roast, vegetables, or smoked fish.

The Ingredients:

¼ cup prepared white horseradish, drained and squeezed dry
1 tablespoon sugar
2 teaspoons Dijon mustard
1 teaspoon white vinegar (or lemon juice)
½ teaspoon salt
Pinch paprika
1 cup heavy cream, whipped

The Steps:

1. Mix the horseradish, sugar, mustard, vinegar, salt, and paprika together until smooth.
2. Gently fold whipped cream into horseradish mixture and chill for 2 hours.

Make-It-Easy Tips:

√ Prepare the day you plan to serve sauce since whipped cream does not keep well.

√ Chill both bowl and beaters to prevent cream from turning, and to produce a lighter and fluffier whipped cream.

Dill Watercress Sauce

YIELD: 2¾ cups
Preparation time: 15 minutes
Chilling time: 2–3 hours

Dill Watercress Sauce accompanies cold poached fish like salmon or halibut, or cold seafood. It can be used by itself as a dip for vegetable crudités.

The Ingredients:

¾ cup chopped watercress
¼ cup freshly snipped dill (or 2–3 teaspoons dried dill to taste)
2 tablespoons freshly chopped parsley
½ teaspoon freshly minced garlic
1 cup mayonnaise
1 cup sour cream
2½ tablespoons fresh lemon juice
½ teaspoon salt, or to taste
¼ teaspoon freshly ground white pepper, or to taste

The Steps:

1. In a food processor or blender, chop watercress, dill, parsley, and garlic, pulsating until just chopped but not pureed.

2. In a bowl, combine chopped ingredients with mayonnaise, sour cream, lemon juice, salt and pepper to taste, and stir until smooth.
3. Chill 2–3 hours.
4. Serve the sauce, chilled, with cold fish, seafood, or as a dip.

Make-It-Easy Tips:

√ The sauce may be prepared 2–3 days in advance. It will keep in the refrigerator for 4–5 days.

√ Leftover watercress wrapped in a towel and placed in a plastic bag will keep fresh for 4–5 days.

Cucumber Dill Sauce

YIELD: 2½–3 cups
Preparation time: 10 minutes
Chilling time: 2 hours

Serve with *Salmon Mousse* or poached fish.

The Ingredients:

1 cup mayonnaise
1 cup sour cream
2 tablespoons freshly snipped dill or 1½ teaspoons dried dill
2 tablespoons lemon juice
½ teaspoon salt, or to taste
Freshly ground white pepper
1 large (or 2 small) cucumbers, peeled, seeded, and chopped

The Steps:

1. In a bowl, combine mayonnaise, sour cream, dill, lemon juice, salt, and pepper until smooth.
2. Fold in chopped cucumber and chill for 2 hours or until ready to use. (Sauce will keep for 2–3 weeks in the refrigerator.)

Make-It-Easy Tips:

√ To seed a cucumber, cut it in half and core with a zucchini corer or with a serrated grapefruit spoon.

√ It is easy to chop cucumbers in a food processor, but remember to pulsate until just chopped, *not* pureed.

√ The European hothouse hydroponic cucumber, which is "burpless" and almost seedless, is especially easy to use since it needs no peeling and little seeding.

Low-Calorie Yogurt Dill Sauce

YIELD: 1¾ cups
Preparation time: 5–10 minutes

Use this dill sauce as a salad dressing, low-calorie dip for vegetable crudités, or as a side sauce for low-calorie fish dishes.

The Ingredients:

2 scallions (green and white parts included)
1 tablespoon freshly snipped dill (or 1 teaspoon dried dill)
1 teaspoon Dijon mustard
½ teaspoon capers, drained (optional)
½ teaspoon lemon juice
½ teaspoon salt, or to taste
¼ teaspoon freshly ground pepper
1¼ cups plain low-fat yogurt

The Steps:

1. In food processor, blender, or by hand chop scallions.
2. Add remaining ingredients, and blend until smooth.
3. Chill until ready to use.

Make-It-Easy Tip:

√ The sauce can be prepared 2–3 days in advance and will keep for 4–5 days in the refrigerator.

Cucumber Raita

YIELD: 3–4 cups
Preparation time: 15 minutes
Marinating time: ½ hour

Raita is a refreshing accompaniment for strong Indian curries. It can be served with any spicy dish as a cooling side sauce. Although the preparation time may seem long, once the cucumbers have been salted to release excess moisture, you can focus your attention on the rest of the meal.

The Ingredients:

2 large cucumbers, peeled, seeded, and grated (or 1 European hothouse hydroponic cucumber, grated)
1 teaspoon salt
1 pint plain yogurt
2 tablespoons minced scallions (green and white included)
¼ teaspoon sugar
¼ teaspoon cumin powder
¼ teaspoon freshly ground white pepper
⅛ teaspoon paprika
Garnish: Freshly chopped coriander or parsley

The Steps:

1. Place cucumber in colander, sprinkle with salt, and allow to stand for 30 minutes; press dry with paper towels.
2. In a bowl, combine yogurt, scallions, sugar, cumin, freshly ground white pepper, and paprika and stir well.
3. Fold in the cucumber; mix well and chill.
4. When ready to serve, taste, and adjust seasoning if necessary. Garnish with chopped coriander or parsley.

Make-It-Easy Tip:

√ When selecting cucumbers, pick unwaxed, slender, firm ones with a bright green color. Fat cucumbers are often soft and mushy on the inside.

Homemade Vanilla Extract

YIELD: 1 pint
Preparation time: 5 minutes

This is especially useful during the Christmas holidays, when pungent vanilla imparts a special flavor to all those holiday baked goodies. It is prepared by mixing brandy with vanilla beans, and letting the mixture marinate for several weeks. This vanilla extract will keep for years, getting just a little bit better each year!

The Ingredients:

2 vanilla beans
1 pint brandy

The Steps:

1. Slice vanilla beans down the center so that seeds are exposed, and drop into the bottle of brandy. Shake, cover, and allow to marinate for several weeks, shaking every few days. (It may be necessary to pour off a small amount of brandy to accommodate the vanilla beans.)
2. Use this homemade vanilla extract whenever vanilla extract is called for in a recipe.

CHAPTER THREE

EGGS AND CHEESE

Frittata
Make-It-Easy Cheese Soufflé
Dutch Babies
Spinach Quiche
Vegetable Cheese Pie

Omelets and baked-egg dishes need not be relegated to the breakfast, brunch, or lunch hour. They make inexpensive and interesting Make-It-Easy suppers when accompanied by a salad and toasted herb bread.

Frittata

SERVES: 4–6
Preparation time: 20–25 minutes
Cooking time: 16–18 minutes

A *frittata* is an Italian vegetable omelet that can be served hot for lunch, brunch, or as a light supper, or served cold the next day as an hors d'oeuvre or snack.

The Ingredients:

2 tablespoons unsalted butter
2 tablespoons olive oil
½ pound mushrooms, thinly sliced
3 shallots or 2 scallions (green and white included), minced
6 eggs
2 tablespoons half-and-half
½ teaspoon salt, or to taste
½ teaspoon freshly ground pepper, or to taste
¼ cup freshly grated Parmesan cheese
1 tablespoon freshly chopped parsley
¼ teaspoon dried oregano, crumbled
¼ teaspoon dried basil, crumbled
3 tablespoons grated Parmesan cheese

The Steps:

1. Preheat broiler.
2. Heat butter and oil together in a 10″ oven-proof skillet; sauté the mushrooms and shallots over medium-low heat until soft and lightly golden, 5–10 minutes.
3. In a bowl, beat eggs with half-and-half, salt, and pepper until well mixed. Add ¼ cup cheese, parsley, oregano, and basil and continue to beat until smooth.
4. Pour egg mixture into skillet, stir once, and then cook without

stirring until the bottom is lightly browned and the eggs are beginning to set; tip skillet to allow eggs to run to the edges.

5. Sprinkle with remaining 3 tablespoons cheese and place under broiler, 5″–6″ from flame for 3–4 minutes to brown top.
6. Serve hot, sliced in wedges, or cold as an hors d'oeuvre.

Accompaniments:

Herbed Pita Toast, Spinach Salad with Creamy Dressing.

Variations:

Additional vegetables can be added or substituted to taste: One 9-ounce package frozen artichokes, cooked and drained; chopped black or green olives; ½ cup frozen chopped spinach, thawed and squeezed dry; sautéed green pepper strips; sautéed minced garlic; diced cooked potatoes; shredded cheese; diced leftover ham, turkey, shrimp, or crabmeat, or even crisp bacon. Be creative and invent your own.

The Frittata may be baked with a topping of tomato sauce or, for a Mexican version, topped with green chile salsa, sprinkled with cheese, and broiled until browned.

Make-It-Easy Cheese Soufflé

SERVES: 6–8
Preparation time: 15 minutes
Cooking time: 50 minutes–1 hour

The advantage of this easy dish is that it is assembled a day ahead. All that's needed is to pop it into the oven for a perfect lunch, brunch dish, or light supper.

The Ingredients:

1 tablespoon unsalted butter for greasing
8 slices bread, crusts removed, and cut into cubes (Pepperidge Farm or similar thin-firm bread)
¾ pound Swiss cheese, cubed (or ½ pound Cheddar cheese and ¼ pound Swiss cheese)

- ¼ cup crumbled bacon bits or ½ cup cooked diced ham (optional)
- 3 tablespoons unsalted butter, melted
- 8 large eggs
- 2 cups whole or low-fat milk
- 1 teaspoon Dijon mustard
- ½ teaspoon Worcestershire sauce
- ½ teaspoon paprika
- ½ teaspoon salt
- ¼ teaspoon freshly ground white pepper
- Pinch cayenne pepper

The Steps:

1. Butter a deep, 10″ round baking dish or a 10″ x 6″ x 2″ rectangular baking dish or other dish of similar size.
2. Beginning with the bread, layer the bread and cheese cubes in the prepared dish until used up. If bacon or ham are to be added, layer them with the cheese.
3. Pour melted butter over layered bread and cheese.
4. Whisk the eggs with the milk. Add mustard, Worcestershire, and seasonings and whisk until combined. Pour over bread and cheese, cover, and refrigerate overnight.
5. The next day, preheat the oven to 350° and bake for 50 minutes to 1 hour or until golden brown and bubbly.
6. Serve immediately, sliced into squares or wedges.

Accompaniment:

Spinach Salad.

Variations:

Cheddar, Monterey Jack, or other cheeses can be substituted for Swiss.

Whole wheat or other whole grain bread, sourdough, or even French bread can be substituted for white bread.

Lightly sautéed mushrooms, onions, and green peppers can be added to the layers in Step 2.

For a spectacular first course, the soufflé can be assembled in 6–8 small au gratin dishes and served individually. The cooking time should be changed to 35–40 minutes for individual small dishes.

Make-It-Easy Tip:

√ The easiest way to grate cheese is in a food processor, but, if grating by hand, make sure the cheese is well chilled and rub a small amount of oil on the grater to prevent sticking.

Dutch Babies

SERVES: 3–4
Preparation time: 15 minutes
Cooking time: 15–20 minutes

"Dutch Babies" is the unusual name given to this oversized puffy pancake, which can be topped with the traditional Hot Swedish Lingonberries or other preserves, or used as a base for sausages, bacon, or other breakfast and brunch meats.

The Ingredients:

3 tablespoons unsalted butter
3 eggs, at room temperature
½ cup sifted all-purpose flour
½ teaspoon salt
½ cup whole milk, at room temperature
Garnish: 2 tablespoons unsalted butter, melted; 1 tablespoon lemon juice; confectioners' sugar

The Steps:

1. Preheat oven to 450°. Butter bottom and sides of a cold, heavy, 10″ skillet with 3 tablespoons butter.
2. In a food processor, blender, or with an electric mixer, beat eggs.
3. Gradually add flour and salt, and continue to beat.
4. Add milk, and beat until smooth.
5. Pour batter into skillet and bake for 15–20 minutes or until golden brown. (The pancake will be uneven and puffy.)
6. Cut into serving pieces, drizzle with melted butter, lemon juice, and a sprinkling of confectioners' sugar, and serve immediately.

Variations:

For sweet variations, top with berries, jelly, jam, honey, nuts, cinnamon, or raisins

For non-sweet variations, serve with butter, sausages, bacon, ham, grated cheese, chilies, or pimientos

Spinach Quiche

YIELD: 2 quiches; 6 servings in each quiche
Preparation time: 15–20 minutes
Cooking time: 30–35 minutes

Quiche is a perfect luncheon, brunch, or supper dish, or it can be cut in thin slivers to use as an hors d'oeuvre.

The Ingredients:

2 tablespoons unsalted butter
¼ cup chopped onion
2 10-ounce packages frozen chopped spinach, thawed and squeezed dry
½ teaspoon salt, or to taste
¼ teaspoon freshly ground white pepper
Fat pinch nutmeg
4 eggs
1 cup half-and-half
1 cup heavy cream
½ cup grated Swiss or Monterey Jack cheese
2 frozen 9″ pie shells, thawed

The Steps:

1. Melt butter in a large skillet. Sauté onions over medium heat until soft, about 5 minutes.
2. Add spinach and continue to cook, stirring often, until no liquid is left in the skillet.
3. Add the salt, pepper, and nutmeg; stir well and allow to cool slightly, about 5 minutes.
4. Preheat oven to 375°.
5. Beat eggs and creams together and gradually add to spinach

mixture, stirring until smooth; add the cheese and stir to combine.

6. Pour mixture into pie shells. Place pie shells on a cookie sheet and bake for 30–35 minutes or until inserted knife comes out clean.
7. Serve the quiche hot or at room temperature.

Accompaniments:

Cold Cucumber-Avocado Soup and sliced tomatoes.

Variations:

Use tiny pie shells for individual quiches and bake 25–30 minutes.

Crisp-fried bacon bits, sautéed mushrooms, or chopped tomatoes can be added for variety.

Make-It-Easy Tips:

√ Spinach Quiche can be frozen once cooked and reheated right from the freezer in a 325° oven for 30 minutes or until hot.

√ Check metal tin holding frozen pie shell to see if there are any tiny holes in the bottom. (This happens occasionally.) If that is the case, place quiches on a foil-lined cookie sheet.

Vegetable Cheese Pie

SERVES: 6–8
Preparation time: 20 minutes
Cooking time: 40 minutes

Vegetable Cheese Pie is a great way to use up leftover cooked vegetables. Combine them with cheese and create an inexpensive vegetarian dinner, lunch, or brunch dish. Choose vegetables with an eye to color as well as taste.

The Ingredients:

1 9″ deep-dish frozen pie crust

3–3½ cups cooked vegetables (carrots, corn, broccoli, green beans, zucchini, peas, etc.)

1½ cups grated Cheddar cheese
6 cherry tomatoes, halved
1 medium onion, finely chopped
1 clove garlic, finely minced
¼ teaspoon salt, or to taste
¼ teaspoon freshly ground pepper, or to taste
¼ cup freshly grated Parmesan cheese
1 tablespoon unsalted butter, diced into bits

The Steps:

1. Preheat oven to 400°.
2. Prick pie crust 3 or 4 times with a fork and bake for 10 minutes.
3. Remove from oven and reduce heat to 350°.
4. Mix cooked vegetables with Cheddar cheese, cherry tomatoes, onion, garlic, salt, and pepper and place in crust.
5. Sprinkle with Parmesan cheese, dot with butter, and bake for 30 minutes or until hot and lightly golden.
6. Serve pie hot, cut into wedges.

Accompaniment:

Tossed Salad with Red Onions.

Variations:

Swiss Gruyère cheese can be substituted for Cheddar, or use half Swiss, half Monterey Jack cheese.

Thawed frozen vegetables can be added if desired.

Make-It-Easy Tips:

√ Cut cherry tomatoes easily with a serrated knife.

√ For a more attractive presentation place the partially thawed pie crust in a glass or ceramic pie plate and proceed with recipe.

CHAPTER FOUR

SOUPS

Beef Barley Soup
Split Pea Soup
Quick and Easy Vegetable Beef Soup
Easy French Onion Soup
Hot Avgolemono Soup
Hot Oriental Mushroom Soup
Stracciatella con Spinaci
Leftover Turkey Soup
Cold Cucumber-Avocado Soup
Cucumber Yogurt Soup
Chilled Dilled Zucchini Soup
Cold Curried Pea Soup
Spanish Gazpacho
Leftover Salad Soup

HOT SOUPS

On cold nights, hot soup is the perfect way to start, and sometimes even complete, a meal. A rich soup such as beef barley or split pea served piping hot with bread on the side can be filling enough for dinner. Prepare the soups in double batches, freeze in family-size containers, and dinner can be ready in a matter of minutes.

When using canned stock, make sure to taste before adding salt since most are high in salt. And, if you want to make canned stock richer, try boiling it with some inexpensive chicken parts like backs and necks, a cut-up onion, a peeled and cut-up carrot, a few sprigs of parsley, and several peppercorns. Strain and use the stock for soups or stews.

Garnishing hot soups, even simple and easy ones, is important even if it's just some toasted almonds, grated cheese, strips of pimiento, sliced mushrooms, chopped green onions, thin-sliced lemons, minced eggs, or the traditional standby, chopped parsley.

Beef Barley Soup

SERVES: 8–10
Preparation time: 20–25 minutes
Cooking time: 2 hours

Beef Barley Soup is so filling it will make a complete dinner when served in deep soup plates with bread and salad as accompaniments.

The Ingredients:

4 pounds beef short ribs or flanken
4 medium onions, coarsely chopped
3 large carrots, sliced
2 10½-ounce cans onion soup plus 2 cans of water
2 10½-ounce cans beef bouillon plus 1 can water
1 10¾-ounce can chicken broth plus 1 can water
1 cup pearl barley
1 bay leaf
½ teaspoon minced garlic
½ teaspoon salt, or to taste
¼ teaspoon freshly ground pepper

The Steps:

1. Place all ingredients in deep soup pot; bring to a boil, skim off accumulated scum from the surface with a large spoon; cover, reduce heat, and simmer slowly for 2 hours or until meat is very tender.
2. Remove bay leaf and discard, taste for seasoning, adjust with salt and pepper if necessary, and serve hot, bones and all, garnished with freshly chopped parsley.

Accompaniments:

Light Beer Bread or hot crusty French bread.

Variation:

If you don't want the bones in the soup, remove from soup and allow to cool; pull off meat and shred into the soup; discard bones and fat.

Make-It-Easy Tips:

√ Double the recipe and freeze the soup in family-size containers for quick and easy dinners.

√ If possible, chill the soup overnight so that the fat will congeal at the top. It can be removed easily the next day.

Split Pea Soup

SERVES: 8–10
Preparation time: 25 minutes
Cooking time: 4 hours

Although the cooking time is long, the ingredients for split pea soup just get tossed in, covered, and cooked until ready. Prepare in large batches and freeze for great winter suppers.

The Ingredients:

6 cups chicken broth
2 cups water
Ham bone, with some meat left on

1 slice thick bacon, chopped
2 stalks celery, coarsely chopped
2 carrots, peeled and coarsely chopped
2 onions, coarsely chopped
1 pound split peas
1 bay leaf
½ teaspoon salt, or to taste
½ teaspoon freshly ground pepper, or to taste
⅛ teaspoon oregano, crumbled
2 tablespoons freshly chopped parsley
2 teaspoons freshly chopped chives or scallion stalks
1 cup diced ham or ½ pound Canadian bacon, cubed (optional)

The Steps:

1. In a large kettle, combine broth, water, ham bone, bacon, celery, carrots, onions, peas, bay leaf, salt, and pepper.
2. Bring to a boil, skim off accumulated scum forming on the top, cover, and simmer 3–4 hours.
3. Remove bone, skim fat off soup, detach meat shreds and return to soup.
4. Add oregano, parsley, chives, and extra ham or Canadian bacon if desired, and simmer covered over very low heat 1 hour longer.
5. Remove bay leaf and discard; taste, and adjust seasoning as necessary; serve as a soup course or even as a whole supper.

Accompaniments:

Sliced knockwurst or hot dogs can be added in the last half hour to create a traditional Split Pea Supper. Serve with herbed crusty French or Italian bread.

Variations:

Ham hocks are a great substitute if you don't happen to have a ham bone on hand. Have the butcher crack one into 3 pieces. Ham hocks will create a layer of scum on the top of the soup as it begins to boil. Skim off the layer and discard.

And . . . if you don't wish to use ham and bacon, use the carcass of a smoked turkey as the basis of the soup.

Substitute dried lentils for the split peas for a hot lentil soup.

Make-It-Easy Tips:

√ Kitchen shears are handy for chopping bacon. Line up the slices and cut across. Turn and cut the other way.

√ If bones are still too hot to shred meat in Step 3, allow to cool or use thick rubber gloves to protect hands.

√ Split Pea Soup is best prepared a day or two in advance to allow the flavors to mellow.

Quick and Easy Vegetable Beef Soup

SERVES: 8–10
Preparation time: 20 minutes
Cooking time: 2½ hours

This soup is more than a first course. It is a full, one-pot dinner for a family, with meat, vegetables, and starch all included. I recommend preparing the soup a day ahead to allow the fat to congeal after refrigeration for easy removal the next day.

The Ingredients:

3½ pounds beef flanken
1 28-ounce can crushed tomatoes packed in puree
2 10½-ounce cans undiluted beef bouillon
1½ cups water
2 large carrots, peeled and roughly chopped
2 stalks celery, roughly chopped
1 large onion, roughly chopped
2 new potatoes, peeled and cut into chunks
Salt and freshly ground pepper to taste
Garnish: *Creamy Horseradish Sauce* (*see* Chapter 2) or grated horseradish

The Steps:

1. Place beef in a large soup pot or deep casserole and cover with tomatoes, bouillon, and water. Bring to a boil, cover and simmer over low heat for 1–1½ hours or until meat is tender.
2. Add carrots, celery, and onion, cover again, and continue to cook over very low heat for 30 minutes.

3. Add potatoes, cover and cook for only 12–20 minutes or until potatoes are just tender but not overcooked. (Prepare soup a day in advance to this point, if possible.)
4. Remove excess grease from top and reheat until just boiling.
5. Taste, and adjust seasoning with salt and freshly ground pepper. If too thick, add additional bouillon or water.
6. Serve soup first, reserving meat. Then follow with meat as a main course, garnished with *Creamy Horseradish Sauce* (*see* Chapter 2) or grated white horseradish.

Accompaniment:

Custardy Corn Bread.

Variations:

For a slightly sweetened flavor, add 2–3 tablespoons ketchup in Step 2.

Flanken is short ribs cut from the ends of the rib roast and the plate. Larger short ribs can be substituted but must be cooked slightly longer.

Add one 10-ounce package frozen mixed vegetables for a chunkier-style soup.

Make-It-Easy Tips:

√ To degrease soups or stews quickly: Skim the surface, and then wrap a few ice cubes in heavy-weight paper towels and run them over the top of the soup. Remove any excess with a wet lettuce leaf.

√ If potatoes are cut in advance, place in a bowl of acidulated water (water with 2 teaspoons lemon juice) to keep from discoloring.

Easy French Onion Soup

SERVES: 8

Preparation time: 20 minutes

Cooking time: 20 minutes for the bread
40 minutes for the soup

The preparation of a traditional French onion soup can be a long and complicated procedure involving long-simmering stocks, homemade breads, and several hand-chopped onions. With a few Make-It-Easy Tips, the help of a food processor to do the chopping, and some canned broth, I've worked out a recipe for an easy French onion soup that may not be totally traditional but is always a success.

The Ingredients:

1 small French bread, cut into 1″ thick slices
4 tablespoons (½ stick) unsalted butter
6 cups thinly sliced onions (3–4 large onions)
1 cup red wine
6 cups strong undiluted beef broth
½ teaspoon salt, or to taste
½ teaspoon freshly ground pepper, or to taste
2½ cups grated Swiss Gruyère cheese

The Steps:

1. Toast bread slices in preheated 350° oven for 20–25 minutes or until golden. (Bread slices can be done a few days in advance and kept in an airtight container or bag until ready to use.)
2. Melt butter in large saucepan; add onions and sauté over medium-low heat until soft and golden, about 15 minutes.
3. Add wine and allow to boil for a minute. Then add broth and bring to a boil again. Cover, reduce heat, and simmer slowly for 15–20 minutes.
4. Preheat oven to 450°.
5. Adjust seasonings in soup with salt and pepper to taste. Place a slice of toasted bread in the bottom of each of 8 onion soup crocks. Pour soup over bread and top with a generous sprinkling of cheese.
6. Place crocks in oven until cheese is melted and bubbly brown, about 5 minutes, and serve immediately.

Variations:

Serve the soup as a complete light supper with a salad and Parmesan melba toast on the side.

For a sweeter flavor, Marsala or port wine can be substituted for red wine.

Sourdough or Italian bread can be substituted for the French bread.

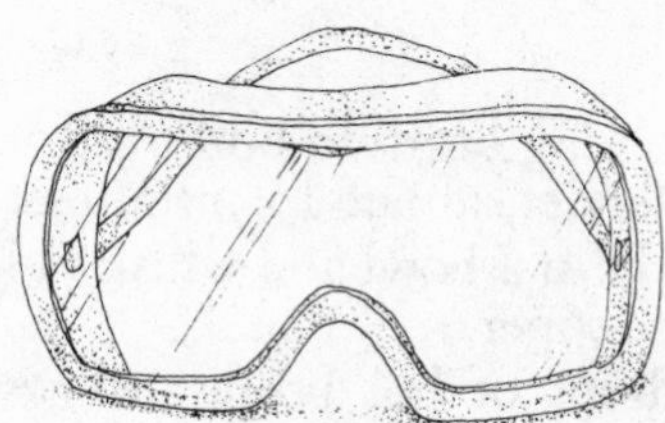

Onion goggles

Make-It-Easy Tips:

√ When chopping or slicing onions, use ski goggles or those funny new onion goggles to ward off tears. As an alternative, freeze onions half an hour before slicing and the funes will not be as strong.

√ If tops don't brown when soup is in oven, run under a hot broiler for 2 minutes, watching carefully.

√ The soup can be cooked ahead through Step 4 and then refrigerated or frozen. When ready to use, reheat and proceed with the recipe.

Hot Avgolemono Soup

SERVES: 4
Preparation time: 10–15 minutes
Cooking time: 20 minutes

Avgolemono is a Greek egg-and-lemon sauce used here as the base for a soup that is flavorful and low in calories. If the egg yolks are at room temperature and the hot liquid is added very gradually there is no danger of curdling.

The Ingredients:

6 cups strong chicken broth, skimmed of fat
¼ cup raw rice
2 egg yolks, lightly beaten, at room temperature
2 tablespoons lemon juice
1 teaspoon arrowroot (or cornstarch)
Pinch cayenne
¼ teaspoon freshly ground white pepper
Garnish: Freshly chopped parsley, thin lemon slices

The Steps:

1. In saucepan, bring broth to boil. Add rice and cook uncovered until rice is tender, about 15 minutes.
2. Place egg yolks in a bowl and whisk in lemon juice, arrowroot, and cayenne pepper.
3. Add a few drops of hot broth to egg mixture and whisk to combine. Continue to add a few drops until egg mixture can be stirred into the broth mixture without curdling.
4. Once the egg mixture is added to the broth, stir over very low heat until slightly thickened. (Do not allow the soup to boil.)
5. Season with freshly ground pepper and serve the soup hot with a generous sprinkling of freshly chopped parsley and thin slices of lemon.

Accompaniment:

Plain melba toast crackers.

Make-It-Easy Tips:

√ The soup can be kept warm in the top of a double boiler for 1–2 hours prior to serving.

√ Leftover egg whites can be frozen in ice-cube trays. After freezing, remove from the trays and store in a sealed plastic bag in the freezer.

√ The starch in the arrowroot helps prevent curdling.

Hot Oriental Mushroom Soup

SERVES: 4–6
Preparation time: 10 minutes
Cooking time: 20 minutes

This clear soup can be served as the beginning of a low-calorie dinner.

The Ingredients:

6 large Chinese or Japanese dried mushrooms, soaked in very hot water to cover for ½ hour
4 cups strong chicken broth
¼ cup Madeira (Marsala or other slightly sweet wine can be used)
Garnish: Chopped scallion stalks

The Steps:

1. When mushrooms are soft, squeeze dry of liquid with your hands. Cut away and discard hard stem portion and slice into julienne strips. (Discard the soaking liquid as well.)
2. Bring broth to a boil, add mushrooms and wine, reduce heat, cover and simmer for 20 minutes.
3. Sprinkle with chopped scallion stalks and serve hot.

Variations:

Soup can be thickened with 1 tablespoon cornstarch, which has been completely dissolved in 2 tablespoons cold water.

An oriental egg-drop soup can be created by bringing the thickened soup to a rolling boil and, while stirring the soup with a fork with one hand, gradually pouring 2 beaten eggs into the boiling soup in a steady stream with the other hand, scrambling with the fork.

Make-It-Easy Tip:

√ Soup can be prepared in advance through Step 2 and reheated just before serving.

Stracciatella con Spinaci

SERVES: 4
Preparation time: 10 minutes
Cooking time: 5–10 minutes

Stracciatella is the Italian version of egg-drop soup, here with spinach added for color and flavor. This clear soup is low in calories.

The Ingredients:

3 cups chicken broth
¼ cup finely chopped spinach leaves or ¼ cup frozen chopped spinach, thawed and squeezed dry
½ teaspoon grated lemon peel
⅛ teaspoon ground nutmeg
¼ teaspoon salt, or to taste

¼ teaspoon freshly ground white pepper, or to taste
2 eggs, lightly beaten
2–3 tablespoons freshly grated Parmesan cheese

The Steps:

1. Bring chicken broth to a boil. Add spinach and cook, stirring, over medium heat for a minute or two.
2. Add lemon peel and nutmeg; stir to combine.
3. Add salt and pepper to taste. (The broth may be heavily salted so you may not need to add salt at all.)
4. While soup is at a rolling boil (be careful to watch that it does not boil over) and, while stirring the soup with a fork with one hand, gradually pour eggs into soup in a stream with the other hand, scrambling with the fork.
5. Quickly stir in cheese and serve immediately with extra cheese on the side.

Accompaniment:

Crusty French bread.

Variations:

Coils of very thin pasta can be cooked in the stock until *al dente.*

For a chinese egg-drop soup variation: Boil the broth with a slice of fresh ginger (if available) and a scallion for 10 minutes. Add 1–2 teaspoons soy sauce in place of the lemon peel and nutmeg and continue with the recipe omitting the Parmesan cheese.

Leftover Turkey Soup

SERVES: 10–12
Preparation time: 25 minutes
Cooking time: 2–3 hours

This is the last gasp for the cooked turkey, when little is left but the bones. It's easy to prepare—just toss in the bones, vegetables, and seasonings, boil and serve.

The Ingredients:

1 turkey carcass, with some meat clinging to the bones
Leftover giblets (if available)

3 large carrots, coarsely chopped
2 large onions, coarsely chopped
2 stalks celery, coarsely chopped
1 parsnip, peeled, coarsely chopped (optional)
Bouquet garni

Bouquet Garni:

4 sprigs parsley
2 celery leaves
2 sprigs fresh dill (optional)
6 peppercorns
¼ teaspoon leaf thyme
1 bay leaf
6 cups chicken broth
Water
½ teaspoon salt, or to taste
½ teaspoon freshly ground pepper, or to taste
1 cup wide noodles or ½ cup raw rice

The Steps:

1. Break up carcass, if necessary, to fit in large soup kettle, adding any leftover giblets. Add carrots, onions, celery, and parsnip.
2. Place parsley, celery leaves, dill, peppercorns, thyme and bay leaf on a small square of cheesecloth, bring corners together and tie securely with string to make a Bouquet garni. Add to soup kettle.
3. Add chicken broth and enough water to cover ingredients, bring to a boil, cover, and cook slowly for 2½–3 hours.
4. Allow to cool slightly, remove carcass, strip meat from bones and return meat to kettle. Remove and discard Bouquet garni, squeezing juices into soup.
5. Adjust seasonings, bring to a boil, add noodles or rice and cook uncovered until rice or noodles are tender.
6. Serve soup hot, sprinkled with freshly chopped parsley.

Variations:

Any vegetables or herbs desired can be added to the soup to taste.

Soup can be served clear without the vegetables; or vegetables can be strained or pureed into the soup for a thick and nutritious treat.

Make-It-Easy Tips:

√ Making a Bouquet garni is easy, and you don't have to go fishing around in hot soup trying to find little pieces of celery or peppercorns. Just remove, squeeze out juice, and toss away. A metal tea ball infuser can also be used to hold the Bouquet garni.

√ Chicken broth is used rather than just water to give extra flavor to the soup; vary the amount of broth and water to taste.

COLD SOUPS

Cold soups are especially refreshing on hot summer days or nights. With the help of a food processor or blender, leftover cooked vegetables and salads can be easily transformed into cold soups. Add some chicken broth, seasoning, curry powder, or cream for a richer soup, if desired. Puree until smooth, and chill. Remember to taste soups after chilling because the cold will diminish the intensity of the seasoning.

Garnishes for cold soups are particularly important; take into account color, texture, and taste. Chopped watercress, chives, basil, and dill are all good toppings, especially when sprinkled over a dollop of regular or reduced-calorie sour cream or yogurt. Chopped vegetables such as radishes, tomatoes, cucumbers, and red and green peppers are also appealing garnishes as are thin slices of lemons, limes, oranges, apples and other fruits.

Cold creamy soups need not be fattening. Yogurt and buttermilk can be used for richness without adding too many extra calories. Even finicky eaters who refuse buttermilk or yogurt will like the light tang these dairy products add to cold soups.

Cold Cucumber-Avocado Soup

SERVES: 4–6
Preparation time: 10–15 minutes
Chilling time: 4–6 hours

A food processor, blender, or hand-held food mill are essential for this recipe.

The Ingredients:

1 large cucumber, peeled, seeded, and cut into 2″ pieces
1 large ripe avocado, peeled
2 scallions (green and white included), chopped
1 cup chicken broth
¾ cup dairy sour cream
2 tablespoons lemon juice
½ teaspoon salt, or to taste
¼ teaspoon freshly ground white pepper
Garnish: A dollop of sour cream and chopped chives or scallion stalks

The Steps:

1. In food processor or blender, combine cucumber, avocado, and scallions until chopped, pulsating on and off.
2. Add broth, sour cream, and lemon juice, and continue to process until smooth.
3. Season with salt and pepper to taste, and chill 4–6 hours.
4. Taste for seasoning after chilling; serve soup in chilled soup bowls garnished with a dollop of sour cream and chopped chives or scallion stalks.

Variation:

European hothouse hydroponic cucumbers, which do not need peeling or seeding, can be substituted.

Make-It-Easy Tips:

√ Wrap cucumbers in plastic and they will keep fresh for about a week in the refrigerator.

√ This soup should not be prepared a day in advance because the avocado will discolor it.

Cucumber Yogurt Soup

SERVES: 4
Preparation time: 10 minutes
Chilling time: 4–6 hours or overnight

A food processor or blender is essential for Cucumber Yogurt Soup.

The Ingredients:

- 2 large cucumbers, peeled, seeded, and roughly chopped or 1 large European hothouse hydroponic cucumber, roughly chopped
- 1 clove garlic, crushed
- 1 cup plain low-fat or whole-milk yogurt
- ⅔ cup dairy sour cream
- 1½ tablespoons freshly snipped dill, or 1½ teaspoons dried dill weed
- ½ teaspoon salt, or to taste
- ½ teaspoon freshly ground white pepper, or to taste
- Garnish: ¼ cup chopped walnuts

The Steps:

1. Place cucumber and garlic in food processor or blender container and process briefly to combine.
2. Add yogurt, sour cream, dill, salt and pepper to taste, and continue to process until smooth.
3. Chill for 4–6 hours or overnight.
4. When ready to serve, taste, and adjust seasoning if necessary; serve the chilled soup garnished with chopped walnuts.

Variations:

For a low-calorie variation, use 2 cups of yogurt instead of yogurt plus sour cream, and substitute chopped dill for the walnut garnish.

Make-It-Easy Tip:

√ To seed cucumbers easily, peel, slice in half horizontally, and seed with a serrated grapefruit spoon.

Chilled Dilled Zucchini Soup

SERVES: 6
Preparation time: 15 minutes
Cooking time: 25 minutes
Chilling time: 6 hours or overnight

Chilled Dilled Zucchini Soup is a very rich soup and should be followed by a light entrée such as roast chicken, and tomatoes with *Laurie's Basic Vinaigrette* dressing.

The Ingredients:

- 4 medium zucchini, cut in slices ½″ thick
- 2 14¼-ounce cans chicken broth
- 1 bunch scallions (green and white included), chopped
- ½ teaspoon salt, or to taste
- ½ teaspoon freshly ground white pepper
- 2 8-ounce bars of cream cheese, softened
- 1 cup dairy sour cream
- 1½ tablespoons freshly snipped dill or 1½ teaspoons dried dill
- 1 tablespoon freshly chopped chives or scallion stalks
- Salt and freshly ground pepper to taste
- Garnish: Dairy sour cream, freshly snipped dill, and paprika

The Steps:

1. Combine zucchini, chicken broth, scallions, salt, and pepper. Bring to a boil in large saucepan. Cover, reduce heat, and simmer slowly for 20–25 minutes or until zucchini is soft. Allow to cool for 10–15 minutes.
2. In a food processor or blender, combine cream cheese, sour cream, dill, and chives and process until smooth.
3. Add the slightly cooled zucchini mixture, liquid and all, and continue to process until smooth.
4. Chill for 6 hours or overnight.
5. Adjust to taste with salt and ground pepper, and serve soup chilled, garnished with a dollop of dairy sour cream, freshly snipped dill, and a sprinkling of paprika.

Variations:

1 teaspoon curry powder can be added in Step 2.

To reduce calories, substitute two 8-ounce packages Neufchatel (low-calorie cream cheese) and 1 cup low-calorie sour cream.

Make-It-Easy Tip:

√ It is important to allow the hot cooked zucchini mixture to cool before adding to the sour cream, which tends to curdle if mixed with boiling liquid.

Cold Curried Pea Soup

SERVES: 4
Preparation time: 10 minutes
Cooking time: 10 minutes
Chilling time: 4–6 hours or overnight

Even if you don't like peas I guarantee you'll like the strong curry flavor of this pea soup.

The Ingredients:

- 1 10¾-ounce can strong chicken broth
- 1 10-ounce package frozen peas
- 1 tablespoon chopped chives or scallion stalks
- 1 teaspoon lemon juice
- 1 teaspoon curry powder, or to taste
- ½ teaspoon salt, or to taste
- ¼ teaspoon freshly ground pepper, or to taste
- ½ cup half-and-half
- Garnish: Chopped chives, scallion tops

The Steps:

1. In a small saucepan, bring broth to a boil. Add peas, bring to a boil again; cover, and simmer for 10 minutes.
2. Add the chives, lemon juice, curry powder, salt, and pepper, and puree in food processor or blender.
3. Chill for 4–6 hours or overnight.
4. Add cream, adjust seasoning, and serve in chilled soup plates garnished with chopped chives or scallion stalks.

Variations:

Fresh or frozen chopped broccoli can be substituted for the peas.

For a lower-calorie version, substitute low-fat buttermilk for the half-and-half.

This pea soup can also be served hot.

Spanish Gazpacho

SERVES: 4–6
Preparation time: 15 minutes
Chilling time: 6 hours or overnight

The Ingredients:

1 medium cucumber, peeled and coarsely chopped
½ green pepper, seeded and coarsely chopped
1 small red onion, coarsely chopped
1 clove garlic, peeled and cut in quarters
1 16-ounce can tomatoes, roughly chopped
1 6-ounce can vegetable juice (I use V-8)
3 tablespoons red wine
2 tablespoons olive oil
2 tablespoons lemon juice
1 egg yolk
1 teaspoon Worcestershire sauce
Salt and freshly ground pepper to taste
Garnish: Croutons, chopped cucumbers, scallions, tomatoes, and green peppers

The Steps:

1. Place cucumber, green pepper, onion, and garlic in food processor or blender and pulsate until finely chopped.
2. Add tomatoes, vegetable juice, red wine, olive oil, lemon juice, egg yolk, and Worcestershire sauce.
3. Process until very smooth, and chill for 6 hours or overnight.
4. Adjust seasoning with salt and pepper to taste and serve soup well chilled, garnished with bowls of croutons, chopped cucumbers, scallions, tomatoes, green peppers, or whatever vegetable desired.

Make-It-Easy Tips:

√ Double the amount of cucumber, green pepper, and onion in Step 1 and use half the chopped amount for garnishes.

√ The soup gets thicker, stronger, and more flavorful as it chills, so be sure to prepare a day or two in advance.

√ If preparing in blender, it is necessary to blend in 2 batches and to strain the soup.

√ If soup is to be served immediately, float an ice cube in each bowl to chill it quickly.

Leftover-Salad Soup

SERVES: 4
Preparation time: 10 minutes
Chilling time: 2–3 hours

It's always a shame to throw away leftover salad but most people don't like it the next day. This recipe takes soggy greens and wilted vegetables along with the dressing and tranforms them into a spicy, cooling soup.

The Ingredients:

2–3 cups leftover salad (greens, tomatoes, onions, bell peppers, cucumbers, etc., complete with dressing)
1 cup chicken broth
Salt and freshly ground pepper to taste
Garnish: Dairy sour cream or plain yogurt, chopped chives or scallion greens

The Steps:

1. Place salad in food processor or blender container with ¼ cup of the broth and process a few times, on and off, to combine.
2. Add remaining broth and continue to process until smooth. (If too thick, add more broth; if too thin, add a few more greens.)
3. Taste at this point. If soup is too bland, vinegar, chopped onions, minced garlic, and salt and pepper will help improve the flavor. Add those to taste, and process until smooth again.
4. Chill for 2–3 hours or until ready to serve.

5. When ready to serve, taste, and add salt and pepper if necessary. Remember that chilling diminishes flavor so always taste cold food just before serving! Serve in chilled bowls garnished with a dollop of sour cream or yogurt and chopped chives or scallions.

Variations:

Add ½ teaspoon minced garlic and ¼ cup minced onion as a flavor booster.

Add any salad vegetables available, as desired.

Make-It-Easy Tip:

√ Refrigerate leftover salad well covered to prevent flavor loss.

CHAPTER FIVE

ENTRÉES

Whole Chicken Cooked in a Clay Pot
Vertically Roasted Chicken
Cuban Chicken
Poulet à Ma Mère
Baked Chicken Chinese Style
Cousin Bette's Chicken
Chicken Breasts Moroccan
Mustard Grilled Boneless Chicken Breasts
Easy Chicken Marengo
Chicken with Artichoke Hearts
Roast Turkey Breast
Turkey Tostados
Turkey and Bulgur
Rock Cornish Game Hens Véronique
Braised Rock Cornish Game Hens
Medium-Rare Roast Beef
Marinated Flank Steak
Broder's Triangle Tip
Brisket Like My Mother Makes
Sweet and Sour Brisket
Spicy Shish Kebab
Deviled Short Ribs
Deviled Beef Bones
Roast Leg of Lamb with Rosemary and Garlic
Marinated Butterflied Leg of Lamb
Lamb with Dill
Rack of Lamb with Fresh Mint Sauce
Barbecued Lamb Riblets
Pork Chops with Mustard Dill Sauce
Sweet and Sour Pork Chops
Pork Loin Polynesian
Potted Pork with Fruit
Special Spareribs
Make-It-Easy Ham
Wiener Schnitzel a la Luchow
Veal and Water Chestnuts
Ragout de Veau
Fluffy Light Meat Loaf
Chinese Ground Beef Loaf
Baked Whole Salmon
Haddock "Blacksmith Shop"
Marinated Grilled Swordfish Steaks
Herb Broiled Fish Fillets
Fish with Butter and Capers en Papillote
Chinese Baked Fish
Fish Fillets Véronique
Braised Fish in Wine and Dill Sauce
Quick and Easy Cioppino
Super-Easy Shrimp Soufflé
Shrimp al Pesto
Curried Scallops
Oriental Flavor Ceviche
Chicken with Hoisin and Nuts
Stir-Fried Beef and Black Bean Sauce
Lamb with Scallions
Ground Pork with Cellophane Noodles, Szechwan-Style
Stir-Fried Shrimp

CHICKEN

We are all aware of the attributes of chicken as a main dish. It is economical, low in calories, low in cholesterol, and exceedingly versatile hot or cold.

Of the many methods of cooking chicken, I find sautéing the easiest when preparing for company. I can sauté the chicken in the morning or the night before, prepare the sauce, and refrigerate until dinner time. The only chore left is to pop the dish into the oven for 10 minutes and serve.

When selecting chickens, look for uniform color. Whether the color is yellow or white makes no difference. Yellow chickens are preferred in the Northeast so they are bred accordingly, whereas other parts of the country demand a white hue. Make friends with the butcher; he (or she) can be a great help. If coaxed, the butcher may even agree to chop up one of the less expensive whole chickens.

Since fresh poultry is extremely perishable, remove it from the store wrapper as soon as you arrive home. The giblets should be removed and refrigerated separately. Wrap the chicken loosely in plastic wrap or waxed paper. Avoid washing until just before using. Moisture and heat create a perfect environment for chickens to go bad. Just before cooking, remove excess fat from the neck area, wash and pat dry with paper towels, and proceed with the recipe.

Whole Chicken Cooked in a Clay Pot

SERVES: 4
Preparation time: 15 minutes
Cooking time: 1¼ hours

Cooking with wet terra-cotta clay dates back to the ancient Etruscans. The unglazed pot is totally immersed in water for about 20 minutes before cooking. When the heat of the oven reaches the clay cooker, the absorbed water heats up causing an instant flush of steam that keeps moisture surrounding the food that is cooking. The food is self-basted and kept moist and juicy so that no extra fats or oils are necessary. No browning of meats in oil or butter is required so the food is low in calories and healthful. The other advantage to clay pot cooking is that a whole one-pot dinner (meat, vegetables, starch) can be assembled in the clay cooker, closed, and totally cooked without basting or watching.

The Ingredients:

- 1 Ovenbrique, Romertopf, Gourmetopf or similar brand unglazed terra-cotta pot large enough to hold a chicken plus vegetables
- 1 whole roasting chicken (3–4 pounds)
- 1 teaspoon *herbes de provence,* crumbled (or combination of crumbled dried basil, oregano, thyme, and chives)
- 1 teaspoon salt (clay cooking requires more salt)
- ½ teaspoon freshly ground pepper
- 3 medium carrots, peeled and sliced
- 2 medium onions, quartered
- ¾–1 cup dry vermouth or white wine
- Salt and pepper to taste

The Steps:

1. Presoak pot, top and bottom, in water for 15–20 minutes.
2. Wash chicken, pat dry with paper towels, and season inside and out with one-half of the herbs, salt, and pepper.
3. Place carrots and onions in bottom of clay pot.
4. Put chicken on top of vegetables and sprinkle with parsley and remaining seasonings.
5. Pour wine around the sides, cover and *place in cold oven.* (Clay pots must be put in a cold oven or they will crack from the intense sudden heat of a preheated oven.) Set oven to 475° and cook for 1 hour and 15 minutes.
6. Remove from oven, baste chicken, and return to oven without lid for 10 minutes if additional browning is desired.
7. Remove chicken and vegetables to a platter and season to taste with salt and pepper.
8. Remove fat from remaining sauce and serve in gravy boat.

Accompaniments:

Plain white rice, and a mixed green salad with *Yogurt Dressing.*

Variation:

Small unpeeled red or new potatoes can be added to the clay pot. They brown well and can be served with a little of the defatted sauce.

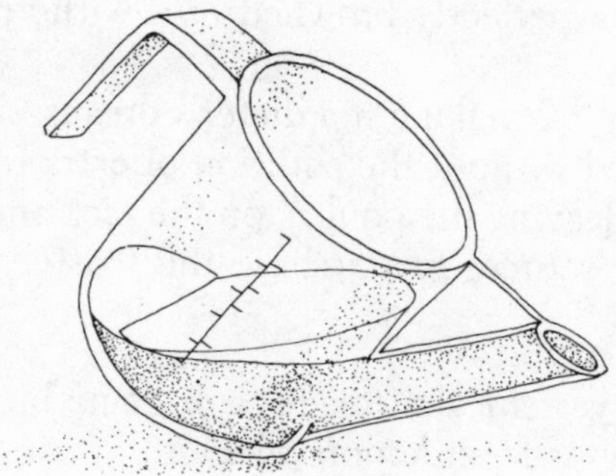

Gravy strainer

Make-It-Easy Tips:

√ When buying a clay cooker, make sure it is large enough to accommodate a large roaster so that you can use it for company as well as family meals. Try the *Potted Pork with Fruit* (*see* page 137) or use your favorite poultry or meat dish and adapt it to clay cookery.

√ The easiest way to remove excess fat from gravy is with a gravy strainer. It is a pitcher with the spout based at the bottom. The gravy is poured in, the fat quickly rises to the top, the gravy is poured off from the bottom and the fat remains in the pitcher.

√ If time is a problem, immerse the clay pot in the morning and leave all day. The meal can then be quickly assembled without additional waiting.

Basic Vertically Roasted Chicken

SERVES: 4
Preparation time: 10–15 minutes
Cooking time: 1 hour

There are many advantages to using the Spanek or any style of vertical roaster for turkey, duck, game hens, or chicken. The fowl is placed in a vertical position on a tempered steel "Eiffel Tower" frame which conducts heat to sear the inside of the bird while allowing the juices to flow downward into the breast area. Poultry is cooked at high temperatures to create a perfectly browned bird without the necessity of turning the bird.

Excess fats drip off making it a dieter's dream, since the birds can be perfectly browned without the addition of extra butter or oil. Carving is facilitated by leaving the poultry on the rack and carving it neatly off the roaster. For sources to purchase the roaster, *see* Appendix A.

The Ingredients:

1 whole fryer chicken (or duck or game bird)
2 tablespoons fresh lemon juice
1 tablespoon unsalted butter, softened (optional)
½ teaspoon minced garlic
½ teaspoon paprika
¼ teaspoon dried oregano, crumbled
¼ teaspoon dried leaf thyme, crumbled
½ teaspoon salt, or to taste
¼ teaspoon freshly ground pepper
¾–1 cup white wine
¾–1 cup chicken broth
2–3 tablespoons unsalted butter, melted (optional)

The Steps:

1. Preheat oven to 450°.
2. Dry chicken inside and out with paper towels and rub with lemon juice. Massage with butter, if desired; season inside and out with minced garlic, paprika, oregano, thyme, salt, and pepper.
3. Remove top ring from the Spanek vertical roaster and place chicken over center hollow section of rack making sure top of roaster fits through neck opening of bird. Put excess skin around neck of bird over top and down inside roaster. Replace the top ring of roaster over skin, which is tucked in. (If using alternate brand of vertical roaster follow manufacturer's instructions.)
4. Mix white wine with chicken broth and pour into roasting pan to a depth of ¼″. This will prevent the juices from cooking away. (Reserve remaining liquid.) Place vertical roaster in pan and place on lower rack of the oven. Cook for 15 minutes at 450° to sear bird, inside and out.
5. Reduce heat to 350° and continue to cook for 15–20 minutes *per pound.*
6. About halfway through roasting process, baste with optional

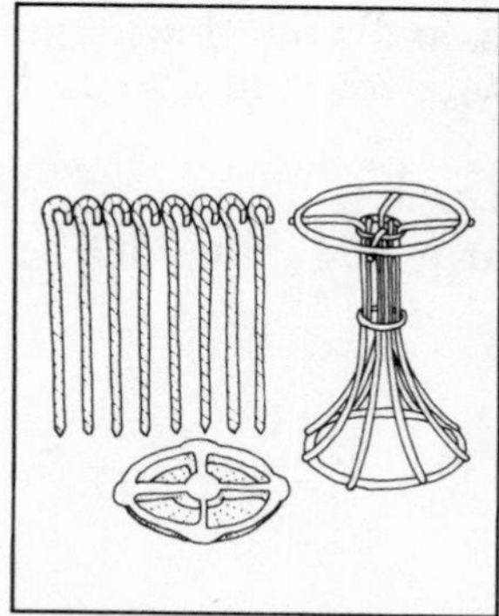

1. The vertical roaster

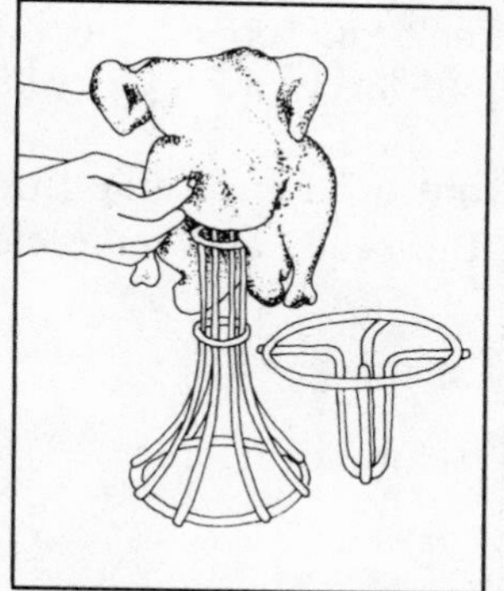

2. Fit the chicken on the roaster.

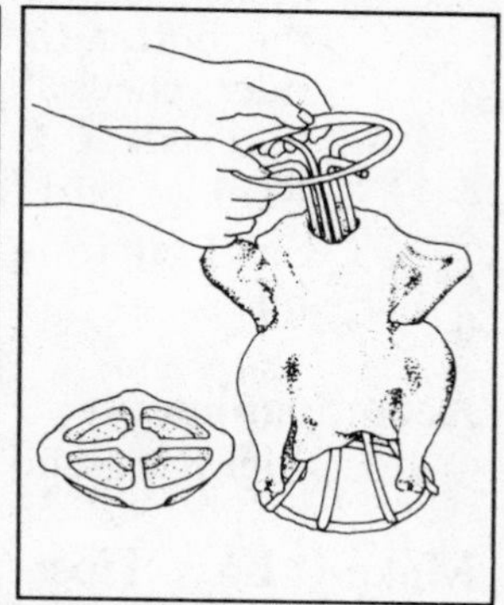

3. Replace the roaster ring.

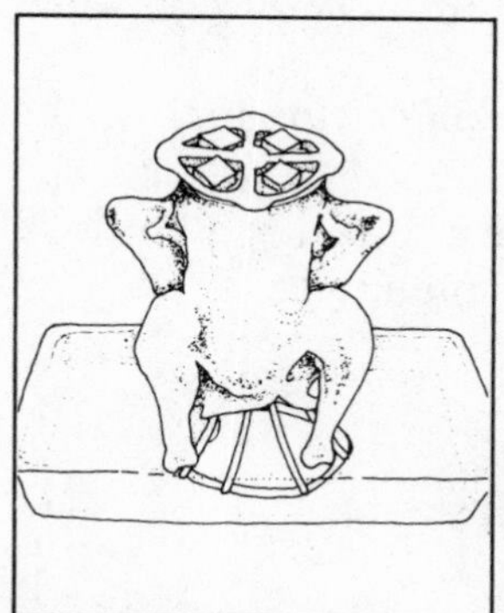

4. Apply baster half way through cooking.

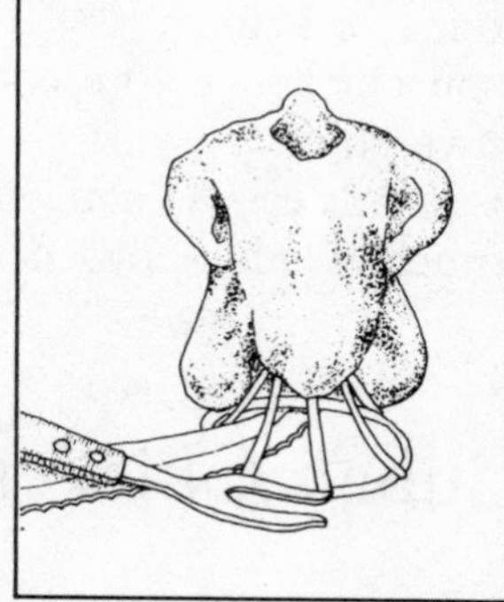

5. The roast is ready for carving.

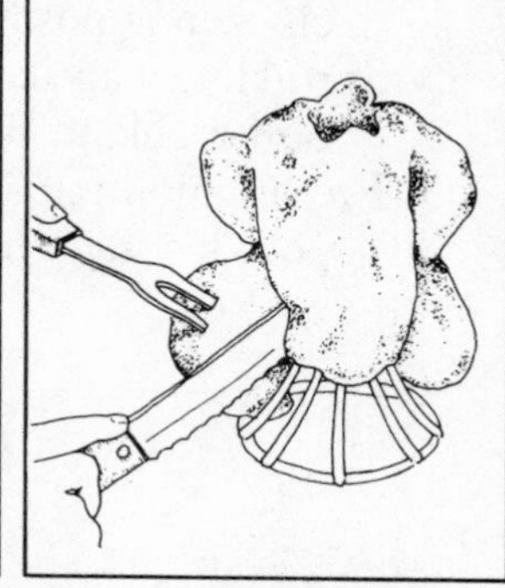

6. Carve the thigh first.

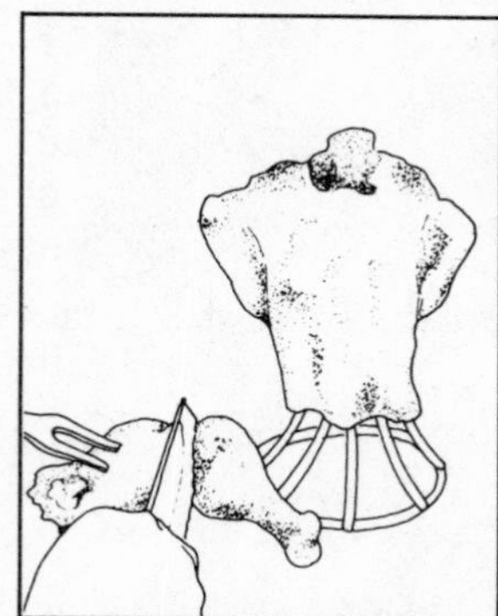

7. Separate the thigh from the leg.

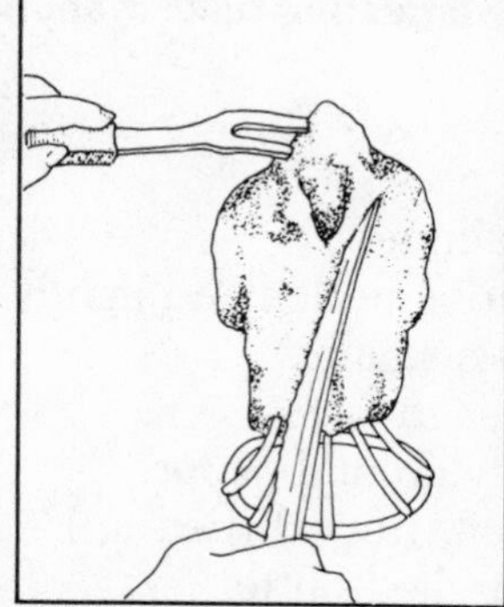

8. Remove the wish-bone.

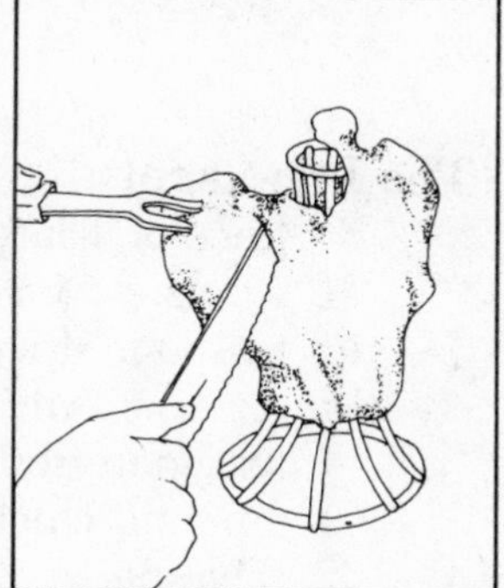

9. Peel down the breast.

melted butter or use the Spanek basting tray, which allows the butter to melt on top of the bird and flow down the sides; check liquid level and replenish with reserved liquid, if necessary.

7. Remove bird from oven and carve from rack.
8. Skim fat from the sauce and serve clear juices alongside the bird.

Accompaniments:

Lemon Rice, and steamed carrots.

Make-It-Easy Tips:

√ This recipe can be used when roasting a chicken on a regular horizontal rack, but the results will not be the same because the juices will not drip down into the breast meat as they do when chicken is positioned vertically.

√ Sprinkling paprika on chicken before cooking helps to give the bird a golden brown color.

√ Fresh lemon juice is just as easy to squeeze as opening a bottle of poor-tasting, chemically laden bottled lemon juice.

Cuban Chicken

SERVES: 4
Preparation time: 10 minutes
Cooking time: 40–45 minutes
Marinating time: 3 hours

The Ingredients:

Juice of 1 large lime
1 whole clove garlic, peeled and lightly crushed but still intact
½ teaspoon dried oregano
½ teaspoon salt, or to taste
¼ teaspoon freshly ground pepper
1 3-pound chicken, trussed (tied up)
2 tablespoons unsalted butter
1 tablespoon olive oil (Spanish is preferable)
½ cup dry white wine

1 large onion, thinly sliced
Garnish: Freshly chopped parsley or watercress

The Steps:

1. In deep bowl, combine lime juice, garlic, oregano, salt, and pepper. Marinate chicken at room temperature for 3 hours, turning occasionally. (If the weather is hot, marinate in refrigerator for 6 hours or overnight and bring to room temperature before cooking.)
2. Remove chicken from marinade, discard garlic, and reserve remaining marinade for sauce.
3. In large deep casserole or Dutch oven, heat butter and oil together and brown chicken on all sides.
4. Reduce heat, add wine, onion, and reserved marinade.
5. Cover and cook over low heat for 40–45 minutes or until tender, basting occasionally.
6. Serve hot, garnished with freshly chopped parsley or watercress.

Accompaniments:

Plain Brown Rice, and a salad of greens, tomatoes, Spanish olives, Spanish onion slices with *Laurie's Basic Vinaigrette* dressing.

Variations:

Cuban Chicken can be prepared with cut-up chicken parts as well but the cooking time should be reduced to 30–35 minutes or until tender.

For a larger crowd, use a 5–6 pound chicken, double the sauce, and cook for 45 minutes to 1 hour, or until tender and the juices run clear when thigh is pierced.

For a reduced calorie count, brown the chicken in a non-stick skillet in only 1 tablespoon oil and use a gravy strainer or similar device to skim off the fat on the sauce before serving.

Make-It-Easy Tips:

√ The easiest way to truss a chicken is with a trussing needle. Just sew the chicken closed with kitchen twine.

√ An easy way to crush and peel garlic is to wrap a whole clove in waxed paper and smash with the side of a cleaver or heavy knife. The peel can be removed easily and the garlic remains intact so it can be removed after marinating.

Poulet à Ma Mère

SERVES: 8
Preparation time: 15–20 minutes
Cooking time: 50 minutes

This particular chicken dish is so named because it came from my mother, Ruth Burrows, who perfected it as the perfect company dish. Although it may appear to have many steps, it is basically a Make-It-Easy recipe.

The Ingredients:

3 tablespoons unsalted butter
1 tablespoon olive oil
2 2½–3 pound chickens, cut into serving pieces and patted dry with paper towels
½ cup port wine (or use Marsala or sweet vermouth)
2 cups chicken broth
1 tablespoon freshly minced tarragon or 1 teaspoon dried tarragon
½ teaspoon salt, or to taste
¼ teaspoon freshly ground pepper
¾ cup dairy sour cream or *Crème Fraîche* (*see* Chapter 2)
Garnish: Parsley sprigs

The Steps:

1. Preheat oven to 350°.
2. In a large skillet, melt butter and oil together; sauté chicken pieces, a few at a time, until golden brown, adding more butter if necessary.
3. Remove browned chicken pieces from skillet. Blot on paper towels to remove excess grease and place in single layer in an oven-proof casserole.
4. When all the chicken has been removed from the skillet, pour off any remaining fat. Add port and stir, scraping up any browned particles on the bottom of the pan.
5. Add broth, tarragon, salt, and pepper; stir, and pour sauce over chicken in casserole.
6. Place casserole in oven and bake uncovered for 40–45 minutes or until tender.

7. Remove casserole from oven, transfer chicken to plate, and allow sauce to cool for 5–10 minutes.
8. Gradually whisk sour cream or *Crème Fraîche* into the sauce until smooth.
9. Return chicken to casserole in single layer and place in oven again just to warm the sauce. (Be careful not to leave casserole in too long or the sour cream may curdle.)
10. Serve chicken hot, garnished with parsley sprigs.

Accompaniments:

Lemon Rice, and *Spinach Salad.*

Make-It-Easy Tips:

√ The chicken can be prepared ahead through Step 7 and refrigerated until ready to serve. Bring sauce and chicken pieces to room temperature before proceeding.

√ *Crème Fraîche,* because of its high butterfat content, will not curdle when heated. *See* Chapter 2 for recipe.

√ To save time and energy, use a very large casserole and prepare sauce in Steps 7 and 8 in a corner of the pan, tipping it towards you.

√ When browning chicken, place a heavy pot lid over the chicken to press it down. This procedure quickens the browning and keeps the grease from splattering all over the stove. If you don't have such a lid, a metal colander inverted over the top of the chicken will serve as a shield but won't assist in the browning.

Baked Chicken Chinese Style

SERVES: 4
Preparation time: 10 minutes
Cooking time: 1 hour

The Ingredients:

3–4 pounds chicken, cut into serving pieces and patted dry with paper towels

2–3 pieces bacon, cut into ½″ pieces (optional)

Sauce:

- ⅓ cup soy sauce
- 2 tablespoons ketchup
- 2 tablespoons dry sherry
- 1 tablespoon peanut oil
- 1 teaspoon dry mustard
- 1 clove garlic, minced
- 1 teaspoon sugar
- 1 large slice gingerroot, minced, or ½ teaspoon ground ginger
- ¼ teaspoon freshly ground pepper
- 2 large scallions (green only) cut into ½″ pieces

The Steps:

1. Place chicken pieces in large roasting pan in single layer.
2. Prepare sauce by combining soy sauce, ketchup, sherry, oil, mustard, garlic, sugar, ginger, pepper, and scallions.
3. Pour the sauce over the chicken, cover, and refrigerate overnight to marinate, turning once.
4. Preheat oven to 375°.
5. Add optional bacon to pan and bake chicken for 30 minutes *per side,* brushing occasionally with the sauce.
6. Serve chicken hot over white rice.

Accompaniments:

Plain White Rice, the Chinese Way, and *Stir-Fried Spinach.*

Variation:

This Chinese Chicken is wonderful served cold the next day for lunch or at a picnic.

Make-It-Easy Tips:

√ To cut down on excess grease and calories, blanch bacon by dropping into boiling water for 2 minutes and then draining.

√ Excess fat can be removed from sauce before serving with a gravy strainer, skimmer, or other type of fat separator.

√ Store peeled ginger, covered with dry sherry, in a jar in the refrigerator. It will keep for several months.

Cousin Bette's Chicken

SERVES: 6–8
Preparation time: 10 minutes
Cooking time: 35–40 minutes

Cousin Bette's Chicken is not from the Balzac novel but comes from a cousin named Bette in Ohio. It is simple to prepare with a three-ingredient sauce.

The Ingredients:

4 chicken breasts, split in half
1 12-ounce jar currant jelly
¼ cup light brown sugar
2 tablespoons orange juice
Salt and pepper to taste
Garnish: Freshly chopped parsley

The Steps:

1. Preheat oven to 375°.
2. Place chicken breasts, skin side up, in a single layer in oven-proof baking dish.
3. In small saucepan, combine currant jelly, brown sugar, and orange juice; heat for 2–3 minutes; paint chicken breasts with mixture. Add any excess to baking dish.
4. Cover pan and bake for 20 minutes; remove cover and continue to bake until chicken is tender and crusty brown on top, 15–20 minutes longer.
5. Taste, and adjust seasoning if necessary. Serve chicken hot with sauce poured over top. Garnish with freshly chopped parsley.

Accompaniments:

Apricot Rice and a mixed green salad with *Laurie's Basic Vinaigrette* dressing.

Make-It-Easy Tip:

√ Chicken can be prepared with boned chicken breasts with skins on but must then be basted often and cooked only 20 minutes, or until tender.

Chicken Breasts Moroccan

SERVES: 6
Preparation time: 20–25 minutes
Cooking time: 20–25 minutes

The Ingredients:

1½ lemons
6 medium-size chicken breasts, halved, washed, and patted dry with paper towels
½ teaspoon salt, or to taste
¼ teaspoon freshly ground pepper
2 tablespoons unsalted butter
2 tablespoons olive oil
4 large shallots, minced (or 4 large scallions, white only, minced)
1 clove garlic, minced
½ cup dry white wine (or dry vermouth)
¼ cup freshly chopped parsley
1 teaspoon dried oregano, crumbled
½ cup chicken broth
Garnish: Fresh coriander or parsley

The Steps:

1. Preheat oven to 350°.
2. Peel the lemons and cut the lemon rind into julienne strips (matchstick size); squeeze juice from lemon and reserve.
3. Sprinkle chicken with salt and pepper.
4. In large oven-proof pan that can go on top of the stove, heat the butter and oil. Brown chicken breasts on both sides over medium high heat until golden; remove with slotted spoon.
5. Sauté shallots and garlic in remaining fat over medium-low heat and cook until soft, about 5 minutes.
6. Deglaze pan with wine by scraping up browned particles from bottom of the pan. Bring to boil and cook over high heat until the wine is reduced to half its volume.
7. Return chicken to pan, sprinkle with parsley and oregano; add chicken broth, lemon juice, and lemon peel strips. Cover and place in oven for 20–25 minutes or until tender (DO NOT OVERCOOK).
8. Serve chicken hot, garnished with coriander or parsley.

Accompaniments:

Couscous, and *Tossed Salad with Red Onions.*

Variations:

A 3–3½ pound whole chicken cut into serving parts can be used or, for a more elegant version, substitute boneless chicken breasts.

Leftover chicken can be served cold the next day accompanied by a lemon mayonnaise.

Make-It-Easy Tips:

√ A lemon "zester," a gadget with 4–5 small openings at the top, will cut the lemon into julienne strips.

√ Peeled lemons are easier to squeeze, and release more juice.

√ Lemons will yield more juice when they are at room temperature.

Mustard Grilled Boneless Chicken Breasts

SERVES: 4
Preparation time: 5 minutes
Marinating time: 10–15 minutes
Cooking time: 8–10 minutes

These boneless chicken breasts are marinated in lemon juice and mustard and then grilled indoors or outdoors until seared on the outside and juicy on the inside without any added butter or fat. The results are delicious and incredibly low-calorie.

The Ingredients:

4 boneless chicken breasts
¼ cup Dijon mustard
¼ cup lemon juice
1 teaspoon Worcestershire sauce
Salt and pepper to taste

The Steps:

1. Paint chicken breasts on both sides with mustard.
2. Sprinkle lemon juice and Worcestershire sauce over chicken

and allow to marinate at room temperature for 10–15 minutes.
3. Preheat broiler or outdoor grill.
4. Grill chicken for 3–4 minutes a side or until just tender.
5. Season to taste with salt and pepper and serve hot.

Accompaniments:

Potatoes Boiled in Jackets, and a mixed green salad with *Low-Calorie Buttermilk Dill Dressing.*

Variations:

Grainy imported mustard, called *Moutarde à l'Ancien,* can be substituted for Dijon mustard. The most popular brand in the U.S. is *Moutarde de Meaux Pommery.*

The leftover chicken can be served cold with *Mustard Mayonnaise.*

Make-It-Easy Tip:

√ Chicken can be marinated for several hours, covered, in the refrigerator.

Easy Chicken Marengo

SERVES: 6–8
Preparation time: 15 minutes
Cooking time: 35–40 minutes

Chicken Marengo is a stew with a delicate flavor that is inexpensive to prepare.

The Ingredients:

- 6 boneless and skinless chicken breasts, cut into 1½″–2″ square pieces
- ½ cup all-purpose flour
- 1 teaspoon dried tarragon, crumbled
- ½ teaspoon salt, or to taste
- ½ teaspoon freshly ground white pepper
- 2 tablespoons unsalted butter
- 2 tablespoons olive oil

½ cup dry white wine
2 cups drained and chopped canned tomatoes (two 16-ounce cans or one 28-ounce can should yield 2 cups drained and chopped tomatoes)
12 mushrooms, sliced
1 2.2-ounce can sliced pitted black olives
1 small clove garlic, minced
Salt and pepper to taste
Garnish: Freshly chopped parsley

The Steps:

1. Preheat oven to 350°.
2. Combine flour with tarragon, salt, and pepper and dip chicken pieces in seasoned flour to coat on all sides.
3. Heat butter and oil in large skillet; brown chicken pieces a few at a time until golden (adding more butter if necessary). Remove to an oven-proof casserole.
4. Add wine to skillet and deglaze by scraping up brown particles from the bottom of the pan.
5. Add tomatoes, mushrooms, olives, and garlic, and stir to combine; pour sauce over chicken pieces, and cover. Place in oven and bake for 35 to 40 minutes.
6. Taste, and adjust seasoning if necessary. Serve chicken garnished with freshly chopped parsley.

Accompaniments:

Rice Pilaf with Pine Nuts, and *Spinach Salad with Creamy Dressing.*

Variation:

Cooked shrimp can be added during the last 10 minutes of cooking.

Make-It-Easy Tips:

√ Chicken Marengo can be reheated successfully and is, therefore, an excellent dish to make in large quantities and freeze for future use in foil or plastic containers.

√ Chicken is more easily cut if semi-frozen.

√ Flour and seasonings can be shaken together in a plastic bag. Add chicken pieces and shake. Remove chicken to a colander or strainer and shake off excess flour.

Chicken with Artichoke Hearts

SERVES: 4–6
Preparation time: 20 minutes
Cooking time: 40 minutes

The Ingredients:

1 3-pound chicken, cut into pieces
½ teaspoon paprika
½ teaspoon salt, or to taste
¼ teaspoon freshly ground pepper
2 tablespoons unsalted butter
1 tablespoon olive oil
2 6-ounce jars marinated artichoke hearts, drained
¼ pound mushrooms, sliced
2 tablespoons all-purpose flour
⅔ cup strong or undiluted chicken broth
⅓ cup dry white wine or dry vermouth
¼ teaspoon dried rosemary, crumbled
Garnish: Freshly chopped parsley

The Steps:

1. Preheat oven to 375°.
2. Sprinkle chicken pieces with paprika, salt, and pepper.
3. Heat butter and oil in a large skillet and brown chicken on both sides over high heat. With slotted spoon, remove chicken pieces to oven-proof casserole, leaving excess fat in the pan.
4. Arrange artichoke hearts in casserole between pieces of chicken.
5. Over medium-low heat, sauté the mushrooms in remaining fat in skillet. Sprinkle flour over mushrooms, stir well, add chicken broth, white wine, and rosemary, stirring until smooth over low heat.
6. Pour mushroom sauce over chicken and artichokes, cover, and bake for 35–40 minutes or until chicken is tender.
7. Taste, and adjust seasoning if necessary. Serve chicken garnished with freshly chopped parsley.

Accompaniments:

Plain White Rice, the Chinese Way, and *Broccoli Florets Vinaigrette.*

Variations:

If desired, 1/4 cup minced onions, shallots, or scallions can be sautéed with mushrooms in Step 5.

For a very elegant dinner, boned chicken breasts with or without skins can be used. Cook these in the casserole only 15–20 minutes, depending on the size, or until tender.

Make-It-Easy Tip:

√ See the tip under *Poulet à Ma Mère* for the best way to brown chicken.

TURKEY

Roast turkey seems destined to be a November holiday dish no matter how you slice it. I find, however, that turkey breasts or thighs can be easily roasted and used as the basis for unusual variations such as Oriental turkey salad or *Mexican Turkey Tostado.*

When selecting a turkey or turkey parts, choose a fresh one if available. Avoid the frozen "butterball" turkeys, which actually contain little or no butter. For the most part, they are injected with saturated fats and are more expensive. The best way to thaw a frozen bird is to refrigerate it 1–2 days, depending on size. If time does not permit, thaw in sealed wrapper outside the refrigerator in a bowl or sink filled with cold water, changing the water often to hasten the procedure.

When trussing a large bird, sew up with a large trussing needle using kitchen twine, or use oversized pins to clip shut.

Roast Turkey Breast

SERVES: 10
Preparation time: 10 minutes
Cooking time: 1½ hours

For those who prefer only white meat of turkey, Roast Turkey Breast is an ideal entrée. It is easy to prepare and serves a large group. The leftovers make fantastic sandwiches as well as the basis for an excellent turkey salad, hot or cold.

The Ingredients:

- 1 5–6 pound turkey breast
- 2 tablespoons unsalted butter
- ½ teaspoon paprika
- ½ teaspoon salt, or to taste
- ¼ teaspoon freshly ground pepper
- 2 shallots or scallions (white part only), minced
- ½ cup dry white wine
- ½–1 cup chicken broth
- Garnish: Orange slices, parsley sprigs

The Steps:

1. Preheat oven to 350°.
2. Rub butter on skin of turkey breast; season with paprika, salt, and pepper, and scatter shallots or scallions over all sides of bird.
3. Place turkey in a roasting pan (lined with aluminum foil to save on clean-ups) and pour wine and broth around the bottom of the pan. (There should be about ½″ of liquid in the pan.)
4. Roast turkey in oven for 1½–2 hours or until juices run clear when meat is pierced. Length of time depends on the size of the bird. In general, roast for 20 minutes per pound or until an inserted meat thermometer registers 160–165°. Using a pastry brush, paint every half hour with the liquids, which can be replenished with additional chicken broth, if necessary.
5. If desired, gravy can be strained, defatted and thickened by boiling down to half its original volume.
6. Serve turkey garnished with orange slices and parsley sprigs.

Accompaniments:

Noodle Pudding, and a mixed green salad with *Laurie's Basic Vinaigrette* dressing.

Variations:

To reduce calories, omit the butter, and baste more often with the natural liquids. Defat gravy, and serve with steamed vegetables and plain white rice.

Leftovers: Cold turkey sandwiches are a favorite around our

house—thin slices of turkey with lots of *Thousand Island Dressing* and some cole slaw on rye bread.

Roast Turkey Breast meat can also be used in casseroles or in the proverbial turkey salad.

Make-It-Easy Tip:

√ Shallots or scallions can be put through a garlic press to extract their juice and crush them.

Turkey Tostados

SERVES: 3–4
Preparation time: 15 minutes
Cooking time: 6–12 minutes

Tostados make a fun dinner where guests or family can help themselves to a variety of toppings.

The Ingredients:

- ¼ cup vegetable oil
- 6 small corn tortillas
- 1½ cups canned refried beans, warmed
- 1½ cups shredded cooked turkey
- ¾ cup Mexican chile sauce with tomatoes (or Jalapeño sauce to taste)
- 2 cups shredded lettuce
- ¾ cup shredded Monterey Jack or Cheddar cheese
- 1 medium onion, finely chopped
- 2 tomatoes, roughly chopped
- 2 pimientos, cut into thin strips
- 1 2¼-ounce can sliced black olives, drained
- 1 ripe avocado, cut into 12 slices
- 1 cup dairy sour cream

The Steps:

1. Heat oil in heavy skillet over medium high heat; fry tortillas on both sides, one at a time, until crisp. (Each should take 1–2 minutes.) Drain on paper towels.

2. On each tostado shell, spread ¼ cup refried beans.
3. Top with ¼ cup shredded turkey and 2 tablespoons Mexican chile sauce.
4. Garnish each tostado with lettuce, cheese, onion, tomatoes, pimientos, black olives, avocado, and sour cream, piling them as high as you want. Serve immediately.

Accompaniments:

Tossed Salad with Red Onions.

Variations:

Guacamole (*see* Chapter 1) can be added to the tostado instead of the avocado slices.

Tostados can be served for supper or lunch.

Make-It-Easy Tips:

√ Crisp tortillas, called tostado shells, are available in supermarkets and can be used, but must be heated in a 350° oven for 3–5 minutes to crisp.

√ A tostado party is a fine idea. Put everyone to work chopping the ingredients and then everyone can enjoy making his or her own tostado.

√ Cover leftover pimientos in jar with vegetable oil and refrigerate to prevent spoilage.

Turkey and Bulgur

SERVES: 6–8
Preparation time: 20 minutes
Cooking time: 1 hour

Bulgur (cracked wheat) adds an unusual and nutty flavor to this casserole.

The Ingredients:

3 tablespoons unsalted butter
1 pound mushrooms, thinly sliced
1 small onion, finely chopped

- 1 cup bulgur (cracked wheat)
- 2½ cups chicken broth, or turkey stock if available
- ½ cup heavy cream
- ½ cup slivered almonds or pine nuts
- 1 tablespoon lemon juice
- 1 tablespoon freshly chopped parsley
- 1 teaspoon chopped chives or scallion stalks
- 1 teaspoon Worcestershire sauce
- ½ teaspoon salt, or to taste
- ½ teaspoon freshly ground pepper
- 3 cups cooked turkey, cubed
- 2 tablespoons unsalted butter

The Steps:

1. Preheat oven to 350°. Generously butter a 2-quart casserole.
2. In large skillet, melt 3 tablespoons butter and sauté mushrooms and onions over medium heat until soft and golden.
3. Add bulgur and stir until grains are coated, about 2 minutes.
4. Add broth, cream, nuts, lemon juice, parsley, chives, Worcestershire, salt, and pepper; stir in turkey.
5. Pour into prepared casserole, cover, and bake for 40 minutes.
6. Remove cover, dot with butter, and bake uncovered 20 minutes.
7. Serve casserole hot. (It can be reheated.)

Accompaniment:

Snow-Pea Salad, or its variation made with sugar snap peas.

Variation:

Brown or white rice can be substituted for the bulgur.

Make-It-Easy Tips:

√ Casserole can be cooked, cooled, and frozen for future use.
√ Use an egg slicer to slice mushrooms quickly and easily.

ROCK CORNISH GAME HENS

Rock cornish game hens are easy to prepare and attractive to serve. They can be stuffed and roasted, braised, or split in half and broiled for a company or family meal. Cornish game hens are readily available frozen but, more recently, fresh ones, which are especially tasty, are appearing on the market.

Whole rock cornish game hens are a great help in Make-It-Easy cooking. Each of these 1-pound birds can be roasted and served without any time-consuming slicing or carving. That chore is left to the guests, except that you'll probably find everyone using his or her fingers!

Rock Cornish Game Hens Véronique

SERVES: 4
Preparation time: 15 minutes
Cooking time: 1 hour

The Ingredients:

4 Rock Cornish Hens, 1 pound or less each (if frozen, thoroughly thawed)
2 medium onions, quartered
1½ teaspoons dried tarragon, crumbled
¼ teaspoon paprika
½ teaspoon salt, or to taste
¼ teaspoon freshly ground pepper, or to taste
3–4 tablespoons unsalted butter, melted
2 cups dry white wine or dry vermouth
Salt and freshly ground pepper to taste
½ pound seedless grapes

The Steps:

1. Preheat oven to 350°
2. Place 2 quarters of onion in cavity of each hen.
3. Sprinkle hens with tarragon, paprika, salt, and pepper and brush with melted butter.
4. Place hens in roasting pan and bake for 20 minutes, basting with the pan juices.
5. Pour wine over hens and continue to cook for 20–30 minutes or until golden and tender, basting often.
6. Remove to a warm platter and discard onions.
7. Heat pan juices on top of the stove; reduce to thicken. Taste, and adjust seasoning with salt and pepper. Add grapes, pour sauce over the hens, and serve hot.

Accompaniments:

Rice Pilaf with Pine Nuts, and *Carrots and Parsnips Combined.*

Make-It-Easy Tips:

√ The onions are added for flavor, but can be eaten at family dinners, or reused to make stock.

√ Frozen hens should be thoroughly thawed overnight in the refrigerator or placed in a bowl of water at room temperature for several hours.

Braised Rock Cornish Game Hens

SERVES: 4
Preparation time: 15 minutes
Cooking time: 35–40 minutes

The Ingredients:

- 2 1-pound Rock Cornish Game Hens, split (if frozen, thoroughly thawed)
- ¼ cup flour seasoned with ½ teaspoon salt and ¼ teaspoon freshly ground pepper
- 2 tablespoons unsalted butter
- 2 tablespoons olive oil
- 1 large onion, finely chopped
- ¼ pound mushrooms, sliced
- ½ cup dry white wine
- ¼ cup chicken broth
- Garnish: Freshly chopped parsley

The Steps:

1. Dredge hens with seasoned flour; shake off excess.
2. In Dutch oven or large casserole, heat butter and oil together; sauté onions and mushrooms over medium heat until soft and golden, 5–7 minutes; remove with a slotted spoon.
3. Brown split hens on both sides in same pan over high heat until golden. Remove hens and set aside with vegetables.
4. Add wine to deglaze the pan, scraping the browned particles into the sauce; return hens, onions, and mushrooms, cover, and simmer slowly for 35–40 minutes or until tender.

5. Serve hens with sauce poured over tops; garnish with a sprinkling of freshly chopped parsley.

Accompaniments:

Lemon Rice, and a mixed green salad with *Green Goddess Salad Dressing.*

Variation:

Chicken parts can be substituted for the game hens.

Make-It-Easy Tips:

√ Hens can be prepared ahead, up to the point where you have deglazed the pan and returned the chicken and vegetables to it. Cool slightly and refrigerate. When ready to proceed with cooking, bring to room temperature and simmer for only 25–30 minutes or until tender.

√ Split the hens open by yourself with a heavy knife or cleaver or ask your friendly butcher to do this for you.

BEEF

After bringing beef home from the market, remove wrapping immediately, and dry meat with paper towls. Wrap loosely in waxed paper or foil before storing to avoid spoilage.

If possible, thaw all frozen meat in the refrigerator to prevent the loss of juices.

When purchasing tougher cuts of meat, try tenderizing them with slices of fresh papaya. The natural enzyme in unripe papaya, called *papain,* is the important ingredient in commercial meat tenderizers. By using fresh papaya you can obtain tender meat without the added salt, sugar, and chemicals that are in packaged tenderizers.

Chopped meat should be ground right before use. The butcher will usually be glad to grind the meat for you while you wait. That way you can be assured of freshness.

Perfect Medium-Rare Roast Beef

SERVES: 4–6
Preparation time: 10 minutes
Cooking time: Depends on size

Variations of this easy method of cooking beef have been suggested by many food authorities in the last few years. It can also be used for leg of lamb cooked to a perfect pink medium rare.

The Ingredients:

Rib roast, 1–2 ribs (brought to room temperature before cooking; this takes about 2 hours)
½ cup chili sauce
1 tablespoon Worcestershire sauce
½ teaspoon salt, or to taste
¼ teaspoon freshly ground pepper
1 tablespoon A-1 Sauce (optional)

The Steps:

1. Preheat oven to 500°.
2. Season roast with a mixture of chili sauce, Worcestershire, salt, pepper, and optional A-1 Sauce.
3. Place roast in pan fat-side up and roast in oven for 36 minutes (which is 18 minutes per rib; a three-rib roast would cook 54 minutes).
4. At the end of that time, turn oven off immediately and do *not* open the door of the oven. Leave the door closed for 2 hours. After that, the roast is done!

Accompaniments:

Tomato Pie, and *Caesar Salad.*

Variations:

Use leftover beef ribs for *Deviled Beef Bones* (*see* p. 124) and use the meat for sandwiches or stir-fry with vegetables Chinese-style.

For leg of lamb, cook for 15 minutes per pound for rare, 18 minutes for medium rare, and 22 minutes for well-done in a preheated 500° oven. Turn oven off and, without opening oven door, allow lamb to cook undisturbed for an additional 3 hours.

Make-It-Easy Tips:

√ The rib roast will keep for an hour after the prescribed 2 hours. To reheat, place in a preheated 200° oven for 10 minutes.

√ If you forget to remove roast from refrigerator beforehand, add 21 minutes to cooking time per rib.

Marinated Flank Steak

SERVES: 6–8
Preparation time: 15 minutes
Marinating time: 12–24 hours
Cooking time: To taste

The Ingredients:

1 cup vegetable oil
½ cup soy sauce
⅓ cup red wine vinegar
¼ cup lemon juice
3 tablespoons Worcestershire sauce
2 tablespoons Dijon mustard
1 teaspoon freshly ground pepper
1 large onion, sliced
1 clove garlic, minced
2 pounds flank steak (or use London broil or Tri-Tip*)

The Steps:

1. Combine oil, soy sauce, vinegar, lemon juice, Worcestershire, mustard, pepper, onion, and garlic in a bowl.
2. Place steak in a shallow dish or bowl, pour marinade over it, cover, and refrigerate. Marinate for 12–24 hours.
3. When ready to cook, preheat broiler or outdoor grill.

* For description of Tri-Tip, see the following recipe.

4. Remove meat from marinade and grill to desired doneness, basting occasionally.
5. Cut meat on the bias into thin slices, and serve hot.

Accompaniments:

Broad Noodles with Spinach, and *Raw Mushroom Salad.*

Make-It-Easy Tips:

√ Two jumbo plastic food-storage bags (not garbage bags) are excellent for marinating meat. Place meat and marinade in bag, tie up with twist tie, place in another bag, tie up again, and feel free to turn the bag at any time without messing up your hands or the refrigerator.

√ If broiling meat indoors, put one or two pieces of dried bread in bottom of pan. They will soak up excess fat and thus cut down on smoking or possible fires.

Broder's Triangle-Tip

SERVES: 4–6
Preparation time: 15–20 minutes
Cooking time: 30–45 minutes

Tri-Tip, sometimes referred to as bottom butt, is a thick, triangular, uneven piece of beef, similar in texture to flank steak. When cut on the bias, it turns into juicy, tender slices of steak. Use the Tri-Tip outdoors on the grill, indoors in the broiler, or braise it, as in the following recipe.

The Ingredients:

2 pounds Tri-Tip
4–6 tablespoons unsalted butter
1 medium onion, thinly sliced
1 green pepper, thinly sliced
8 medium mushrooms, sliced

2 cups red wine
2 tablespoons Worcestershire sauce
½ teaspoon freshly minced garlic
½ teaspoon salt, or to taste
¼ teaspoon freshly ground pepper
⅛ teaspoon dried oregano, crumbled
⅛ teaspoon dried basil, crumbled
⅛ teaspoon dried thyme, crumbled
Garnish: Toasted French bread, freshly chopped parsley

The Steps:

1. Heat Dutch oven or deep skillet; sear Tri-Tip, fat side down. Turn and brown on other side. Remove.
2. Add butter to pan, reduce heat and, when butter is melted, sauté onions and peppers until soft and translucent, about 8–10 minutes.
3. Add mushrooms, and continue to sauté for 4–5 minutes or until golden.
4. Add wine, Worcestershire, garlic, salt, pepper, and dried herbs and stir to combine.
5. Return Tri-Tip to pan, fat side down, bring liquid to a boil, cover, and simmer slowly for 30–45 minutes, depending on desired degree of doneness. Baste occasionally.
6. Remove meat from pan, slice, and serve over toasted, buttered French bread garnished with chopped parsley. Taste sauce, adjust seasoning, and pour over meat slices.

Accompaniments:

Italian Zucchini Bake, and a mixed green salad with *Laurie's Basic Vinaigrette* dressing.

Variation:

Tri-Tip is almost better the next day, sliced and served on toasted sourdough or rye bread.

Make-It-Easy Tip:

√ In the morning, when thawing meat for dinner, first wrap in plastic wrap and then in several sheets of newspaper. When you arrive home later in the day the meat will still be chilled instead of mushy and warm.

Brisket Like My Mother Makes

SERVES: 8
Preparation time: 15 minutes
Cooking time: 3–4 hours

Brisket is one of the best meats to use for potting. The first cut, also called a flat or thin cut, is less fatty and tends to be drier. It should be cooked a shorter time than the second cut, which is also called the front, point, or thick cut. The second cut is fattier, juicier, and less expensive.

The Ingredients:

- 3 tablespoons unsalted butter
- 2 large onions, coarsely chopped
- 2 carrots, peeled and coarsely chopped
- ½ teaspoon salt, or to taste
- ¼ teaspoon freshly ground pepper
- ¼ teaspoon freshly minced garlic
- ¼ teaspoon paprika
- 4–5 pound brisket
- ¾ cup dry red wine
- Salt and freshly ground pepper

The Steps:

1. Heat butter in Dutch oven or deep skillet; sauté onions and carrots over medium-low heat for 10–15 minutes, or until soft; remove vegetables with a slotted spoon.
2. Increase heat; rub salt and pepper, garlic, and paprika onto both sides of brisket, and sear on all sides.
3. Add wine to deglaze skillet, scraping up browned particles from bottom of pan. Return vegetables to pan; reduce heat to simmer, cover, and cook slowly for 3–4 hours or until fork tender, turning every hour.
4. Remove meat from gravy, cool slightly, and cut in thin slices.
5. Defat gravy and puree in a food processor, blender, or through a strainer or food mill until smooth; taste, adjust seasoning if necessary, and serve with sliced meat.

Accompaniments:

Barley Casserole, and *Spinach Salad.*

Variations:

Similar cuts of meat for potting can be substituted for brisket, such as chuck or rump roast.

Although my mother does not approve, I occasionally add ¼ cup chili sauce along with the wine.

Serve the brisket hot, or cold without gravy but with white horseradish or *Creamy Horseradish Sauce* (*see* Chapter 2). For those watching their caloric intake, serve it with strong mustard.

Make-It-Easy Tips:

√ Prepare the brisket 1–2 days ahead. When ready to serve, slice the cold meat (it's easy to slice when cold), pack the slices back together in heavy-duty foil, and heat the foil-wrapped meat for 10 minutes in a 325° oven. The cold gravy can be defatted easily and reheated.

√ If time is a problem, sauté the brisket and transfer it to a crock pot, which will continue to cook the meat unattended.

√ Store onions separately from potatoes. Onions release a gas that hastens the spoilage of potatoes.

Sweet and Sour Brisket

SERVES: 6
Preparation time: 20 minutes
Cooking time: 3 hours

This brisket is best prepared a day in advance and reheated, sliced, in the gravy.

The Ingredients:

4–5 pound first-cut brisket
½ teaspoon salt
¼ teaspoon freshly ground pepper
¼ teaspoon freshly minced garlic

¼ teaspoon paprika
1 tablespoon unsalted butter
1 tablespoon vegetable oil
1 large onion, finely chopped
1 8-ounce can tomato sauce
½ cup beef broth
½ cup water
6 ginger snap cookies, crushed

The Steps:

1. Season meat with salt, pepper, garlic, and paprika.
2. Heat butter and oil in large Dutch oven or casserole, brown meat over high heat on all sides.
3. Before last side is completely brown, add onions to bottom of pan and allow to soften as meat continues to brown.
4. Add tomato sauce, beef broth, and water. Cover, reduce heat to simmer, and cook slowly for 3 hours, turning every 45 minutes.
5. Remove meat and cool for 20 minutes before slicing.
6. Add crushed ginger snaps to gravy and heat through.
7. Serve brisket slices in warmed gravy.

Accompaniments:

Potatoes Boiled in Jackets, and *Carrot Puree in Artichoke Bottoms.*

Variation:

Second-cut brisket can be used but should be cooked slightly longer.

Make-It-Easy Tips:

√ Turn the meat with wooden spoons or tongs so as not to pierce it and thus lose precious juices.

√ Brisket is best prepared a day in advance and reheated in gravy.

Spicy Shish Kebab

SERVES: 4–6
Preparation time: 15 minutes
Cooking time: 15 minutes

This Spicy Shish Kebab has a Middle-Eastern flavor. The easiest way to cook shish kebab is to place the meat and vegetables on separate skewers. This way the meat cooks to desired doneness and the vegetables don't overcook and fall off.

The Ingredients:

2½ pounds boneless sirloin (or similar tender cut of beef)

Marinade:

Juice of 2 lemons
¼ cup olive oil
2 tablespoons grated onions
2 tablespoons chili powder
2 teaspoons curry powder
1 teaspoon ground coriander
1 teaspoon ground ginger
½ teaspoon salt, or to taste
1 clove garlic, minced

Skewer Vegetables:

2 tomatoes, quartered
Red or green pepper
Large mushroom caps
Garnish: Coriander or parsley sprigs

The Steps:

1. Combine all ingredients for marinade in large bowl. Add beef and marinate for *only* 2 hours at room temperature. (The marinade is very spicy, so timing is important.)
2. Remove meat from marinade and thread on skewer(s); thread vegetables on separate skewer(s).
3. Preheat broiler or outdoor grill.
4. Grill meat for 5–7 minutes a side for medium rare, and grill vegetables for 3–4 minutes a side.
5. Serve meat and vegetables together garnished with sprigs of coriander or parsley.

Accompaniments:

Apricot Rice, and *Cucumber Raita.*

Variation:

Boneless lamb can be substituted for beef.

Make-It-Easy Tip:

√ Onions are not included as a vegetable because they require parboiling and peeling which are tedious chores. If you have the time, by all means include onions with your vegetables.

Deviled Short Ribs

SERVES: 4
Preparation time: 15 minutes
Cooking time: 2 hours

These Beef Short Ribs are braised in a spicy chili-and-onion-flavored sauce.

The Ingredients:

1–2 tablespoons vegetable oil
3 pounds short ribs, cut into serving-size pieces
2 medium onions, chopped
½ cup chili sauce
½ cup beef broth
3 tablespoons cider vinegar
1½ tablespoons light brown sugar
1 teaspoon Dijon mustard
2 teaspoons Worcestershire sauce
1 clove garlic, minced
1 teaspoon dry mustard
1 teaspoon chili powder
1 teaspoon paprika
½ teaspoon salt, or to taste
¼ teaspoon freshly ground pepper

The Steps:

1. Preheat oven to 350°.
2. In large Dutch oven or deep casserole, heat oil; brown ribs all over; discard accumulated fat.
3. In large bowl, combine onion, chili sauce, broth, vinegar, sugar, Dijon mustard, Worcestershire, garlic, dry mustard, chili powder, paprika, salt, and pepper; pour over ribs, tossing to combine.
4. Cover and bake for 2 hours, removing the cover for the last ½ hour so meat will brown.
5. Taste, and adjust seasoning, if necessary. Serve ribs hot with sauce.

Accompaniments:

Southern-Style Cheese Grits, and *String Bean Salad.*

Make-It-Easy Tips:

√ Double the recipe and freeze in foil containers in family-size portions for future use.

√ To peel a clove of garlic easily, crush it lightly with the flat side of a cleaver or heavy knife and skin will separate.

Deviled Beef Bones (For Beef or Pork Ribs)

SERVES: 4–6
Preparation time: 15 minutes
Cooking time: 20 minutes

The Ingredients:

¼ cup (½ stick) unsalted butter, melted
2 tablespoons white vinegar
6 cooked beef ribs or 8–10 cooked pork ribs
1½ cups fine dry bread crumbs
water

Sauce:

½ cup mustard (¼ cup spicy brown plus ¼ cup Dijon)
3 tablespoons molasses

2 tablespoons white vinegar
3 tablespoons Worcestershire sauce
½ teaspoon Tabasco
½ teaspoon salt, or to taste
¼ teaspoon freshly ground pepper

The Steps:

1. Preheat broiler to hot. Line a broiling pan with foil.
2. In a small saucepan, melt butter with vinegar and dip bones in mixture to coat.
3. Then dip bones in crumbs coating all over, and place in prepared pan. Pour water into pan to a depth of ½ inch to prevent smoking.
4. Combine sauce ingredients together in bowl.
5. Broil bones for 5 minutes, 6″–8″ from heat; then begin basting with sauce, continuing to baste and broil for 20 minutes, or until golden brown.
6. Serve ribs hot or at room temperature.

Accompaniment:

Rice Salad Niçoise.

Variation:

Any combination of mustards can be used.

LAMB

Several years ago, all our lamb was cooked well done. It was greyish looking and often tough. Lately we have come to appreciate lamb cooked rare (slightly red), or medium rare (rosy pink)—lamb that is moist and flavorful, with an attractive appearance.

Although chops are still very popular, they are more expensive and fattier than leg of lamb. The leg can be roasted whole or cut into "lamb steaks," which are chops from the leg that are less expensive than loin or rib chops and much leaner. The leg can also be butterflied (deboned by the butcher), producing a piece of meat similar in shape to a thick steak. Butterflied lamb is particularly tasty when marinated and grilled outdoors.

When buying lamb, look for the tender young lamb that has pink meat versus the dark red meat of old lamb. Young lamb also has white fat versus the yellow fat of older lamb, and young lamb has redder bones versus the whiter, drier ones of older lamb.

Roast Leg of Lamb with Rosemary and Garlic

SERVES: 8
Preparation time: 10–15 minutes
Cooking time: 1½–1¾ hours

The flavor of fresh rosemary and garlic make this super-easy roast leg of lamb delicious.

The Ingredients:

- 1 5–6 pound leg of lamb, with fell (the tough outer skin) and most of fat removed
- 2 tablespoons lemon juice
- 1–2 tablespoons olive oil
- ½ teaspoon salt, or to taste
- ½ teaspoon freshly ground pepper, or to taste
- 2 cloves garlic, peeled and thinly sliced
- 6–8 sprigs fresh rosemary (if unavailable, use 1 teaspoon dried rosemary)

The Steps:

1. Preheat oven to 350°.
2. Wipe lamb with paper towels, rub with lemon juice, massage in olive oil, and sprinkle with salt and pepper.
3. Using tip of sharp knife, make slashes in flesh of lamb and insert slices of garlic and sprigs of rosemary.
4. Place lamb on an oiled rack in a roasting pan; insert a meat thermometer into meatiest part of leg, avoiding the bone. Place in oven for 1½–1¾ hours or until a meat thermometer registers 130°–135° for pink, medium-rare, lamb. (Remove the lamb from oven and allow to stand for 10 minutes at room temperature.) If you prefer lamb more well done, continue to cook to desired degree of doneness. However, I think lamb is at its best served pink. Try it once, you just might like it.

5. Remove garlic and rosemary sprigs, carve the lamb, and serve sliced.

Accompaniments:

Orzo with Mushrooms and Onions, and *Greek Salad.*

Make-It-Easy Tips:

√ If using dried rosemary, crumble the dried leaves between your fingers to release flavor and insert in the slits in the meat.

√ A rosemary herb plant can be grown indoors, adding a fresh scent to the kitchen.

√ Squeeze additional lemon juice to rub on your fingers to remove garlic smell.

Marinated Butterflied Leg of Lamb

SERVES: 6–8
Preparation time: 15 minutes
Marinating time: 24–48 hours
Cooking time: 30–40 minutes

There are many recipes for butterflied leg of lamb—lamb that has been boned and left open so that the meat resembles a steak. It may look jagged and lopsided but, after marinating and grilling, it provides incredibly tasty meat slices. This recipe is adapted from one by the late Michael Field, noted cooking teacher and cookbook author, who serves the lamb with a Greek avgolemono sauce (egg and lemon). I serve *Hot Avgolemono Soup* first, and then the lamb.

The Ingredients:

1 6–7 pound leg of lamb, butterflied, with fell (tough outer skin) removed

Marinade:

⅔ cup olive oil
3 tablespoons lemon juice
2 large onions, thinly sliced
2 cloves garlic, finely minced

2 tablespoons freshly chopped parsley
2 bay leaves, crushed
1 teaspoon dried oregano, crumbled
½ teaspoon salt, or to taste
½ teaspoon freshly ground pepper
Garnish: Sprigs of fresh mint or parsley

The Steps:

1. Place lamb in a plastic jumbo food storage bag. (Don't use garbage bags.) Combine marinade ingredients in large measuring cup, pour over lamb in the bag, tie up securely. Place in another bag and tie up. (The storage bag keeps marinade closely around meat and allows you to turn it easily.)
2. Marinate lamb for 24–48 hours, turning twice a day.
3. Preheat broiler or outdoor grill and bring lamb to room temperature.
4. Broil or grill lamb for 15–20 minutes a side, basting occasionally, or until medium rare (light pink).
5. Slice lamb on the bias and serve hot, garnished with sprigs of fresh mint or parsley.

Accompaniment:

Pasta al Pesto, and *Greek Salad.*

Variations:

Leftover medium-rare lamb can be used on sandwiches with spicy mustard, stir-fried with Chinese vegetables, or dipped in mustard and then bread crumbs and broiled until golden.

Make-It-Easy Tips:

√ The lamb can be marinated in a shallow, nonmetallic baking dish, if desired.

√ If pressed for time, marinate lamb for 12 hours. It will not be as tender or juicy, but still satisfactory. If dinner is put off, it can easily marinate for three days.

Lamb with Dill

SERVES: 8
Preparation time: 15 minutes
Cooking time: 3 hours, 18 minutes

Lamb with Dill is juicy, flavorful, and low in calories. The dill flavor comes from the seed, rather than the leaves of the dill plant. The lamb is cooked in a very hot oven for the first 18 minutes, and then the oven is turned off and the lamb cooks undisturbed for the remaining 3 hours.

The Ingredients:

1 5–6 pound leg of lamb, with fell (tough outer skin) and most of fat removed
1 large onion, thinly sliced
1 clove garlic, minced
½ teaspoon salt, or to taste
½ teaspoon freshly ground pepper
1 quart buttermilk
1 tablespoon dill seed
2 large onions, thinly sliced
8–10 small red or new potatoes, scrubbed but unpeeled
⅓ cup beef broth
⅓ cup red wine
Salt and pepper to taste

The Steps:

1. Place lamb in large deep bowl, and cover with 1 onion, garlic, salt, and pepper. Pour buttermilk over the lamb, sprinkle with dill seed, cover, and marinate in refrigerator for 2–3 days, turning twice a day, if possible.
2. When ready to cook, preheat oven to 500°.
3. Lay 2 sliced onions in bottom of roasting pan, remove lamb from marinade, draining off excess, and place on bed of onions and surround with potatoes.
4. Add broth and wine to pan, place in oven, and roast for 18 minutes.
5. Turn oven off immediately and allow lamb to stand undis-

turbed in oven for 3 hours *without* opening the door of the oven. (This amount of time will produce medium-rare lamb; for rare, cook only 15 minutes in hot oven and, for well done, cook 20 minutes.)

6. Strain gravy and remove excess fat. Taste, and adjust seasoning with salt and pepper. Serve alongside carved lamb with roasted potatoes and onions.

Accompaniment:

Perfect Baked Potatoes and, shredded cabbage with *Low-Calorie Buttermilk Dill Dressing.*

Variation:

Carrots and celery can be added to bed of onions when roasting lamb.

Make-It-Easy Tips:

√ When marinating lamb, it is easy to do tied up in 2 plastic jumbo food storage bags where the meat can conveniently be turned without messing up hands or utensils.

√ Once the lamb has been cooked at a high temperature for 18 minutes, the oven is turned off and you can forget about dinner until ready to serve. The lamb can sit an additional 1–2 hours after the prescribed 3 hours and then can be reheated for 10 minutes in a 325° oven.

Rack of Lamb with Fresh Mint Sauce

SERVES: 4–6
Preparation time: 15 minutes
Cooking time: 30–35 minutes

This is an expensive and elegant dinner dish that I reserve for very special occasions, serving the lamb with a refreshing mint sauce on the side. A rack is a section of rib or loin chops all in one piece—uncut.

The Ingredients:

2 racks of lamb (1¾–2 pounds each), well trimmed (rib or loin section)

Marinade:
- ¼ cup brandy
- ½ teaspoon dried thyme, crumbled
- ¼ teaspoon dried oregano, crumbled
- ¼ teaspoon dried basil, crumbled
- ½ teaspoon salt, or to taste
- ¼ teaspoon freshly ground pepper

Dip:
- ¼ cup flour
- 1 egg lightly beaten with 1 tablespoon milk or half-and-half
- 1 cup dry bread crumbs

Sauce:
- ½ cup olive oil
- ½ cup red wine vinegar
- 6–8 fresh mint leaves
- ½ teaspoon salt, or to taste
- ¼ teaspoon freshly ground pepper

The Steps:

1. Place lamb in shallow dish. Combine marinade ingredients and pour over lamb; cover and marinate at room temperature for 2–3 hours or in refrigerator overnight. Bring to room temperature before cooking.
2. Preheat oven to 450°.
3. Dip lamb in flour, shaking off excess, then dip in egg mixture and, finally, roll in bread crumbs, coating evenly.
4. Bake lamb, fat side up, for 30–35 minutes or until top is crusty and golden brown (meat will be medium rare).
5. While meat is cooking, combine ingredients for sauce in blender or food processor and process until just smooth but with the mint in chunky pieces.
6. Carve lamb into chops and serve hot, with sauce on the side.

Accompaniments:

Potatoes Boiled in Jackets, and *Tomatoes Filled with Peas.*

Variation:

If fresh mint is unavailable, use mint jelly as an accompaniment.

Make-It-Easy Tip:

√ Have butcher cut through bone connecting ribs so that chops can be easily cut after roasting.

Barbecued Lamb Riblets

SERVES: 4–6
Preparation time: 15 minutes
Cooking time: 1 hour

Lamb Riblets are "spareribs" from the breast of lamb. They are an inexpensive and juicy substitute for pork or beef spareribs.

The Ingredients:

3 pounds breast of lamb, well trimmed of fat
1 clove garlic, smashed

Sauce:

¾ cup ketchup
2 teaspoons Dijon mustard
½ teaspoon minced garlic
2 teaspoons Worcestershire sauce
½ teaspoon chili powder
2 tablespoons corn oil
2 tablespoons vinegar
1 tablespoon soy sauce
½ teaspoon salt, or to taste
¼ teaspoon freshly ground pepper

The Steps:

1. Preheat oven to 350°.
2. Rub lamb all over with garlic; place lamb, fat side up, in a roasting pan and bake for ½ hour.
3. Combine sauce ingredients in bowl and stir until smooth.
4. Turn lamb, brush lightly with sauce, and return to oven for 20 minutes.
5. Increase heat to broil, lavish on sauce, and broil, not too close to the heat source, until crisp and meat is tender, basting occasionally.
6. Slice lamb riblets into serving pieces and serve hot.

Accompaniments:

Sweet Potato Soufflé, and *Spinach Salad.*

Variations:

This recipe can be used for pork or beef ribs; adjust cooking times accordingly.

To remove excess grease, parboil lamb for 20 minutes, drain, and proceed with Step 3.

Make-It-Easy Tips:

√ Lamb can be cooked earlier in the day, wrapped in foil, refrigerated, and reheated in a low-temperature oven.

PORK

Pork is often neglected as a main course because it is thought to have a high calorie count. Actually, today's pork is much leaner and has almost the identical fat content and calorie count as beef.

Pork is easy to prepare, either as chops, roasted whole as a loin, or cooked as spareribs on the barbecue. When cooking pork roasts, rely on a meat thermometer to determine for health reasons whether it is fully cooked. The old recommended 185°F. temperature is no longer necessary, and the new leaner pork will be dried out if cooked that long. An internal temperature of 165°F. for lean loin roasts, or 170°F. for more marbled cuts of pork, should be sufficient.

Pork Chops with Mustard Dill Sauce

SERVES: 4–6
Preparation time: 20 minutes
Cooking time: 1 hour

The chops are coated with a creamy dill sauce to make a very elegant dinner entrée.

The Ingredients:

- 6 pork chops, cut 1″ thick
- 3–4 tablespoons Dijon mustard
- 2 tablespoons unsalted butter
- 1 large onion, thinly sliced

- 3 tablespoons all-purpose flour
- 1½ cups beef or chicken broth
- ¾ cup heavy cream
- 1 teaspoon freshly snipped dill or ⅓ teaspoon dried dill
- ½ teaspoon salt, or to taste
- ½ teaspoon freshly ground white pepper
- Garnish: Freshly snipped dill or chopped parsley

The Steps:

1. Lay chops on sheet of waxed paper and brush 1 side generously with Dijon mustard.
2. Melt butter in a large heavy skillet; add chops, mustard side down, and cook over medium-high heat until lightly browned; brush top side with mustard, turn the chops, and brown on the other side; remove the chops from skillet with slotted spatula.
3. Add onions to pan and cook over medium heat until golden brown, about 5 minutes. (It may be necessary to add a tablespoon of butter if no fat remains in the skillet.)
4. Remove skillet from direct heat and add flour, stirring well to combine.
5. Add broth, and return to heat, stirring constantly; when boiling, add cream.
6. Add dill, salt, and pepper; return chops to pan, cover, reduce heat, and simmer slowly for 50–60 minutes or until tender. Turn once during cooking.
7. Taste, and adjust seasoning if necessary. Serve chops hot, with sauce poured over them.

Accompaniments:

Baked Potato Skins, and *Raw Mushroom Salad.*

Variations:

Veal chops can be substituted for pork chops but should be cooked only 20 minutes or until just tender.

Make-It-Easy Tip:

√ Dried dill can be substituted, but fresh is better. To ensure having fresh dill year 'round, chop large bunches when available and freeze in small plastic bags or containers.

Sweet & Sour Pork Chops

SERVES: 4–6
Preparation time: 20 minutes
Cooking time: 45 minutes

This is an easy pork chop recipe that can be assembled a day ahead and reheated.

The Ingredients:

- ¼ cup all-purpose flour
- ½ teaspoon salt, or to taste
- ½ teaspoon freshly ground pepper
- ½ teaspoon ground ginger
- 6 pork chops, cut 1″ thick, trimmed of fat
- 1 tablespoon unsalted butter
- 1 tablespoon vegetable oil
- 1 small onion, finely chopped
- 1 clove garlic, finely minced
- ½ cup hot beef broth
- ¼ cup chili sauce
- 3 tablespoons cider vinegar
- 1½ tablespoons light brown sugar
- Garnish: Freshly chopped parsley

The Steps:

1. Combine flour, salt, pepper, and ginger; dip chops in flour mixture, shaking off any excess.
2. In large Dutch oven or deep skillet, heat butter and oil together and brown chops on both sides over high heat.
3. Add onions and garlic and cook over medium heat until they are soft, about 5 minutes.
4. Pour off excess accumulated fat in skillet; add beef broth, chili sauce, cider vinegar, and brown sugar. Stir to combine, bring to a boil, cover, and simmer slowly for 45 minutes or until chops are tender. (It may be necessary to add additional beef broth. Check the liquid level periodically and add broth when necessary.)
5. Taste, and adjust seasoning as necessary. Serve chops hot, garnished with freshly chopped parsley.

Accompaniments:

Green Rice, and a mixed green salad with *Laurie's Basic Vinaigrette* dressing.

Variations:

Sweet & Sour Pork Chops can be baked, covered, in a 375° oven for 45 minutes instead of cooking on top of range.

½ teaspoon freshly grated ginger can be substituted for dried ginger.

Make-It-Easy Tips:

√ The chops can be cooked earlier in the day, and then refrigerated or frozen.

√ Garlic should be cooked only until golden. When browned or burned, it develops a bitter and unpleasant taste.

Pork Loin Polynesian

SERVES: 6
Preparation time: 15 minutes
Cooking time: 1½–2 hours

The Ingredients:

Half a loin of pork (3–4 pounds), boned, and tied securely
½ teaspoon salt
¼ teaspoon freshly ground pepper
¼ teaspoon ground rosemary
Sauce:
¼ cup soy sauce
¼ cup ketchup
2 tablespoons honey
1 large clove garlic, finely minced
¼ teaspoon powdered ginger
Garnish: Preserved kumquats and sprigs of watercress

The Steps:

1. Preheat oven to 350°.

2. Place pork on rack in shallow roasting pan and sprinkle with salt, pepper, and rosemary and roast for 20 minutes.
3. Combine sauce ingredients in bowl and mix together; baste the pork loin frequently with mixture to give it a caramel glaze; cook for an additional 1½ hours or until a thermometer registers 160°F.
4. Transfer pork to a platter and allow to stand for 10 minutes; this will increase the temperature to 165°F. Serve sliced, garnished with preserved kumquats and sprigs of watercress.

Accompaniments:

Baked Spinach with Cheese, and *Curried Brown Rice Salad with Fruit.*

Variations:

Leftover pork can be shredded in an *Oriental Salad* (*see* Chapter 7, Braised Daikon, Variations) with vegetables.

The glaze is also wonderful on roast leg of lamb.

Freshly ground ginger (½ teaspoon) can be substituted for powdered ginger.

Make-It-Easy Tips:

√ The easiest way to grind rosemary is with a mortar and pestle. If unavailable, wrap the rosemary leaves in waxed paper and crush with a rolling pin.

√ To prevent sticking, oil the rack with a brush before roasting pork.

√ When measuring sticky liquids, such as honey, syrup, or molasses, lightly oil the inside of the measuring cup before using and easily rinse out with very hot water after measuring.

Potted Pork with Fruit

SERVES: 4–6
Preparation time: 20 minutes
Cooking time: 1½ hours

As discussed in the recipe for *Whole Chicken Cooked in a Clay Pot*, the wet terra-cotta clay keeps natural cooking juices in, the food is self-basted, fats are kept to a minimum, and a one-pot, no-fuss dinner is created.

The Ingredients:

1 Ovenbrique, Romertopf, Gourmetopf or similar brand unglazed terra-cotta pot
1 loin of pork (3½ pounds) well trimmed of fat, with bones cracked for easy carving
1 clove garlic, crushed but still intact
1 teaspoon salt, or to taste
½ teaspoon freshly ground pepper
¼ teaspoon freshly grated ginger
1 large onion, thinly sliced
2 large carrots, peeled and thinly sliced
¾–1 cup port wine
12 pitted prunes
3 ounces dried apples (soaked in boiling water, optional step)
¼ cup heavy cream

The Steps:

1. Presoak a clay pot, top and bottom, in water for 20 minutes.
2. While the pot is soaking, rub the trimmed loin of pork well with garlic. Sprinkle both sides with salt, pepper, and ginger.
3. Place onion in bottom of pot. Add pork, fat side up, and surround with carrots. Pour wine around meat and vegetables and insert a meat thermometer into thickest part of the meat.
4. Cover with the presoaked top and place in a *cold* oven. (Clay pots will crack from the sudden heat of a preheated oven.) Set oven to 475° and cook pork for 1 hour.
5. After 1 hour of cooking time, remove pot from oven and distribute prunes and apples around meat. Re-cover pot and continue to cook for an additional ½ hour or until meat thermometer registers done.
6. Remove meat and vegetables to a platter, and keep warm. Skim fat from gravy (or use device to remove fat) and place defatted gravy in small saucepan. Add cream, and stir until slightly thickened. Serve sauce with pork, vegetables, and fruit.

Accompaniments:

Plain Brown Rice, and a mixed green salad with *Laurie's Basic Vinaigrette* dressing.

Variations:

A boneless loin of pork may be substituted for the loin with ribs attached.

Additional dried fruits, such as peaches or apricots, can be added.

Make-It-Easy Tips:

√ A small amount of ginger can be grated easily by using the smallest holes of a kitchen grater or a small lemon- or nutmeg-grater.

√ Use a Gravy Strain or similar brand of fat-straining pitcher to remove fat. It is a pitcher with the spout based at the bottom. The gravy is poured in, the fat rises quickly to the top, the gravy is poured off from the bottom, and the fat remains in the pitcher.

Special Spareribs

SERVES: 6
Preparation time: 15 minutes
Cooking time: 1½ hours

The Ingredients:

4 pounds small, meaty, pork spareribs

Basting Glaze:

¼ cup Bourbon
¼ cup soy sauce
¼ cup brown sugar
¼ cup orange juice
1 tablespoon Dijon mustard
1 tablespoon vinegar
¼ teaspoon minced garlic

The Steps:

1. Preheat oven to 350°.
2. Place spareribs in foil-lined roasting pan (to save on clean-ups) and bake, fat side up, for 15 minutes; turn and bake an additional 15 minutes; pour off accumulated fat.
3. Meanwhile, combine glaze ingredients in saucepan; cook over low heat, stirring constantly, until smooth.

4. Generously glaze ribs with sauce and return to oven for ½ hour, basting after 15 minutes; turn and lavish remaining sauce on ribs and bake for 30 minutes longer or until glazed and golden.
5. Glaze once again, and serve spareribs hot.

Accompaniments:

Southern-Style Cheese Grits, and sliced tomatoes with *Spinach Mayonnaise.*

Variations:

Beef ribs can be substituted for pork ribs.

Make-It-Easy Tips:

√ Store brown sugar in a sealed container in the refrigerator to prevent caking.

√ Use a thick brush to baste ribs.

Make-It-Easy Ham

SERVES: 6–8
Preparation time: 10 minutes
Cooking time: 1 hour

The recipe for this ham comes from a friend in the South who insists that the real secret is the Coca Cola. I've tried ginger ale, diet colas and even Dr. Pepper with success, proving that the secret is in the bubbles.

The Ingredients:

1 3–pound ham
¼ cup Dijon mustard
6–8 whole cloves
⅓ cup apricot preserves, orange marmalade, or peach preserves
¼ cup maple syrup
1 cup red wine
⅓ cup cola drink

2 tablespoons cider vinegar
Garnish: *Mustard Mayonnaise* (*see* Chapter 8)

The Steps:

1. Preheat oven to 350°. Line baking pan with foil.
2. Place ham in pan, fat side up; coat with mustard and stud with cloves.
3. Mix preserves and syrup together and spread on ham.
4. Combine wine, cola, and vinegar; pour over ham, and bake ham for 1 hour, basting every 15 minutes.
5. Remove ham from oven, allow to rest 15 minutes, and serve with *Mustard Mayonnaise.*

Accompaniments:

Baked Acorn Squash, and *Cabbage Salad with Caraway Seeds.*

Variations:

Ham can be served as a luncheon entrée with *Spinach Quiche* or *Frittata* (*see* Chapter 3).

Leftover ham can be stir-fried with Chinese vegetables or used as a base for pâtés or simply in sandwiches with *Mustard Mayonnaise.*

Make-It-Easy Tips:

√ Make sure to line the pan with foil because the glaze on the ham will stick forever to your pan.

√ When purchasing a canned ham, select only a refrigerated one. Hams must be refrigerated at all times, although some supermarkets ignore this fact.

VEAL

Veal is a wonderful and versatile meat. It is easy to prepare either sautéed as scaloppine, or braised in stews; it is also delicious as a roast. Veal adapts itself to a wide variety of sauces. Of all the meats, it is the lowest in both calories and cholesterol.

The only drawback is that veal is very expensive. Scaloppine has become a luxury dinner. However, a pound of veal can serve four people. Veal stews are much less expensive than scaloppine and veal provides a lighter flavor than beef. Ground veal is even less expensive and can be used for meat loaves, meatballs, or even burger patties.

Wiener Schnitzel à la Luchow

SERVES: 4
Preparation time: 15 minutes
Cooking time: 10 minutes

This recipe is an easy variation of the Wiener Schnitzel served at the famous New York restaurant, Luchow's. The traditional topping for Schnitzel à la Holstein is a fried egg and anchovy fillets. Luchow's uses scrambled eggs and asparagus.

The Ingredients:

3 tablespoons unsalted butter
4 8-ounce veal cutlets, pounded thin and wiped dry
1 cup beef broth
6 eggs
1 tablespoon chopped chives (or finely minced scallion greens)
½ teaspoon salt, or to taste
½ teaspoon freshly ground pepper, or to taste
2 tablespoons unsalted butter
10 medium-size mushrooms, sliced
Garnish: Hot cooked asparagus, 16 stalks (optional)

The Steps:

1. In a large skillet, heat 3 tablespoons butter; brown veal over high heat for only a minute on each side. (Do not overcook.) Remove to a warm platter.
2. To make gravy, add broth to pan, scraping up browned particles from the bottom; taste for seasoning and adjust.
3. In small bowl, beat eggs with chives, salt, and pepper.
4. In another skillet, heat 2 tablespoons butter and sauté mushrooms for 4–5 minutes until golden.
5. Add egg mixture to mushrooms and cook over moderate heat, scrambling the eggs until just soft but not overcooked.
6. Pour the eggs over the browned cutlets and top with the broth gravy.
7. Garnish platter with asparagus and serve immediately, good and hot.

Accompaniment:

Potatoes boiled in Jackets.

Variations:

Boned and skinned chicken breasts or pork tenderloins can be used for a less expensive version, but they must be cooked longer.

Make-It-Easy Tip:

√ Wiener Schnitzel a la Luchow must be prepared at the last minute.

Veal and Water Chestnuts

SERVES: 6
Preparation time: 25 minutes
Cooking time: 1⅓ hours

Veal and Water Chestnuts is a very rich and creamy entrée to be served over plain white rice with only a simple green salad.

The Ingredients:

4 tablespoons (½ stick) unsalted butter
2 pounds boneless veal, cut into 1″ cubes
1 pound mushrooms, sliced
1 medium onion, finely chopped
1 clove garlic, finely minced
¼ cup dry white wine
1 cup beef broth
2 8-ounce cans sliced water chestnuts, drained
½ teaspoon salt, or to taste
¼ teaspoon freshly ground pepper
Pinch of nutmeg
Pinch of cayenne
1 cup heavy cream
Garnish: Freshly chopped parsley

The Steps:

1. Preheat oven to 375°.
2. Melt butter in a Dutch oven or large, deep skillet; brown veal on all sides over high heat; remove with slotted spoon.
3. Add the mushrooms, onion, and garlic, and sauté over medium heat until golden.
4. Add wine to deglaze pan, scraping browned particles from bottom of pan.
5. Return veal to pan; add broth, water chestnuts, salt, pepper, nutmeg, and cayenne. Bring to boil; cover, and place in oven for 1¼ hours or until tender.
6. Stir in cream and continue to cook, uncovered, for 20 minutes longer.
7. Taste, adjust seasoning if necessary, and serve hot, garnished with freshly chopped parsley.

Accompaniments:

White rice, and tossed green salad with *Laurie's Basic Vinaigrette* dressing.

Variations:

Whole or quartered water chestnuts can be substituted for sliced.
Beef can be substituted for the veal.

Make-It-Easy Tips:

√ This dish can be prepared a day or two in advance, or even frozen and reheated before serving.

Ragoût de Veau (Casserole of Veal)

SERVES: 6–8
Preparation time: 20 minutes
Cooking time: 1½ hours

The Ingredients:

2 tablespoons unsalted butter
1 cup thinly sliced onions
1 clove garlic, minced
⅓ cup all-purpose flour

½ teaspoon salt, or to taste
½ teaspoon freshly ground pepper, or to taste
¼ teaspoon paprika
3 pounds boneless veal (veal stew meat), cut into 1½″–2″ cubes
2 tablespoons unsalted butter
1 tablespoon olive oil
½ cup port, Marsala, or other sweet red wine
1 16-ounce can tomatoes, drained and roughly chopped
½ cup chicken broth
½ teaspoon thyme, crumbled
18 pitted olives, 9 black, 9 green (or use only black olives)
Salt and freshly ground pepper to taste
Garnish: Freshly chopped parsley

The Steps:

1. Preheat oven to 325°.
2. In Dutch oven or large casserole, heat butter; sauté onions and garlic over medium heat until soft and lightly golden; remove to a bowl and set aside.
3. Combine flour, salt, pepper, and paprika; add veal cubes and toss to coat all over.
4. Add remaining butter and oil to casserole; sauté veal over medium/high heat until golden.
5. Add wine to deglaze pan, scraping brown particles up from bottom; add tomatoes, broth, and thyme. Bring to boil, cover, and bake for 1½ hours or until veal is tender.
6. Add olives, cover, and continue to bake for 10 minutes longer to heat through.
7. Taste, and adjust seasoning with salt and pepper. Serve garnished with freshly chopped parsley.

Accompaniments:

White rice, and Salad of Asparagus Tips with Mustard Dressing

Variation:

Beef can be substituted for the veal.

Make-It-Easy Tips:

√ This Ragout can be prepared up through Step 5 and refrigerated for 2–3 days, or frozen for several months.

√ To avoid tears when slicing onions, place onion in freezer for 20 minutes prior to slicing.

MEAT LOAVES

The announcement of "meat loaf tonight" is generally not going to bring down the house. As a matter of fact, it might bring down the spirits of the diners if it's of the all too common variety—heavy, mealy, a real loser. The following easy recipes, however, are guaranteed to clear meat loaf's bad name forever!

When buying meat for a meat loaf, ask your butcher (whenever possible) to grind the various meats together. If he can't, do so yourself in a meat grinder or food processor—you'll taste the difference!

Meat loaf is an economical, easy to prepare meal for family or company. Take a test run on your family. You'll see how easy it is to make and how great it is the next day as leftovers!

For variety, bake the meat loaf in muffin tins or mini-loaf pans for individual loaves. Remember that the smaller loaves take only one-half to three-quarters of the time to bake.

Fluffy Light Meat Loaf

SERVES: 3–4

Preparation time: 15 minutes
Cooking time: 50 minutes–1 hour

Fluffy Light Meat Loaf is light in texture and yet high in fiber. If time permits, prepare it in the morning, cover, and allow the flavors to mellow until ready to cook.

The Ingredients:

- 1 pound ground beef
- 1 6-ounce can tomato paste
- ½ cup oatmeal
- 3 tablespoons finely chopped green pepper or celery
- 2 tablespoons bran
- 2 tablespoons wheat germ
- 1 small onion, finely chopped
- 1 tablespoon freshly chopped parsley
- 1 egg, lightly beaten
- ¼ teaspoon finely chopped garlic

½ teaspoon salt, or to taste
¼ teaspoon freshly ground pepper
Chili sauce

The Steps:

1. Preheat oven to 350°.
2. Combine all loaf ingredients, using your hands.
3. Form into loaf and place in a 9″ x 5″ x 3″ loaf pan, cover with a layer of chili sauce (or ketchup if desired), and bake for 50 minutes to 1 hour. (Do not overbake since part of the secret of fluffiness is shorter cooking time.)
4. Serve the meat loaf sliced and hot.

Accompaniments:

Perfect Baked Potatoes, and *Broccoli Florets Vinaigrette.*

Variations:

Half ground veal and half ground beef can be used for a meat loaf lower in calories.

Leftover cold meat loaf is a favorite lunch sandwich with ketchup on dark rye bread.

Make-It-Easy Tips:

√ Chop the onion, garlic, parsley, and green pepper or celery together in food processor.

√ A new gadget called a "fat-free meat loaf pan" is currently available. It consists of two pans, one fitting inside the other. The inner pan has holes in it to allow fat to drip off into the other pan. *See* Appendix A.

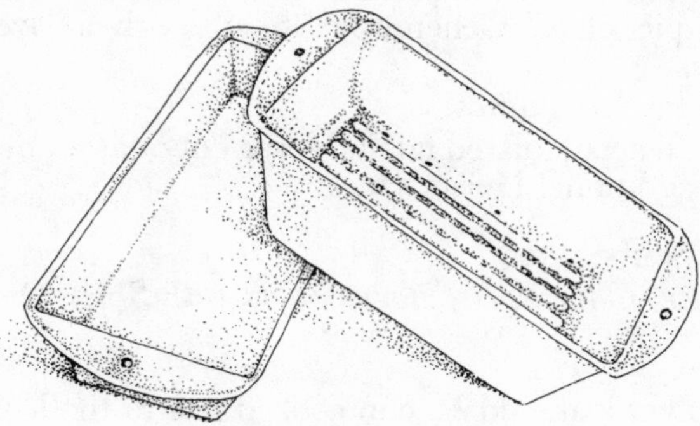

Low-fat meat loaf pan

Chinese Ground Beef Loaf

SERVES: 6
Preparation time: 15 minutes
Cooking time: 45 minutes

This oriental-flavored loaf can be served as a main course or chilled and served as a pâté.

The Ingredients:

1 pound ground beef
1 tablespoon peanut oil
1 tablespoon oriental sesame oil
¼ teaspoon sugar
2 tablespoons soy sauce
1 tablespoon dry sherry
2 scallions (white and green included), finely minced
¼ teaspoon minced garlic
2 eggs, lightly beaten
½–¾ cup Hoisin sauce (available at oriental grocery stores and by mail order, *see* Appendix A)

The Steps:

1. Preheat oven to 350°. Lightly oil, or spray with non-aerosol vegetable shortening, an 8″ x 4″ x 2″ loaf pan or glass pie plate.
2. Combine all ingredients, except Hoisin sauce, using hands or pulsating in a food processor.
3. Form into a loaf and place in pan, or into a circular mound in glass pie plate. Generously "frost" with a layer of Hoisin sauce.
4. Bake for 45 minutes.
5. Discard accumulated fat and serve hot or at room temperature with additional Hoisin sauce.

Accompaniments:

Fried Rice, Chinese Asparagus Salad with Spicy Dressing.

Variations:

For a fluffier loaf, add ½ cup cooked rice to the loaf.

Pork can be substituted for the beef. If using pork, increase cooking time to 1 hour, and decrease the amount of oil since ground pork often has a higher fat content.

Serve the loaf cold the next day as a pâté or in a Pita bread sandwich with additional Hoisin sauce.

Make-It-Easy Tip:

√ Prepare the Chinese Beef Loaf in muffin tins, cook only 30–40 minutes, and serve as a first course.

FISH AND SEAFOOD

Fish is adaptable to almost any form of cooking. It can be grilled, sautéed, pan-fried, baked, braised or even stir-fried in a matter of minutes for a quick and easy entrée.

When buying fish for a particular recipe note the length of cooking time. Thicker, fleshy fish, such as haddock, halibut, or bass, are more adaptable to baking or broiling, and thin fillets of flounder or sole are best suited for sautéing.

Try to buy fish or seafood at a fish store rather than at a supermarket. You can be a little more certain of freshness. Get to know the people who sell at your fish market since they can advise you on the freshest local fish to buy. They will also provide information about the ideal seasons for shrimp, clams, mussels, scallops, or other seafood, thus reducing your costs.

Freshness is of the utmost importance when purchasing fish. Use odor as the main criterion. If there is an unpleasant or "fishy" smell, the fish is not fresh. Whole fish should have bright and clear bulging eyes. The flesh should be firm and resilient to the touch, and the gills should be reddish and intact. Freezing masks most of these criteria so, if possible, buy fresh fish. If you freeze fresh fish yourself, thaw well wrapped for 12–24 hours in the refrigerator.

Fish is low in calories and low in cholesterol, a perfect dietetic main course. It can be grilled with fresh lemon juice and herbs for a simple, easy entrée to please family and friends, who all seem to be conscious of burgeoning waistlines. For another low-calorie variation, try cooking fish *en papillote* (wrapped in parchment paper), to steam in fresh juices and flavor, avoiding the often dried-out taste of many low-calorie fish recipes.

Baked Whole Salmon

SERVES: 6
Preparation time: 15 minutes
Cooking time: 45–60 minutes
Chilling time: 4–6 hours or overnight

This Make-It-Easy recipe enables you to cook a whole salmon when you don't own a large poacher and you wish to avoid tying up the fish in cheesecloth. The salmon is baked in foil, steaming in flavor and juices.

The Ingredients:

- 1 whole salmon, 6–7 pounds, cleaned and scaled
- 2 large lemons, thinly sliced
- 1 medium onion, thinly sliced
- ½ cup dry white wine or dry vermouth
- 2 tablespoons freshly chopped parsley
- ½ teaspoon freshly ground pepper

Garnish: Watercress, lemon wedges, and *Cucumber Dill Sauce* or *Spinach Mayonnaise*

The Steps:

1. Preheat oven to 350°.
2. Place salmon on large sheet of *heavy-duty* foil.
3. Layer lemon and onion slices over fish; add wine, sprinkle with parsley and pepper. Seal well.
4. Bake for 45–60 minutes or until fish is flaky and tender.
5. Remove from oven, open foil package, arrange salmon on platter, cover, and chill for 4–6 hours or overnight.
6. Serve salmon chilled, garnished with watercress and lemon wedges and *Cucumber Dill Sauce* or *Spinach Mayonnaise.*

Accompaniments:

Rice Salad Niçoise, and *Broccoli Florets Vinaigrette.*

Variations:

Poached fish is low in calories but the *Cucumber Dill Sauce* or *Spinach Mayonnaise* is not. If concerned about calories, substitute *Yogurt Dill Sauce* or Cucumber Dressing and serve the salmon with tomatoes with *Spicy Tomato Dressing with No Oil.*

Additional fresh herbs such as dill or chives can be added to the salmon before baking.

Salmon can also be served hot with a hollandaise sauce or sprinkled with melted butter.

Leftover salmon makes a wonderful salad with mayonnaise, herbs, and lemon juice.

Make-It-Easy Tip:

√ To transfer salmon easily from foil package to platter, roll carefully, gently pulling the foil away.

Haddock "Blacksmith Shop"

SERVES: 4
Preparation time: 15 minutes
Cooking time: 20 minutes

This recipe comes from The Blacksmith Shop, a restaurant on Cape Cod.

The Ingredients:

2 tablespoons Dijon mustard
2 tablespoons lemon juice
2 teaspoons Worcestershire sauce
2 pounds haddock or similar filleted fish such as scrod
1 large onion, thinly sliced
1½ pints dairy sour cream
Garnish: Watercress sprigs, lemon slices

The Steps:

1. Preheat oven to 400°.
2. Combine mustard, lemon juice, Worcestershire, and spread completely over fish in a baking dish.
3. Cover with onion and top with a thick blanket of sour cream.

4. Bake for 20 minutes or until fish is flaky and top is golden at edges.
5. Serve hot, garnished with sprigs of watercress and lemon slices.

Accompaniments:
Lemon Rice, and *String Bean Salad.*

Make-It-Easy Tips:
√ The fish can be prepared earlier in the day by marinating in refrigerator in mustard, Worcestershire, and lemon juice.
√ To avoid "fishy" smells while cooking, boil a separate pot of water with 3 or 4 whole cloves for a pleasant aroma.

Marinated Grilled Swordfish Steaks

SERVES: 4
Preparation time: 10 minutes
Cooking time: 14–18 minutes

The Ingredients:
4 swordfish steaks
2 tablespoons unsalted butter, melted
2 tablespoons olive oil
¼ teaspoon salt, or to taste
¼ teaspoon freshly ground white pepper
Pinch of paprika

Sauce:
2 tablespoons olive oil
1 tablespoon lemon juice
2 teaspoons freshly chopped parsley
¼ teaspoon finely minced garlic

The Steps:
1. Place fish in dish. Combine butter and oil and pour over fish; sprinkle with salt, pepper, and paprika and allow to marinate for ½ hour at room temperature, turning once or twice.
2. Preheat broiler or outdoor grill.

3. Broil fish for 6–9 minutes per side or until just flaky, basting occasionally. (Do not overcook or the fish will dry out.)
4. While fish is broiling, combine sauce ingredients in bowl.
5. Place fish on platter, pour a little sauce over each piece, and serve immediately.

Accompaniments:

August Pasta, and *Caesar Salad.*

Variations:

Other firm fleshy fish or fish steaks such as halibut or salmon can be substituted.

Mash leftover fish with mayonnaise, a little lemon juice, chives or scallions, and seasoning to use as a fish salad the next day.

Make-It-Easy Tip:

√ If cooking outdoors, it is easier to turn fish if it is placed in a flat-grid hamburger or hot dog grill.

Herb Broiled Fish Fillets

SERVES: 4
Preparation time: 10–15 minutes
Cooking time: 8–10 minutes

It is not necessary to use the specific herbs I have listed in the ingredients. Select one herb, or make up a combination of fresh herbs that you prefer equal to one tablespoon.

The Ingredients:

½ cup mayonnaise
1 tablespoon lemon juice
1 teaspoon freshly snipped dill
1 teaspoon freshly chopped chives (or scallion stalks)
1 teaspoon freshly chopped parsley
½ teaspoon salt, or to taste
¼ teaspoon freshly ground pepper

2 pounds fish fillets or fish sticks (e.g., flounder, halibut, haddock, bass, red snapper, swordfish)
Garnish: Freshly grated lemon peel

The Steps:

1. Preheat broiler.
2. Combine mayonnaise, lemon juice, and herbs and mix until smooth.
3. Sprinkle salt and pepper over both sides of fish and place on broiling pan.
4. Spread ½ mayonnaise-herb mixture on fish and broil for 3–5 minutes a side, depending on thickness of fish.
5. Turn fish, spread on remaining mayonnaise-herb mixture, and continue to broil until fish is flaky.
6. Serve fish hot, garnished with freshly grated lemon peel.

Accompaniments:

Stir-Fried Straw and Hay Summer Squash, and crusty French bread.

Variation:

Leftover Tip: Any remaining fish can be eaten cold as a fish salad the next day.

Make-It-Easy Tips:

√ Chop fresh herbs in food processor or blender and keep extra fresh herbs frozen in small containers or plastic bags.

√ If using dried herbs, remember that 1 teaspoon of dried herbs = 1 tablespoon of fresh herbs.

Fish with Butter and Capers en Papillote

SERVES: 2
Preparation time: 15 minutes
Cooking time: 10–15 minutes

Cooking in parchment paper (available at cookware shops and department stores) steams in flavors and keeps very thin fish from drying out while baking.

The Ingredients:

- 2 pieces of parchment paper (about 18″ in length)
- 2 fish fillets, ½ pound each (e.g., sole, flounder, snapper, or sand dabs)
- 2 tablespoons unsalted butter, melted
- 2 teaspoons fresh lemon juice
- 2 tablespoons capers
- 1 tablespoon freshly chopped parsley
- ½ teaspoon salt, or to taste
- ¼ teaspoon freshly ground pepper
- 1 lemon, thinly sliced

Garnish: Lemon slices, freshly chopped parsley, capers

The Steps:

1. Preheat oven to 350°.
2. Prepare parchment and fish according to instructions in the figures.
3. Brush fish with a little melted butter, and then drizzle a teaspoon of lemon juice on each. Distribute capers and parsley evenly over fish and season with salt and pepper.
4. Finally, place a few thin slices of lemon on each portion. Fold paper over and seal by crimping edges all around (see figure).
5. Place packet on a baking sheet and bake for 10–15 minutes or until fish is tender and flaky. (Timing depends on thickness of the fish.)
6. Serve fish garnished with additional lemon slices, chopped parsley, and capers.

Accompaniments:

Rice Pilaf with Pine Nuts, and *Snow Pea Salad.*

Variations:

For a low-calorie steamed fish, omit butter and garnish with lots of lemon juice and some grated lemon rind.

For another low-calorie version, top 2 pounds fish fillets with one 10-ounce package frozen chopped spinach, 4 mushrooms sliced, 2 tablespoons lemon juice, 2 scallion stalks, salt and pepper to taste, and a sliced lemon, and proceed as above.

Make-It-Easy Tips:

√ Lemons will yield more juice if they are at room temperature when squeezed.

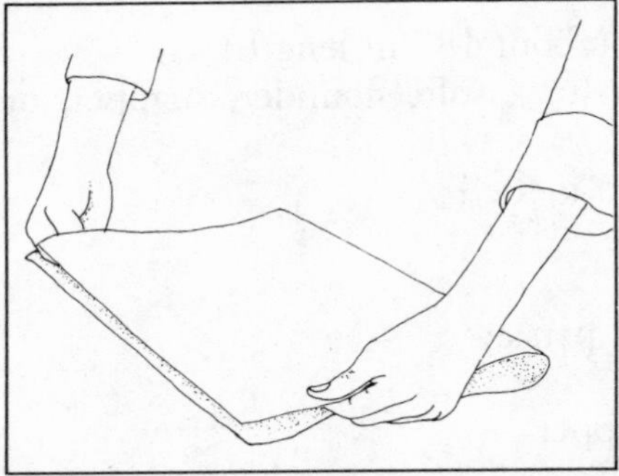

1. To cook en papillote, cut a large rectangular piece of parchment paper. Fold the rectangle in half.

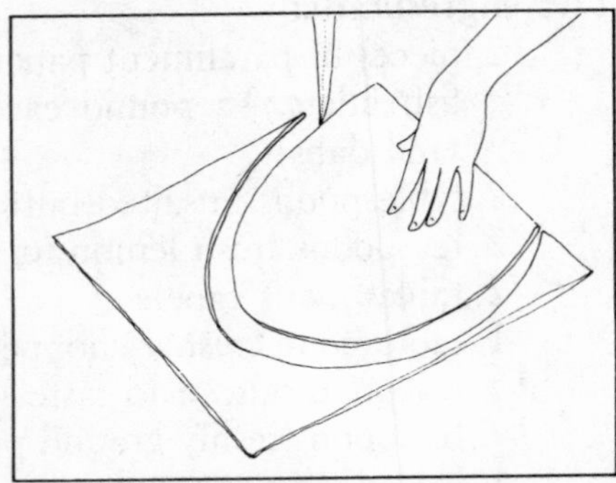

2. Using scissors or a knife, start cutting from the folded side, following an imaginary line that resembles a heart.

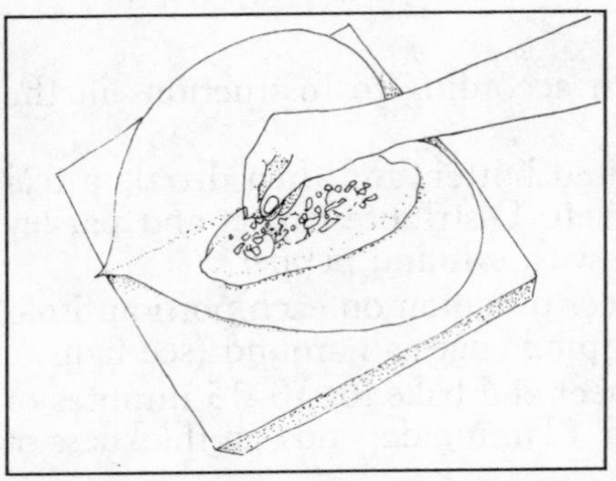

3. Place the fish fillet on top and add seasonings.

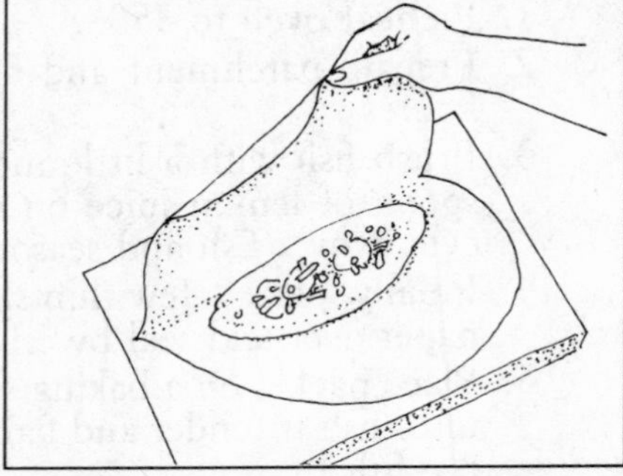

4. Cover the fish with the other half of the paper.

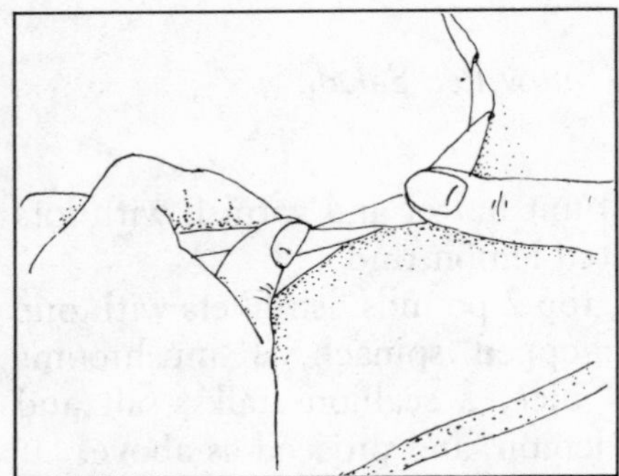

5. Seal edges of paper by folding the edges over and crimping them all the way around from the fold. If the edges aren't tightly sealed, the paper won't puff.

6. An individual papillote after baking.

√ Foil can be used in place of parchment paper, but the paper produces a better result.

√ Parchment paper is a useful kitchen tool for baking, too. Line cookie sheets with it and cookies will slide off easily.

Chinese Baked Fish

SERVES: 3–4
Preparation time: 15 minutes
Cooking time: 20 minutes

Rather than setting up a steamer basket, use this recipe to make cooking fish easy by simply baking it with Chinese herbs.

The Ingredients:

Peanut oil
1½ pounds thick, firm, fleshy fish (sea bass, snapper, halibut), cut 1″–1¼″ thick
3 tablespoons soy sauce
3 tablespoons dry sherry
3 scallion stalks, cut into ¼″ pieces
½ teaspoon freshly minced ginger root (or ¼ teaspoon powdered)
½ teaspoon freshly minced garlic
¼ teaspoon sugar
2 teaspoons oriental sesame oil

The Steps:

1. Preheat oven to 350°. Lightly oil a baking dish with peanut oil.
2. Arrange fish in dish. Sprinkle evenly with soy sauce, sherry, scallions, ginger, garlic, and sugar.
3. Bake for 20 minutes or until flaky, basting occasionally. (The cooking time depends on the thickness of the fish, so adjust accordingly.)
4. Drizzle sesame oil over fish and serve immediately.

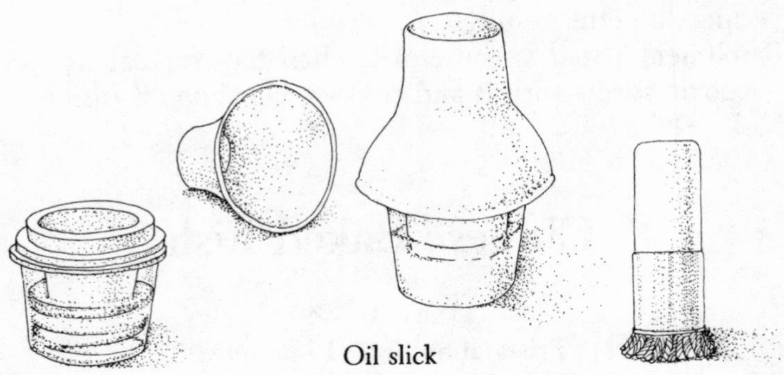

Oil slick

Accompaniments:

Plain White Rice, the Chinese Way, and *Oriental Zucchini Salad.*

Variation:

Leftover fish can be served cold as a fish salad the next day, sprinkled with a few teaspoons of Japanese rice vinegar.

Make-It-Easy Tips:

√ An "oil slick," the small gadget that keeps a brush soaked and ready in oil, can be conveniently used to oil the pan.

√ Sea bass, snapper, and halibut are all lean fish that work better than mackerel or striped bass, which are fat fish.

√ Do not substitute sweet sherry. If necessary, use sake (Japanese wine).

Fish Fillets Véronique

SERVES: 4–6
Preparation time: 15 minutes
Cooking time: 6–7 minutes

No butter is necessary on the Fish Fillets Véronique, making this a low-calorie main course.

The Ingredients:

1 cup seedless grapes, sliced in half
2 tablespoons dry white wine or vermouth
2 pounds fish fillets (sole, flounder, snapper, sand dabs)
1 teaspoon grated lemon peel
2 tablespoons lemon juice
½ teaspoon salt, or to taste
¼ teaspoon freshly ground pepper, or to taste
Garnish: Lemon slices, parsley sprigs

The Steps:

1. Preheat broiler.
2. Combine grapes and wine in bowl and toss.
3. Place fish in foil-lined broiling pan; sprinkle with lemon peel and juice. Season with salt and pepper.
4. Broil fish 3″–4″ from heat until golden, about 5 minutes.
5. Arrange grapes, cut side down, over top of fish and broil 1–2 minutes longer.
6. Taste, and adjust seasoning to taste. Serve fish hot, garnished with lemon slices and parsley sprigs.

Accompaniments:

Perfect Baked Potatoes, and a mixed green salad with *Low-Calorie Buttermilk Thousand Island Dressing.*

Variations:

Tiny julienne strips of sweet red pepper, thin slices of fresh ginger, and freshly chopped parsley can be sprinkled over fish in Step 3 for an attractive confetti-like appearance.

If desired, 1–2 tablespoons butter can be added in Step 3, but then the calorie content is increased.

Make-It-Easy Tip:

√ The grapes can be marinated earlier in the day, if desired.

Braised Fish in Wine and Dill Sauce

SERVES: 4–6
Preparation time: 15 minutes
Cooking time: 15–20 minutes

The Ingredients:

1½ tablespoons unsalted butter
1 small onion, finely chopped
½ cup dry vermouth or dry white wine
¼ cup Madeira (Marsala or port can be substituted)
1 cup chicken broth
2 tablespoons tomato paste
1 teaspoon Dijon mustard
1 teaspoon freshly snipped dill or ⅓ teaspoon dried dill
2 pounds flaky fish fillets (e.g., halibut, snapper, sea bass)
Garnish: Freshly snipped dill, freshly chopped parsley

The Steps:

1. In large skillet melt butter; sauté onions over medium heat until soft, about 5 minutes.
2. Add vermouth and Madeira and allow to boil a minute or two, stirring well.
3. Add broth, tomato paste, mustard, and dill; stir until mixed.
4. Add fish, season to taste with salt and pepper. Bring to boil; then reduce heat and simmer, partially covered, for 10–15 minutes or until fish is flaky and tender.
5. Adjust seasoning if necessary, and serve hot in deep soup bowls, garnished with freshly snipped dill and/or freshly chopped parsley.

Accompaniments:

Crusty French bread, and a mixed green salad with *Laurie's Basic Vinaigrette* dressing.

Variation:

Fish can be cut up into small chunks, broth increased to 2 cups, and the recipe turned into a fish stew.

Make-It-Easy Tip:

√ The new Italian tomato paste available in tubes is a convenient way to obtain a small amount without opening a large can.

Quick and Easy Cioppino

SERVES: 6
Preparation time: 25 minutes
Cooking time: 20–25 minutes

Cioppino is an Italian shellfish stew that can be served as a complete meal in deep soup plates with lots of Italian bread for dunking. Use any variety of fresh shellfish or fish that is in season and reasonably priced. As a one-pot supper, it is low in calories yet very filling.

The Ingredients:

1 tablespoon olive oil
1 medium onion, finely chopped
¾ cup dry vermouth
2 cups marinara sauce (*see* Chapter 2 for fresh, or use prepared sauce)
2 8-ounce bottles clam juice
½ teaspoon salt, or to taste
¼ teaspoon freshly ground pepper
16 small cherrystone clams, scrubbed clean
1 pound raw, medium shrimp, shelled and cleaned
1 pound fresh, firm, fleshy fish [i.g., monk fish (*lotte*), halibut, haddock, bass, or snapper]
½ pound sea scallops, cut in half
Garnish: One loaf Italian, French, or sourdough bread, toasted; freshly chopped parsley

The Steps:

1. In a Dutch oven or deep skillet, heat olive oil; sauté onion over medium heat until soft and golden, 10 minutes.
2. Add wine, stir well, then add marinara sauce and clam juice until consistency is soupy but still thick.

3. Add salt and pepper to taste, and bring to a boil.
4. Add clams, cover, and cook 5 minutes.
5. Add shrimp, fish, and scallops, cover again and cook for 5–6 minutes longer or until clam shells open.
6. Place a slice of toasted bread in a deep soup bowl, pour hot soup over, and garnish with lots of freshly chopped parsley.

Accompaniment:

Mixed green salad including artichoke hearts, red onions, black olives, and Parmesan cheese, with *Laurie's Basic Vinaigrette* dressing.

Variations:

Mussels can be added with clams. They, too, must be washed and scrubbed thoroughly. If you're lucky and lobsters are in season, use a small, cut up lobster and cook with the clams in Step 4.

If buying prepared marinara sauce, read the list of ingredients carefully. There are many available without chemicals, preservatives, salt, or sugar.

For a less expensive version, use only local, seasonal fresh fish.

Red wine can be substituted for dry vermouth.

Make-It-Easy Tips:

√ Have the fishman clean the shrimp for you or it will add an extra 15–20 minutes to preparation time. If this is not possible, substitute extra fish.

√ The stock and sauce may be assembled through Step 4 and reheated when adding the seafood.

√ When selecting clams or mussels at the market, pick out only ones that are completely closed, which indicates they are alive. After cooking and before serving, discard any clams that fail to open.

√ To clean clams easily, soak in cold water with a tablespoon of oatmeal. The clams will take in the oatmeal and spit it out along with the sand. Scrub well with a vegetable brush or strong wire brush.

Super-Easy Shrimp Soufflé

SERVES: 4–6
Preparation time: 20 minutes
Cooking time: 45 minutes to 1 hour

This is one soufflé that will not fall. It can be served as a lunch dish, light supper main course, or even as a spectacular first course.

The Ingredients:

½ cup mayonnaise (not salad dressing)
¼ cup all-purpose flour
2 teaspoons curry powder (or more to taste) dissolved in
1 tablespoon lemon juice
½ teaspoon salt, or to taste
¼ teaspoon freshly ground pepper
¼ cup half-and-half
1 pound cooked tiny bay shrimps
4 egg whites

The Steps:

1. Preheat oven to 350°. Generously butter a 1½-quart soufflé dish or straight-sided casserole.
2. Mix together the mayonnaise, flour, curry powder dissolved in lemon juice, salt, and pepper.
3. Gradually add the cream and whisk until smooth.
4. Stir in the shrimp and toss well.
5. Beat the egg whites until stiff with an electric beater or by hand and gently fold into mixture.
6. Pour batter in prepared soufflé dish and bake for 45 minutes to 1 hour until puffed up and golden brown on top.
7. Serve the soufflé immediately.

Accompaniments:

Serve as a first course by itself, or for a luncheon or supper with *Tabbouleh.*

Variation:

Flaked crabmeat can be substituted for the bay shrimp.

Make-It-Easy Tips:

√ Egg yolks can be reserved for *Zabaglione* or *Quick Chocolate Mousse.* To keep yolks, cover with water and refrigerate for 1–2 days.

√ For greater volume, allow egg whites to come to room temperature before whipping.

√ Do not whip egg whites in an aluminum bowl; it will tint them slightly grey. Use copper, glass, china, or stainless steel. Plastic tends to retain moisture and the water will prevent the egg whites from whipping properly. To increase volume add ¼ teaspoon cream of tartar after egg whites are foamy and begin to stiffen.

√ If egg whites overbeat try saving them by adding another white and beating again.

Shrimp al Pesto

SERVES: 4
Preparation time: 10 minutes
Cooking time: 5 minutes

The Ingredients:

2 tablespoons unsalted butter
2 tablespoons olive oil
1½ pounds raw medium shrimp, cleaned and shelled
2 tablespoons fresh lemon juice
3–4 tablespoons Pesto (*see* Chapter 2)
¼ teaspoon freshly ground white pepper
Garnish: White rice, Parmesan cheese

The Steps:

1. In large skillet, heat butter and oil together; sauté the shrimp, stirring constantly, until they just begin to turn pink.
2. Add lemon juice, stir to combine, cover, and cook for 2 minutes or until shrimp are tender.
3. Add Pesto and stir to coat shrimp.
4. Taste, and adjust seasoning if necessary. Serve shrimp hot, with sauce, over white rice. Serve Parmesan cheese on the side.

Accompaniments:

White rice, and sliced tomatoes with *Laurie's Basic Vinaigrette dressing,* and *Garlic Bread.*

Variations:

Substitute sea scallops, cut in half, or bay scallops, if available, and cook for only 1 minute, in Step 1.

Curried Scallops

SERVES: 3–4
Preparation time: 10 minutes
Cooking time: 5 minutes

The Ingredients:

- 2 tablespoons unsalted butter
- 1 tablespoon olive oil
- 1 pound sea scallops, cut in half, or 1 pound bay scallops
- 2 teaspoons curry powder, or to taste
- ¼ cup dry white wine or dry vermouth
- 1 tablespoon lemon juice
- ½ teaspoon salt, or to taste
- ½ teaspoon freshly ground pepper
- Garnish: Freshly chopped parsley

The Steps:

1. In large skillet, heat butter and oil; sauté scallops over medium heat, stirring constantly, for 2 minutes.
2. Sprinkle curry powder over scallops, toss well, and cook for an additional 2 minutes, stirring constantly.
3. Deglaze with wine and lemon juice by scraping up browned particles from bottom of pan into sauce.
4. Season to taste with salt and pepper and serve hot, garnished with freshly chopped parsley.

Accompaniments:

White rice, and *Spinach Salad with Creamy Dressing.*

Variation:

Fish fillets cut in strips can be substituted for the scallops for a less expensive version of the dish.

Make-It-Easy Tips:

√ Curried Scallops can be easily cooked in a wok.

√ When selecting scallops, choose ones that are translucent and shiny in appearance and have a sweetish aroma.

Oriental Flavor Ceviche

SERVES: 2–3

Preparation time: 15 minutes

Chilling time: 6 hours or overnight

Ceviche is raw fish or seafood that is prepared by marinating. Ceviche is traditionally a South American or Mexican specialty but in this recipe it has an oriental flavor. Serve it as a main course on a hot night or as an appetizer served on little plates with toothpicks.

The Ingredients:

1 pound bay scallops or sea scallops, cut in bite-size pieces
½ cup fresh lime juice
2 teaspoons soy sauce
1 teaspoon sugar
¼ teaspoon salt, or to taste
1 tablespoon minced scallions
½ teaspoon freshly grated ginger
Salt and pepper to taste
Garnish: Lettuce leaves, coriander or parsley, thin lime slices

The Steps:

1. Place scallops in a small, deep bowl. Combine lime juice, soy sauce, sugar, and salt, and pour over scallops. Cover and chill in refrigerator 6 hours or overnight.
2. Drain scallops and discard lime juice; combine with scallions, ginger, salt, and pepper to taste.

3. Place scallops on a lettuce-lined platter garnished with coriander or parsley and slices of lime.

Accompaniment:

Oriental Noodle Salad.

Variations:

For a less expensive meal, any firm fleshy fish can be substituted for the scallops. Be sure the fish is non-parasite bearing.

Ceviche can be part of a luncheon menu served with a hot quiche and *Spinach Salad.*

Make-It-Easy Tips:

√ Scallops can be prepared through Step 2 and chilled for several hours before serving.

√ Red leaf lettuce, Boston, or Romaine are particularly attractive as liners for platters.

STIR-FRIED ENTREES

Chinese cooking appears to be complicated, involving lots of chopping, slicing, stirring, mixing, and other tedious work. What takes longest in cooking a Chinese meal is the preparation—the cutting and chopping that must go on before the meal can be cooked. But this cutting and chopping can be done ahead of time so that, when it comes time to cook the dish, it's a simple, fast procedure.

The meat, poultry, or fish can be purchased fresh, cut into family-size portions and frozen. Just before a meal, a portion can be removed from the freezer, thawed for 20 minutes to half an hour, and easily sliced in that semi-frozen state.

Canned beef or chicken broth can be kept on hand. Minced fresh garlic can be kept in a jar covered with peanut oil, and minced fresh ginger can be kept in a jar covered with dry sherry.

In order to make stir-frying easy, you must be well organized. The 15–20 minute preparation time should be spent getting all the ingredients in small dishes or bowls around the stove. Once this preparation is done, completing the recipe takes only a few minutes.

Remember to have *all* ingredients assembled because, once you've started stir-frying, it's impossible to stop and chop some garlic.

By all means, use a food processor or hand chopping gadgets to simplify these chores.

When adding cornstarch paste (cornstarch mixed with a liquid), make sure to stir it again just before adding because the paste tends to thicken and gum up when standing.

Chinese stir-frying does not have to be a mysterious gourmet skill. It can be an easy way to prepare fabulous meals in a few minutes. It is an economical, healthful way to cook, and the finished product looks appealing because the vegetables retain their brilliant colors. And, it tastes wonderful because the textures, flavors, and nutrients of the foods are retained.

The Equipment and Its Preparation

If I had to choose only one pot to do all my cooking in, I would definitely select a wok.

1. A wok can be used for all kinds of cooking from French to American—it's not just for Chinese cooking!
2. A wok is so versatile it can be used for all types of kitchen chores; deep-frying, steaming (on a rack or with a bamboo steamer), boiling, sautéing, poaching, braising, parboiling, simmering and, of course, stir-frying.
3. A wok is an inexpensive investment—you need only one pot.
4. A wok is durable; if cared for properly, it will last forever.
5. A wok is easily cleaned; once "seasoned," it needs only a rinsing, brushing, drying, and light coating with oil.
6. A wok is perfect for low-calorie cooking; it needs only a little oil, a little poultry, and lots of fresh vegetables for a perfect dietetic meal.
7. A wok allows the true flavors of foods to come out because foods are seared in hot oil, keeping natural juices and favors within.

Woks come in iron, aluminum, copper, brass, and stainless steel. You can also purchase an electric version. The wok I recommend is made of rolled, tempered steel. This type retains heat well, is easy to care for, and is low in price. I find that the heat in electric woks cannot be controlled well enough to accommodate the quick changes necessary for Chinese cooking. You just can't remove an electric wok from the heat!

Woks range in sizes from 12″ to 26″. I prefer a 14″ wok, which will allow a large amount of food to be cooked and still retain a high heat level. Conventional cooktops cannot handle the heat necessary for an oversized wok.

There are a few utensils that make wok cooking easy:

Bamboo scrubber (or stiff brush): For easy clean-ups without scratching the surface of the wok.

Flat lifter: Spatula shaped for stir-frying.

Ladle: For stir-frying, braising, soups, and serving.

Chopsticks: For stir-frying, scrambling, and to use as tongs.

Mesh strainer: For deep frying.

Dok (or ring) on which to set the wok: Originally, the wok was designed for wood-burning and charcoal-style Chinese stoves. The dok helps to adapt the wok's round bottom to the American stove. Use upright on gas stoves

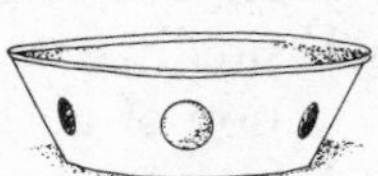

and upside down on electric stoves.

Cleaver: For chopping.

Bamboo steamer (or steaming rack): To convert the wok into a steamer.

Seasoning a Wok

Seasoning a wok used to be a lengthy procedure involving lots of steps (and lots of snob appeal). You can make the seasoning of a wok a very easy procedure, taking only a few simple steps. Once seasoned, you need only rinse it, scrub with a stiff brush, dry well, and rub with a light coating of vegetable oil to keep it in great condition and keep food from adhering to it.

Remember to follow the manufacturer's instructions and remove the tough layer of machine oil in which the wok is packaged.

1. Wash the new wok well in hot, soapy water, and rinse. (This is the one time you will use soap—to remove the tough layer of machine oil.)
2. Grease the inside of the wok with vegetable oil.
3. Heat the oiled wok over high heat in the ring for a minute and then rinse well.
4. Repeat the procedure.
5. Rinse the wok carefully, with hot water only.

Stir-frying is the cooking technique most associated with Chinese wok cookery. The secret to successful stir-frying is to cook quickly at maximum heat. That way, meat juices are sealed in and vegetables retain their color, vitamins, and crispness. Stir-fried main dishes are usually a combination of complementary meats and vegetables.

Chicken with Hoisin and Nuts

SERVES: 6
Preparation time: 15 minutes
Cooking time: 10 minutes

This recipe was taught to me by the noted Chinese cooking expert and teacher, Madame Grace Zia Chu.

The Ingredients:

- 6 large Chinese or Japanese (dried) mushrooms
- 1 small green pepper or 1 small sweet red pepper (or a combination of both)
- 1 8-ounce can water chestnuts, drained and sliced (or use presliced water chestnuts, which are now available in cans)
- 1 tablespoon cornstarch
- 2 tablespoons dry sherry
- 2 large, whole chicken breasts, skinned, boned, and cut into 1″ pieces
- 1 tablespoon peanut or vegetable oil
- ½ teaspoon salt, or to taste
- 3 tablespoons peanut or vegetable oil
- 1 tablespoon granulated sugar
- 3 tablespoons Hoisin sauce (available at some supermarkets, oriental groceries, or by mail, *see* Appendix A)
- ¼ cup split unsalted raw cashew nuts (or use unsalted, natural almonds, pecans, or peanuts)

  Garnish: Coriander sprigs (Chinese parsley) or regular parsley sprigs

The Steps:

1. Soak mushrooms in water for 20 minutes; drain, squeeze dry, cut away hard stem ends, and slice into quarters.
2. Cut pepper in similar-size wedges, add to water chestnuts, and set aside.
3. Combine cornstarch and sherry and add to chicken cubes; stir and set aside.
4. Heat the wok or large heavy skillet until very hot; add 1 table-

spoon oil and stir-fry mushrooms for 1 minute; add peppers and water chestnuts and continue to stir-fry another minute.
5. Add salt, mix, and remove vegetables; set aside.
6. Heat the wok again; add 3 tablespoons additional oil and stir-fry chicken pieces for about 3 minutes or until the chicken turns opaque.
7. Add sugar and Hoisin sauce, toss well, return the cooked vegetables, and continue to mix.
8. Add nuts and serve immediately with white rice garnished with coriander sprigs (Chinese parsley) or regular parsley sprigs.

Accompaniments:

Plain White Rice, the Chinese Way, and *Eggplant Szechwan-Style.*

Variation:

Bamboo shoots, cut in strips, can be added to the dish.

Make-It-Easy Tips:

√ Although it may lose a slight amount of texture, I prepare the chicken earlier in the day and reheat it when ready to serve.

√ Hoisin sauce is now available at many supermarkets along with a wide variety of oriental groceries. Opened jars will keep for quite a while stored in the refrigerator.

Stir-Fried Beef and Black Bean Sauce

SERVES: 4
Preparation time: 20 minutes
Cooking time: 5–6 minutes

This is a non-spicy Chinese dish flavored with the distinctive taste of Chinese fermented black beans.

The Ingredients:

½ pound flank steak, sirloin, or other tender cut of beef
1 tablespoon fermented black beans (available at some supermarkets, most oriental grocery stores, or by mail order, *see* Appendix A)

1 large red pepper (or, if not in season, use green pepper), roughly chopped
1 onion, roughly chopped
1 slice ginger, minced
1 clove garlic, minced
1 tablespoon sherry
1 tablespoon water
1 tablespoon cornstarch
½ cup beef broth
3 tablespoons peanut oil

The Steps:

1. Slice beef across the grain into thin slices, about 2″ square.
2. Soak black beans for 10 minutes in warm water; drain and mash with side of cleaver or knife.
3. Place peppers and onions in a bowl near cooking area.
4. Combine ginger and garlic in bowl near cooking area.
5. Mix sherry, water, and cornstarch together until it forms a paste. Set near range along with beef broth.
6. Heat a wok or large heavy skillet; add 2 tablespoons of oil and, when hot, stir-fry ginger and garlic for 30 seconds; add beef and continue to stir-fry for about 2 minutes. Remove and set aside.
7. Add remaining 1 tablespoon oil and, when hot, stir-fry pepper and onions for 2 minutes.
8. Add black beans and stir-fry 30 seconds; stir and add sherry/water/cornstarch paste, and broth.
9. Return beef, stir until smooth and slightly thickened; serve over white rice.

Accompaniment:

Snow Pea Salad.

Variations:

Boneless chicken, cut into dice, shrimp, or even pork can be substituted for the beef in this recipe.

Make-It-Easy Tips:

√ It is easier to cut the beef when it's in a semi-frozen state. Cut on the bias into strips.

√ Chop onions, garlic, ginger, and pepper in food processor, pulsating until just barely chopped. Do not over-process!

√ Remember to stir the sherry/water/cornstarch mixture just before adding in Step 8.
√ Use old margarine tubs or paper plates as containers for ingredients for less clean-up afterwards.
√ Fresh ginger can be peeled, placed in a jar, covered with dry sherry, and stored in refrigerator for several months.

Lamb with Scallions (Ts'ung Pao Yang Jou)

SERVES: 4
Preparation time: 15 minutes
Cooking time: 5 minutes

The Ingredients:

1½ pounds boneless lean lamb, cut into 2″ x 2″ x ⅛″ slices

6 scallion stalks, cut into ½″ slices
1 clove garlic, finely minced

3 tablespoons peanut oil

Marinade:

2 tablespoons soy sauce
2 tablespoons cold water
4 teaspoons cornstarch
1 teaspoon sugar

Sauce:

2 tablespoons soy sauce
2 tablespoons dry sherry
2 teaspoons rice vinegar (or white wine vinegar)
1 tablespoon sesame oil

The Steps:

1. Combine marinade ingredients in medium bowl; add lamb and set near cooking area to marinate for 10–15 minutes while preparing rest of ingredients.
2. Place scallions and garlic near cooking area; mix sauce ingredients together and set near range.
3. Heat wok or large heavy skillet, add peanut oil and, when hot,

stir-fry garlic for 30 seconds; add lamb and continue to stir-fry until lamb loses its pink color.

4. Add scallions and stir-fry; add sauce and continue to stir until smooth.
5. Serve lamb hot over white rice.

Accompaniment:

Bean Sprout Salad.

Variations:

Beef (flank steak or sirloin or other tender cut of meat) can be substituted for the lamb in this recipe.

Make-It-Easy Tip:

√ It is easier to cut the lamb when it's in a semi-frozen state.

Ground Pork with Cellophane Noodles, Szechwan-Style

SERVES: 4
Preparation time: 15 minutes
Cooking time: 5–7 minutes

The spiciness of this Szechwan pork dish can be altered to taste.

The Ingredients:

2 ounces (1 package) oriental dry cellophane noodles (available in oriental grocery stores or by mail order, *see* Appendix A)
1 pound lean ground pork
2 scallion stalks, minced
8 water chestnuts, minced
2 tablespoons dry sherry
2 tablespoons soy sauce
½ teaspoon salt, or to taste
½ teaspoon sugar
1 teaspoon chili paste with garlic, or more to taste (available at oriental groceries or by mail order, *see* Appendix A)
1 cup beef broth
2 tablespoons peanut oil

The Steps:

1. Soak cellophane noodles in warm water for 20 minutes to soften; drain and snip with kitchen shears, chef's knife, or Chinese cleaver, into 2" sections.
2. Assemble noodles, ground pork, scallions, and water chestnuts in separate containers near the range; mix sherry, soy sauce, salt, sugar, and chili paste together and set near stove; place beef broth near cooking area.
3. Heat wok or large heavy skillet, add oil and, when hot, stir-fry scallions for 30 seconds.
4. Add half the ground pork and break up until crumbly; push cooked pork to the sides of wok, add the remaining pork and continue to stir-fry until all pork is separated and crumbly.
5. Add water chestnuts and sherry mixture and stir to combine.
6. Add noodles and broth; cover and cook over medium heat until much of liquid has been absorbed.
7. Serve pork hot over white rice.

Accompaniments:

Chinese Asparagus Salad with Spicy Dressing.

Variation:

If you prefer beef to pork, substitute ground round for the pork and increase the peanut oil to 3 tablespoons.

Make-It-Easy Tip:

√ Pork with Cellophane Noodles can be cooked a few hours earlier and reheated.

Stir-Fried Shrimp

SERVES: 4
Preparation time: 15 minutes
Cooking time: 5 minutes

Serve the shrimp hot or cold as a first course or cold as hors d'oeuvres before a Chinese or American dinner.

The Ingredients:

1 pound raw, cleaned shrimp
2 scallion stalks cut into 1″ pieces
2 slices fresh ginger
1 large clove garlic
2 tablespoons soy sauce
1 tablespoon dry sherry
2 tablespoons ketchup
1 teaspoon sugar
3 shakes Tabasco
3 tablespoons peanut oil

The Steps:

1. Rinse shrimp and pat dry on paper towels.
2. Place scallions in a small container; mash ginger and garlic together and place in another container; put both containers near cooking area.
3. Combine soy sauce, sherry, ketchup, sugar, and Tabasco together and set near range.
4. Heat a wok or heavy skillet, add oil and, when hot, add ginger/garlic; stir-fry for 30 seconds.
5. Add shrimp and stir-fry for 3 minutes or until pink.
6. Add scallions, stir-fry 30 seconds; add soy sauce mixture, stir, and continue to cook.
7. Taste, and adjust seasoning if necessary. Serve immediately with rice, or refrigerate if you plan to serve shrimp cold.

Accompaniments:

Oriental Roast Pork and Snow Pea Salad.

Make-It-Easy Tips:

√ Shrimp can be cooked in advance, which is a great help when more than one stir-fried dish is to be prepared.

√ Ask the fishman to clean the shrimp for you—it saves a lot of time.

√ Tabasco should be added at the end of cooking. If cooked too long, it can become bitter tasting.

CHAPTER SIX

PASTA, RICE AND THEIR MORE EXOTIC RELATIVES

August Pasta
Fettuccine Carbonara
Linguini with Smoked Salmon
Pasta al Pesto
Linguini con Piselli (Pasta with Peas)
Pasta with Broccoli
Chicken Pasta Alfredo
Broad Noodles with Spinach
Noodle Pudding
Plain White Rice—The Chinese Way
Plain Brown Rice
Rice Pilaf with Pine Nuts
Lemon Rice
Curried Rice
Apricot Rice
Fried Rice
Green Rice
Bulgur Baked with Onions and Mushrooms
Kasha
Barley Casserole
Southern Style Cheese Grits
Orzo with Mushrooms and Onions
Couscous

QUICK & EASY PASTA DISHES

Quick and easy pasta dishes are the answer to what to serve to unexpected company. If ingredients are kept on hand, the meal can be assembled in just a few minutes.

Pasta is lower in calories than people think. If you cut down on rich sauces, you can have a fabulous low-calorie pasta feast. Pasta dishes are also inexpensive, especially when garnished with simple sauces.

Leftover hot pasta makes a splendid salad when served cold the next day. Add a sprinkling of vinegar or lemon juice for extra flavor or toss in some leftover cooked, chopped vegetables.

The general rules for cooking dried pasta are:

1. Bring a large pot of water with a teaspoon of salt to a boil.
2. Add 1 teaspoon vegetable oil to keep the pasta from sticking.
3. Cook according to package directions but test periodically so the pasta does not overcook. It should be *al dente,* just tender, a phrase translated from the Italian meaning "to the teeth."
4. Drain the pasta and toss immediately with the sauce. There are those who maintain that it is necessary to rinse the pasta with cold water after draining to remove excess starch and stop the cooking immediately. I find this an unnecessary step and prefer the pasta to be as hot as possible before mixing with the sauce.

Fresh pasta is now available at many specialty stores in large cities throughout the country. It can be used fresh or can be frozen successfully. When preparing fresh pasta, cook it for only 2–3 minutes, depending on the thickness of the noodle. It overcooks easily, so watch carefully. If cooking frozen fresh pasta, do not defrost it. Simply drop it frozen into the water and cook for 3–4 minutes, or until *al dente.*

A spaghetti pot filled with a built-in colander is a helpful Make-It-Easy tool for cooking pasta—cook the pasta, lift up, drain, and serve. Pasta measures are now available, designed to calculate perfect portions of uncooked spaghetti. Remember to consider the richness of the sauce before deciding the amount of pasta to cook. In general, one pound of pasta will serve three ravenous or four moderate diners as a main course.

If available, purchase imported Italian brands of dried pasta, such as de Cecco, Mennucci, Carmine Russo or del Verde. By law, Italian dried pasta has less water than the American brands and is made of the heart of durum wheat. Italian dried pasta holds its shape better and cooks up *al dente,* tender and firm. The American brands use a different flour and, because they have a higher water content, tend to become gummy and soft if not properly cooked.

If dinner is postponed and pasta must be reheated, place in a colander over a pot of simmering water. Cover the pot and the pasta will keep for a short while. Or, drain the pasta, toss it with oil, cover, and refrigerate. Before serving, plunge into boiling water, drain, and toss with sauce.

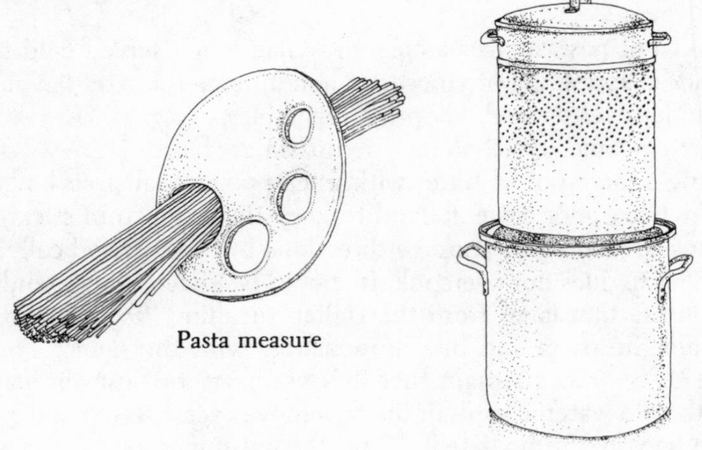

Pasta measure

Pasta pot

August Pasta

SERVES: 6
Preparation time: 15 minutes
Cooking time: 10–12 minutes

August Pasta is so named because the tomatoes used in the sauce are at their ripest and juiciest, and basil is at its most plentiful, in the month of August.

The Ingredients:

4 large or 6 medium very ripe, juicy tomatoes, cut into small chunks
2 zucchini, cut in thin julienne strips (matchstick shape)
2 tablespoons olive oil
1 tablespoon freshly chopped parsley

- 1 tablespoon freshly chopped basil (or 1 teaspoon dried basil, crumbled)
- 1 teaspoon freshly minced garlic (or more to taste)
- ½ teaspoon salt, or to taste
- ½ teaspoon freshly ground pepper
- 1 pound fusilli or similar-size spaghetti twists
- 2–3 tablespoons freshly grated Parmesan cheese

The Steps:

1. In large serving bowl, combine tomatoes, zucchini, oil, parsley, basil, garlic, salt and pepper to taste.
2. Cook pasta in salted boiling water until just tender, *al dente.*
3. Drain in colander and immediately toss drained pasta with sauce.
4. Sprinkle with grated Parmesan cheese, taste, adjust seasoning if necessary, and serve immediately.

Accompaniments:

Cheese-Garlic Bread (*see* Garlic Bread, Variations), and *Raw Mushroom Salad.*

Variations:

Substitute linguini or spaghetti for the fusilli.

Serve as a cold pasta salad the next day by adding a tablespoon of red wine vinegar plus extra salt and pepper to taste after chilling.

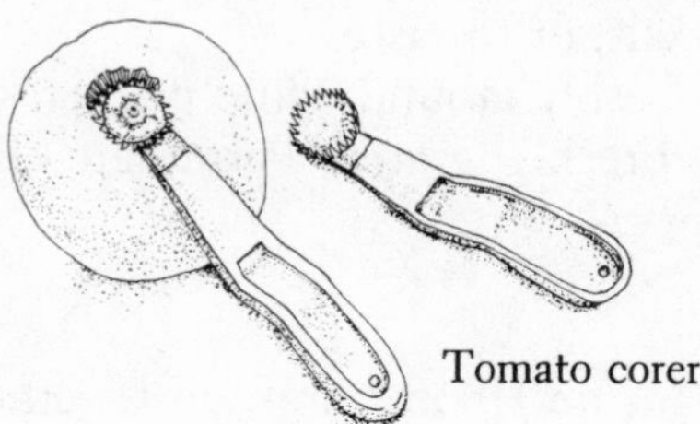

Tomato corer

Make-It-Easy Tips:

√ A tomato corer will lift the core out of the tomato making it easier to cut the tomato into small chunks with a serrated tomato knife.

√ Since fresh basil is available only in the summer months, chop it in large bunches and freeze in small containers or plastic bags for use year 'round.

√ In the off-season, when ripe tomatoes are very expensive, substitute canned Italian tomatoes, drained, with the addition of a pinch of sugar to cut acidity.

Fettuccine Carbonara

SERVES: 4–6
Preparation time: 20 minutes
Cooking time: 15–20 minutes

Fettuccine Carbonara is a super-rich dish—so rich that it only needs a light Italian salad to make a whole meal.

The Ingredients:

1 tablespoon unsalted butter
1 teaspoon olive oil
4 large shallots, minced, or 4 scallions, white part only, minced
6 strips bacon, sliced crosswise into julienne strips
1 pound fettuccine noodles
3 egg yolks, at room temperature
¼ cup heavy cream
½ cup freshly grated Parmesan cheese
½ teaspoon salt, or to taste
½ teaspoon freshly ground white pepper
Garnish: Freshly grated Parmesan cheese, freshly ground white pepper

The Steps:

1. In saucepan, heat butter and oil together; sauté shallots over medium heat until soft, about 5 minutes. Add bacon and continue to cook over medium heat for an additional 10 minutes or until bacon begins to brown; set aside.
2. Drop pasta into pot of boiling salted water and cook until *al dente,* just tender.
3. In the meantime, beat egg yolks with cream until smooth with a wire whisk; add cheese.
4. Drain pasta in colander; return to warm pot.

5. Pour bacon sauce over noodles, then add egg mixture, tossing well so that hot pasta "cooks" the other ingredients.
6. Add salt and pepper to taste, and serve with extra cheese and a pepper mill on the side.

Accompaniment:

Italian salad (*see* Greek Salad, Variations).

Variations:

Leftover cubed ham or prosciutto can be added to the sauce.

Spinach fettuccine is a nice variation in color and taste.

Spaghetti or other thin noodles can be substituted for fettuccine.

Make-It-Easy Tips:

√ The preparation of Fettuccine Carbonara is similar to that of Chinese dishes because all ingredients should be assembled in advance near cooking area ready for last-minute cooking.

√ To set up in advance, cook bacon sauce and ready eggs and cheese mixture. When ready to cook, boil pasta, and toss.

√ Use kitchen scissors to julienne bacon easily. Cut width-wise across package of uncooked bacon.

Linguini with Smoked Salmon

SERVES: 4
Preparation time: 15 minutes
Cooking time: 10–12 minutes

This is an unusual and very rich pasta dish that should be served with light accompaniments.

The Ingredients:

1 pound linguini
3 tablespoons unsalted butter
¼ pound thinly sliced smoked salmon, cut into julienne strips
½ cup heavy cream
2 tablespoons cream cheese, cut into bits
Salt and freshly ground white pepper to taste

½ cup freshly grated Parmesan cheese
Garnish: Freshly chopped parsley

The Steps:

1. Drop pasta into boiling salted water and cook until *al dente*, just tender. Drain in colander.
2. In the meantime, melt butter in saucepan; add salmon and toss to warm, but do not sauté.
3. Add cream and cream cheese and cook until boiling and smooth, stirring often.
4. Season to taste with salt and pepper, taking into account the saltiness of salmon.
5. Mix pasta with sauce; stir in Parmesan cheese and serve immediately, garnished with freshly chopped parsley.

Accompaniment:

Raw Mushroom Salad.

Variations:

A 10-ounce package of frozen tiny peas, thawed, can be added to pasta with sauce in Step 5.

Cappellini, very, very thin spaghetti, also called "Angel's Hair," can be substituted for linguini.

Pasta al Pesto

SERVES: 4
Preparation time: 10 minutes
Cooking time: 12 minutes

The Ingredients:

1 pound linguini, spaghetti, or spaghettini
4–5 tablespoons Pesto sauce (*see* Chapter 2)
½ cup freshly grated Parmesan cheese
¼ teaspoon freshly ground white pepper, or to taste
Garnish: Extra Parmesan cheese

The Steps:

1. Drop pasta into salted boiling water and cook until *al dente*, just tender.
2. Drain pasta in colander. Toss with Pesto, cheese, and pepper to taste.
3. Serve hot with extra Parmesan cheese on the side.

Accompaniments:

Marinated Butterflied Leg of Lamb, and a mixed green salad with *Laurie's Basic Vinaigrette* dressing.

Variation:

Two tablespoons of heavy cream can be added for a richer sauce.

Make-It-Easy Tip:

√ Toss drained pasta with 1 tablespoon butter first to keep noodles from sticking.

Linguini con Piselli (Pasta with Peas)

SERVES: 4–6
Preparation time: 20 minutes
Cooking time: 12 minutes

Linguini con Piselli is a wonderful accompaniment to veal or chicken dishes, or can stand on its own as a vegetarian main dish, or can even be served as a first course.

The Ingredients:

- 2 tablespoons unsalted butter
- 1 tablespoon olive oil
- 1 large onion, finely chopped
- ½ pound prosciutto, cut into thin julienne strips (if prosciutto is unavailable, use 2 slices minced bacon and eliminate the butter and oil)

2 tablespoons freshly chopped parsley
2 tablespoons freshly chopped basil or 2 teaspoons dried basil, crumbled
Pinch of nutmeg
½ teaspoon salt, or to taste
½ teaspoon freshly ground white pepper
1 cup strong chicken broth
1 cup heavy cream
1 pound linguini, or spaghetti, or vermicelli
20 ounces frozen tiny peas, thawed and drained (or use 20 ounces regular green peas, cooked 2 minutes)
¾–1 cup freshly grated Parmesan cheese

The Steps:

1. In large skillet, heat butter and oil together; add onion and prosciutto and cook over medium heat until soft, 5–7 minutes.
2. Add parsley, basil, nutmeg, salt, and pepper; stir to coat with butter.
3. Add broth and cook until smooth; add cream and continue to cook until slightly thickened.
4. In the meantime, cook linguini in boiling salted water until just tender, *al dente.* Drain in colander.
5. Toss pasta with peas; sprinkle with Parmesan cheese and serve piping hot.

Accompaniments:

Basic Vertically Roasted Chicken, and *Garlic Bread.*

Variations:

Linguini con Piselli can be transformed into an easy *pasta primavera* (pasta with vegetables in a creamy sauce) with the addition of frozen broccoli florets, cooked until just tender, some cooked zucchini, carrots, asparagus, or whatever other crunchy, but cooked, vegetables are available.

Cappellini, the very fine "Angel's Hair" pasta, makes a good substitute for linguini.

Pasta with Broccoli

SERVES: 4
Preparation time: 10–15 minutes
Cooking time: 12 minutes

Pasta with Broccoli is brimming with garlic flavor; it is recommended for a non-romantic dinner or one where you're sure everybody will have some!

The Ingredients:

1 large head fresh broccoli, about 2 pounds, broken into small florets, stalks reserved for another use
2 tablespoons unsalted butter
3 tablespoons olive oil
2 cloves garlic, finely minced
¼–½ teaspoon hot red pepper flakes, or to taste
1 pound spaghetti or linguini
½ teaspoon salt, or to taste
¼ teaspoon freshly ground pepper
3–4 tablespoons freshly grated Parmesan cheese
Garnish: Freshly grated Parmesan cheese

The Steps:

1. Drop broccoli into boiling salted water and cook uncovered 2–3 minutes or until just tender, *al dente;* drain in colander and run under cold water.
2. In saucepan, heat butter and oil together; add garlic and cook for 2 minutes. Add hot pepper flakes and set aside.
3. In the meantime, cook pasta in boiling salted water until just tender, *al dente,* and drain in colander.
4. In large bowl, toss spaghetti with garlic-butter sauce.
5. Add broccoli, salt, pepper, and cheese; toss to coat spaghetti well.
6. Serve hot, with additional Parmesan cheese on the side.

Accompaniments:

Can be served as a vegetarian main course by itself, or as an accompaniment to plain broiled chicken or fish, with *Tomato and Onion Salad* and crusty Italian bread.

Variations:

Sliced zucchini or asparagus tips can be substituted for the broccoli, and fettuccine can be used in place of the linguini.

Make-It-Easy Tips:

√ Broccoli is cooked in boiling water and then drained with cold water to maintain the bright green color.

√ Base of stalk closest to florets can be peeled with a sharp paring knife, thinly sliced, and cooked as a vegetable. Tough, woody base of stem should be discarded.

Chicken Pasta Alfredo

SERVES: 4–6
Preparation time: 20 minutes
Cooking time: 12 minutes

The addition of chicken to the traditional Alfredo cream sauce makes this pasta a full main course.

The Ingredients:

- ⅛ pound (½ stick) unsalted butter
- ⅔ cup heavy cream
- ⅔ cup freshly grated Parmesan cheese
- 1 pound spinach fettuccine (if unavailable, use plain fettuccine)
- 1 whole skinned and boned chicken breast, poached and shredded
- ⅓ cup freshly grated Parmesan cheese
- Pinch of ground nutmeg
- ½ teaspoon salt, or to taste
- ½ teaspoon freshly ground white pepper, or to taste
- Garnish: Additional grated Parmesan cheese, and ground white pepper

The Steps:

1. In large skillet, melt butter over medium heat, and stir in cream; as sauce begins to thicken, add ⅔ cup Parmesan cheese; stir and set aside.

2. In the meantime, cook the fettuccine in boiling salted water until just tender, *al dente*, and drain in colander.
3. In large bowl, immediately toss noodles with the butter/cream cheese mixture.
4. Add chicken, additional ⅓ cup Parmesan cheese, nutmeg, salt and pepper to taste.
5. Serve immediately with additional cheese on the side and a generous sprinkling of ground white pepper.

Accompaniment:
Snow Pea Salad.

Variation:
Diced baked ham can be substituted for the chicken.

Make-It-Easy Tips:
√ Poach chicken in broth to cover for 20 minutes at a simmer or until just tender. Baked chicken can be substituted but it is not as juicy or flavorful as poached chicken. For an easy method to poach chicken, *see Madame Chu's Szechwan Peppercorn Chicken Salad.*

Broad Noodles with Spinach

SERVES: 4
Preparation time: 10 minutes
Cooking time: 10 minutes

The Ingredients:
1 10-ounce package frozen chopped spinach, thawed and squeezed dry
1 8-ounce package broad noodles
1 cup dairy sour cream
2 tablespoons unsalted butter
1 teaspoon lemon juice
Fat pinch of ground nutmeg

½ teaspoon salt, or to taste
¼ teaspoon freshly ground white pepper, or to taste

The Steps:

1. In large pot of boiling salted water, cook noodles until just tender; drain in colander and return noodles to hot pot.
2. Immediately toss noodles with sour cream, spinach, butter, lemon juice, nutmeg, salt and pepper to taste; pour into a serving bowl and serve immediately.

Accompaniments:

Marinated Flank Steak or any other grilled meat or poultry dishes.

Variation:

One 10-ounce package frozen chopped broccoli can be substituted for spinach.

Make-It-Easy Tip:

√ Spinach does not have to be cooked, just thaw well, squeeze dry, and toss with hot noodles.

Noodle Pudding

SERVES: 6–8
Preparation time: 5–10 minutes
Cooking time: 60 minutes

This sweet noodle pudding, sometimes called a Kugel, is a perfect accompaniment for *Brisket Like My Mother Makes* or *Basic Vertically Roasted Chicken.* It can be served hot, at room temperature, or cold.

The Ingredients:

1 8-ounce package medium-wide egg noodles
1 cup whole milk
1 cup (8 ounces) dairy sour cream
1 cup (8 ounces) cottage cheese
2 eggs

½ cup granulated sugar
1 teaspoon vanilla
¾ cup golden seedless raisins
1–2 teaspoons cinnamon
⅔ tablespoon butter

The Steps:

1. Preheat oven to 350°. Generously grease a 9″ x 12″ baking dish.
2. Cook noodles according to package directions. Drain and rinse with cold water in colander.
3. While noodles are cooking, place milk, sour cream, cottage cheese, eggs, sugar, and vanilla in the blender or food processor. Blend for 10–15 seconds.
4. Pour blended ingredients into prepared baking dish.
5. Add raisins and noodles, spreading evenly.
6. Dust top generously with cinnamon, dot with small pieces of butter, and bake for 60 minutes.
7. Allow Kugel to cool for 15 minutes and serve hot, or cool longer and serve at room temperature.

Accompaniments:

Roast poultry or potted beef dishes.

Variations:

Substitute 1 cup of drained, canned, juice-packed pineapple cut in small pieces for the raisins.

Low-fat cottage cheese and low-fat milk can be substituted for the cottage cheese and whole milk.

Make-It-Easy Tip:

√ Substitute 2 smaller baking dishes for large one and freeze one of the puddings for a family dinner.

RICE

Rice is a staple of Make-It-Easy cooking. White rice takes only 20 minutes to cook, can be reheated and, once cooked, can be used in a variety of dishes.

For plain white rice, I use the Chinese method of cooking rice (*see Plain White Rice, the Chinese Way*). I find this to be the easiest way to produce perfect, separated grains.

For rice dishes that include sautéed vegetables, the easiest and most successful method of cooking is to sauté the onions or other vegetables in 3–4 tablespoons of butter. Add the rice, coating the grains well with the butter, which will keep the grains separate when cooked. Finally, add hot broth in the ratio of 2 cups broth to 1 cup rice. Cover, reduce to a simmer, and cook over very low heat for 20–25 minutes or until liquid is absorbed and rice is tender.

There are many varieties of rice but, to simplify, they divide into two categories—long grain and short grain. Long grain is best for plain white rice or for use in casseroles, whereas short grain cooks down to a softer consistency that's better for puddings.

Brown rice is unpolished rice in which only the husks have been removed. Brown rice is nutritionally superior to white rice, richer in vitamins, minerals, and fiber.

Wild rice is really not rice at all. It is the seed of a wild plant called water grass. It is high in nutrition and fiber content but is expensive.

Plain White Rice, the Chinese Way

YIELD: 3 cups

This is the easiest and most successful method for preparing plain white rice.

The Ingredients:

1 cup long-grain rice
1¾ cups cold water

The Steps:

1. Put rice in a 2-quart saucepan with a tight-fitting lid, add water, bring to a boil, cover, reduce to a simmer, and cook very slowly for 20 minutes.
2. Turn off heat and allow rice to sit, covered and undisturbed, for an additional 20 minutes.
3. Fluff up with a fork or chop sticks and serve hot.

The term "converted rice," also called "parboiled," "precooked," or "pre-fluffed" is rice that has been steam-treated so that the grains become tender without gumming up. "Quick-cooking" or "minute rice" is tasteless and should be avoided.

All of the rice recipes in this section can be prepared with nutritionally higher brown rice. When substituting brown rice for white rice, increase the cooking time by 30 minutes.

Raw Rice	*Water*	*Saucepan Size*
1½ cups rice	2⅝ cups water	3-quart pan
2 cups rice	3¼ cups water	3-quart pan
3 cups rice	4 cups water	4-quart pan
4 cups rice	5 cups water	6-quart pan
10 cups rice	11 cups water	large stock pot

Note: The proportion of water to rice decreases as the amount of rice increases.

Regardless of the amount of rice cooked, once the rice comes to a boil, the 20 minutes' simmering time and the 20 minutes' sitting time remain the same.

Make-It-Easy Tips:

√ *Reheating Instructions:* Cook rice the regular length of time or a little less. When ready to reheat, fluff up rice and place in a colander. Bring 2–3 inches of water to a boil in a large pot and place colander in pot so that colander is above the water. Steam for only 10–15 minutes. Mix once during that time.

Plain Brown Rice

SERVES: 6–8
Preparation time: 5 minutes
Cooking time: 35–45 minutes

The Ingredients:

4 cups water
2 cups brown rice

½ teaspoon salt, or to taste
Garnish: Freshly chopped parsley

The Steps:

1. In large saucepan, bring water to boil; add rice but do not stir.
2. Sprinkle with salt, cover; reduce heat to simmer and cook slowly for 35–40 minutes, or until liquid is absorbed and grains are tender.
3. Fluff rice and serve garnished with freshly chopped parsley.

Variations:

Substitute boiling chicken, beef, or vegetable broth for water; eliminate salt.

Make-It-Easy Tip:

√ 1 cup raw brown rice yields about 3 cups cooked brown rice.

Rice Pilaf with Pine Nuts

SERVES: 4–6
Preparation time: 15 minutes
Cooking time: 25 minutes

This is the basic recipe I use for a side dish of rice flavored with broth.

The Ingredients:

3 tablespoons unsalted butter
1 medium onion, finely minced
1 small clove garlic, finely minced
1¼ cups long-grain rice
⅓ cup pine nuts (*pignoli*) or slivered almonds
2½ cups chicken or beef broth
½ teaspoon salt, or to taste
¼ teaspoon freshly ground pepper
Garnish: Freshly chopped parsley

The Steps:

1. In small, heavy saucepan, melt butter over medium heat, add onion and garlic, and sauté until soft, about 5 minutes.

2. Add rice and pine nuts and stir until all grains are coated.
3. Add broth, salt, and pepper; bring to boil, cover, lower heat, and simmer slowly without lifting lid for 25 minutes.
4. Allow to rest 5 minutes; fluff with 2 forks and serve garnished with freshly chopped parsley.

Variations:

Use beef or chicken broth, depending on the main course.

Make-It-Easy Tip:

√ The rice should be coated well with butter so that the grains remain separate and tender.

Lemon Rice

SERVES: 4
Preparation time: 15 minutes
Cooking time: 25–30 minutes

The Ingredients:

2 tablespoons unsalted butter
1 tablespoon olive oil
1 small onion, finely chopped
1 cup long-grain rice
1¾ cups chicken broth
¼ cup fresh lemon juice
1½ teaspoons freshly grated lemon rind
½ teaspoon salt, or to taste
¼ teaspoon freshly ground pepper, or to taste
Garnish: Freshly chopped parsley, freshly grated lemon peel

The Steps:

1. Preheat oven to 350°.
2. Heat butter and oil together in small casserole; add onion, and sauté over medium heat until soft, about 5 minutes.
3. Add rice and stir to coat with butter and oil.

4. Add broth, lemon juice, lemon rind, salt and pepper to taste; bring to a boil, cover, and bake for 25–30 minutes or until liquid is absorbed and grains are tender.
5. Serve rice hot, garnished with freshly chopped parsley and freshly grated lemon peel.

Variations:

This rice can be cooked successfully on top of range at a slow simmer if oven is in use.

Orange juice and orange rind can be substituted for lemon juice and rind, and mixed with a teaspoon of curry powder and some raisins for a curried orange rice variation.

Make-It-Easy Tip:

√ Grate lemon rind first, and then squeeze lemon at room temperature to obtain the optimum amount of juice.

Curried Rice

SERVES: 4–6
Preparation time: 10 minutes
Cooking time: 25 minutes

Curried Rice goes very well with roast lamb, poultry, or pork dishes.

The Ingredients:

3 tablespoons unsalted butter
1 small onion, finely chopped
1 cup long-grain rice
2 cups hot chicken or beef broth
¼ cup golden seedless raisins
1 teaspoon curry powder
Garnish: Dairy sour cream, chutney (optional)

The Steps:

1. In heavy saucepan, melt butter; sauté onion over medium heat until soft, 5–7 minutes.
2. Add rice, and stir to coat grains with butter.
3. Add broth, raisins, and curry powder; bring to a boil, cover,

and cook for 25 minutes or until rice is tender and liquid absorbed.

4. Serve rice hot with sour cream, and chutney, if desired.

Variations:

Toasted slivered almonds can be added during last few minutes of cooking.

The rice can also be baked in a 325° oven for 25 minutes.

Apricot Rice

SERVES: 6
Preparation time: 15 minutes
Cooking time: 20–25 minutes

Apricot Rice makes a great accompaniment to roast pork or roast turkey.

The Ingredients:

- 3 tablespoons unsalted butter
- 1 small onion, finely chopped
- ½ cup chopped celery
- ½ teaspoon freshly minced ginger (or ¼ teaspoon powdered ginger added with broth)
- 1 cup long-grain rice
- 2 cups chicken broth
- 1 cup diced dried apricots
- ¼ cup chopped chutney
- ½ cup toasted slivered almonds
- Garnish: Freshly chopped parsley

The Steps:

1. In a deep saucepan, melt butter; sauté the onions, celery, and ginger over medium heat until soft, about 5 minutes.
2. Add rice, and continue to sauté until grains are coated.
3. Add broth, apricots, and chutney; bring to a boil, reduce heat, cover, and simmer slowly for 20–25 minutes or until rice is tender.
4. Add nuts and serve hot, garnished with freshly chopped parsley.

Variations:

⅓ cup golden seedless or dark raisins can be substituted for the chutney.

Dried peaches, pineapple, apples, or other dried fruits can be substituted for the apricots.

Make-It-Easy Tip:

√ Toast nuts easily in a toaster-oven or under the broiler for 1–2 minutes, turning once with a spatula and watching carefully.

Fried Rice

SERVES: 6–8
Preparation time: 20–25 minutes
Cooking time: 5–7 minutes

Fried Rice is a great way to use up leftover rice and . . . leftover poultry, meat, fish, or vegetables.

The Ingredients:

- 3 eggs, lightly beaten
- ⅓ cup chopped scallion stalks
- ½ teaspoon minced fresh ginger
- ½ teaspoon minced garlic
- 3 cups cold cooked rice
- ¼ teaspoon salt, or to taste
- ¼ teaspoon sugar
- 1½ tablespoons dark soy sauce
- ⅓ pound baked ham, finely diced
- ½ cup frozen tiny peas, thawed
- 3 tablespoons peanut oil
- 1 teaspoon oriental sesame oil

The Steps:

1. Place the eggs, scallions, ginger, garlic, rice, salt, sugar, soy sauce, ham, and peas in small containers or on paper plates near the cooking area.

2. Heat wok or large heavy skillet; add 1 tablespoon of peanut oil and, when hot, scramble eggs very loosely; remove from pan and set aside.
3. Heat remaining 2 tablespoons peanut oil and, when hot, stir-fry scallions, ginger, and garlic for 30 seconds.
4. Add rice, stir-fry until tossed with ingredients.
5. Add salt, sugar, soy sauce, and ham and stir-fry to combine.
6. Add reserved scrambled eggs, breaking them up to distribute evenly.
7. Gently fold in peas, glaze with sesame oil, and serve immediately.

Variations:

Dark soy sauce is available at oriental grocery stores (*see* Appendix A) but regular, light soy sauce, the kind found in supermarkets, can be substituted.

Any leftover meats or vegetables can be added to fried rice: bacon bits, cooked chicken strips, roast pork, roast beef, bean sprouts, water chestnuts, bamboo shoots, button mushrooms, or any cooked vegetable desired.

Leftover Fried Rice can be refrigerated and reheated. It can even be frozen.

Make-It-Easy Tips:

√ This is fast Chinese wok cookery, so remember to have all ingredients assembled and ready to go.

√ The rice must be cold before stir-frying in order to obtain the best texture and taste.

Green Rice

SERVES: 8–10
Preparation time: 15–20 minutes
Cooking time: 45 minutes

This Green Rice casserole dish is a great way to use up leftover cooked rice. The addition of cheese, mentioned in the Variations, and the eggs make this dish substantial enough to serve as a main dish for lunch.

The Ingredients:

- 6 cups cooked white rice (2 cups raw rice)
- 4 eggs
- 2 cups half-and-half
- 1 10-ounce package frozen chopped spinach, thawed and squeezed dry
- ½ cup freshly chopped parsley
- ½ cup freshly grated Parmesan cheese
- ¼ cup finely chopped onion
- 3 tablespoons unsalted butter, melted
- 1 tablespoon Worcestershire sauce
- ½ teaspoon salt, or to taste
- ½ teaspoon freshly ground pepper, or to taste
- Garnish: Freshly chopped parsley

The Steps:

1. Preheat oven to 325°. Generously butter 2-quart casserole or soufflé dish.
2. In large bowl, combine the cooked rice, eggs, half-and-half, spinach, parsley, Parmesan cheese, onion, butter, Worcestershire, salt, and pepper; mix well, and pour into prepared casserole.
3. Bake for 45 minutes or until hot and bubbly.
4. Serve rice dish hot, garnished with additional freshly chopped parsley.

Variations:

Add ½ cup grated Swiss Gruyère or Monterey Jack cheese to transform Green Rice into a vegetarian main course.

Brown rice can be substituted for white rice.

Make-It-Easy Tip:

√ Green Rice can be assembled well in advance, refrigerated, and baked just before serving.

ALTERNATIVES TO RICE

Innovative and healthy alternatives to the routine white rice/noodles side-dish slump are available, only their names aren't as familiar: bulgur, couscous, barley, kasha, grits, orzo. All of these offer the chance to mix tastes and cuisines creatively; try Armenian bulgur with *Cuban Chicken.* Your meal will be anything but dull.

Bulgur Baked with Onions and Mushrooms

SERVES: 4–6
Preparation time: 15 minutes
Cooking time: 50 minutes

Bulgur (Bulghur, Burghul, Bulgar), the staple of Middle Eastern cooking, is cracked wheat that has been hulled and parboiled, a process that makes the grain easier to cook and gives it a pronounced flavor and lighter texture. Serve as a side dish in place of rice or use in the Lebanese salad *Tabbouleh* in which bulgur is mixed with mint, onions, and parsley. Bulgur Baked with Onions and Mushrooms goes well with brisket and other pot roasts.

The Ingredients:

2 tablespoons unsalted butter
1 small onion, finely chopped
6 mushrooms, finely chopped
1 cup bulgur
2 cups hot chicken or beef broth
½ cup toasted pine nuts (or toasted almonds)
Salt and freshly ground pepper to taste
Garnish: Freshly chopped parsley

The Steps:

1. Preheat oven to 350°.
2. In small oven-proof casserole, melt butter; sauté the onions and mushrooms over medium heat until soft and golden, about 5 minutes.
3. Add bulgur to casserole, toss to coat grains with butter and vegetables. Add hot broth, bring to a boil, reduce heat, cover, and bake for 40 minutes.
4. Remove from oven, top with pine nuts, and return to oven for an additional 10 minutes.
5. Taste, adjust seasoning with salt and pepper, and serve bulgur hot, garnished with freshly chopped parsley.

Variation:

The use of chicken or beef broth should depend on the main dish.

Make-It-Easy Tip:

√ It is easy to toast nuts; brown in a toaster-oven or under the broiler for 1–2 minutes, turning once with a spatula and watching carefully.

Kasha

SERVES: 4
Preparation time: 15 minutes
Cooking time: 15 minutes

Kasha is a dish of braised buckwheat groats that is served as a side dish or used in soups.

The Ingredients:

2 tablespoons unsalted butter
1 small onion, chopped
1 egg
½ teaspoon salt, or to taste
¼ teaspoon freshly ground pepper
1 cup kasha
2 cups hot chicken or beef broth, depending on main course
1 8-ounce can water chestnuts, drained and chopped
Garnish: Freshly chopped parsley

The Steps:

1. Melt butter in saucepan; sauté onion over medium heat until translucent, 5–7 minutes.
2. In a small bowl, beat egg with salt and pepper, add kasha, stir with a fork until combined, pour into saucepan, and stir well.
3. Add broth and bring to boil, reduce heat, cover, and simmer for 10 minutes.
4. Add water chestnuts, cover again, and cook for 5 minutes longer.
5. Taste for seasoning, adjust if necessary, and serve hot, garnished with freshly chopped parsley.

Variations:

Rendered chicken fat can be substituted for butter.
Chopped celery can be sautéed with onions.

Cashews, pine nuts, or almonds can be added with water chestnuts for additional crunchiness.

Barley Casserole

SERVES: 6–8
Preparation time: 15 minutes
Cooking time: 1¼ hours

The Ingredients:

4 tablespoons unsalted butter
2 medium onions, finely chopped
½ pound mushrooms, sliced
1½ cups pearl barley
3 cups chicken or beef broth, depending on the main course
1 4-ounce jar pimientos, drained and coarsely chopped
¼ teaspoon salt, or to taste
¼ teaspoon freshly ground pepper, or to taste
Garnish: Freshly chopped parsley

The Steps:

1. Preheat oven to 350°.
2. Melt butter in a large casserole; sauté onions for 2 minutes over medium heat, add mushrooms and continue to sauté until soft, 5–7 minutes.
3. Add barley and cook until lightly browned. Add 2 cups of the broth, pimientos, salt, pepper, and stir; bring to a boil, cover, reduce heat, and bake for 45 minutes.
4. Add remaining 1 cup broth, return to oven and cook 30 minutes longer.
5. Serve hot, garnished with freshly chopped parsley.

Variations:

Toasted egg barley, called *farfel,* can be substituted for pearl barley.

Drained roasted Italian red peppers in jars or cans are a nice substitute for pimientos.

Make-It-Easy Tip:

√ If oven is in use, barley can be cooked on top of range at a very slow simmer.

Southern-Style Cheese Grits

SERVES: 6
Preparation time: 15 minutes
Cooking time: 30–40 minutes

Grits, also called hominy grits or corn grits, are coarsely ground cornmeal. In the southern United States, grits are popular served either as a breakfast cereal or as a substitute for potatoes.

This recipe adapts grits for use as an alternative to rice, a side dish flavored with garlic-cheese that is great with barbecued spareribs or chicken.

The Ingredients:

1 cup quick-cooking grits, cooked according to package directions
1 4-ounce package garlic-and-herb cheese (Boursin, Rondele, or Alouette)
1 egg, lightly beaten
4 tablespoons (½ stick) unsalted butter
¼ cup whole milk

The Steps:

1. Preheat oven to 375°. Lightly butter a 1½-quart baking dish.
2. In large bowl, combine grits, cheese, egg, butter, and milk and stir well until combined.
3. Pour into prepared baking dish and bake 35–45 minutes or until golden brown on top and center is set.
4. Serve grits piping hot.

Variation:

One cup grated Cheddar, Swiss, or Jack cheese can be substituted for the garlic cheese.

Make-It-Easy Tip:

√ The easiest way to cook quick grits is to stir 1 cup grits into 4 cups boiling salted water, reduce heat to a simmer, cover, and cook 4–5 minutes, stirring occasionally. This recipe yields 4 cups of cooked grits.

Orzo with Mushrooms and Onions

SERVES: 6–8
Preparation time: 15 minutes
Cooking time: 10–15 minutes

Orzo is rice-shaped pasta. It's available in Greek or Armenian grocery stores.

The Ingredients:

4 tablespoons unsalted butter
1 large onion, finely chopped
8 mushrooms, thinly sliced
1 16-ounce box orzo
½ cup freshly grated Parmesan cheese
½ teaspoon salt, or to taste
¼ teaspoon freshly ground pepper
Garnish: Freshly chopped parsley

The Steps:

1. In large skillet, melt the butter; sauté onions over medium heat until soft, about 5 minutes.
2. Add mushrooms and continue to cook for an additional 5 minutes or until golden.
3. Cook orzo in boiling salted water, according to directions on box; drain in colander.
4. Toss orzo with onion/mushroom mixture; sprinkle cheese on top. Season to taste with salt and pepper and serve hot, sprinkled with freshly chopped parsley.

Variations:

Tiny Italian noodles can be substituted for orzo.

Chopped water chestnuts can be added with the orzo for a crunchy texture.

Couscous

SERVES: 6–8
Preparation time: 5 minutes
Cooking time: 5 minutes

Couscous is a traditional Moroccan dish made with steamed grains of semolina. It can be served as the basis for a main course, accompanied by soups, sauces, stews, or vegetables, or served alone as a side dish.

The Ingredients:

1 16-ounce package couscous, pre-cooked medium grain (Near East brand is good)
2 cups boiling broth, beef or chicken (or water)
2 tablespoons unsalted butter (or oil), or to taste
Garnish: Freshly chopped coriander or parsley

The Steps:

1. Combine couscous with boiling broth or water (if using less than 16 ounces, combine equal amounts of couscous, by volume, and boiling broth or water); cover, and allow to stand for 5 minutes.
2. Add 2 tablespoons butter, or to taste, stir well, and fluff with a fork.
3. Place couscous in a serving dish, garnish with freshly chopped coriander or parsley, and serve hot.

Variations:

Use chicken or beef broth, depending on the main course.

Couscous is traditionally cooked in a Couscousier, a double boiler-like pot with a steamer attachment. To simulate a Couscousier, complete preparation through Step 1 and place couscous in strainer or colander over pot of boiling broth. Do not let broth come in direct contact with the strainer. Allow the steam to penetrate the couscous for 5 minutes and then complete Step 2 as above.

CHAPTER SEVEN

VEGETABLES

Crisp Fresh Asparagus
Baked Asparagus
Carrots and Parsnips Combined
Carrot Purée in Artichoke Bottoms
Sautéed Chayote with Tomatoes
Braised Daikon
Eggplant Szechwan-Style
Baby Lima Beans and Prosciutto
Petite Peas Française
Potatoes Boiled in Jackets
Perfect Baked Potatoes
Baked Potato Skins
Stir-Fried Spinach
Baked Spinach with Cheese
Stir-Fried Straw and Hay Summer Squash
Baked Acorn Squash
Banana Squash Purée
Baked Spaghetti Squash
Sweet Potato Soufflé
Cherry Tomatoes Flavored with Dill
Tomatoes Filled with Peas
Tomato Pie
Dilled Zucchini
Italian Zucchini Bake

Once thought of as an unimportant side dish, vegetables are now considered an important part of any meal. In fact, they are occasionally the main course. We appreciate their taste, their versatility, and especially their nutritional benefits. Color, texture, and flavor are all being taken into consideration in modern vegetable cookery.

Steaming and boiling are the simplest methods of preparing fresh vegetables. Steaming is the most advantageous, preserving vitamins, minerals, and other nutrients. The only drawback to steaming is the loss of the vibrant green color. Boiling vegetables uncovered retains the bright color, but some nutrients are lost in the water.

Several years ago it was popular to add baking soda to the cooking water to retain the bright color of vegetables. We now realize that, although the color is retained, many of the vitamins are destroyed and the vegetables become mushy.

Fresh vegetables are definitely preferable to canned. Canned vegetables, high in salt content and often filled with preservatives, are a poor substitute for fresh, no matter how much time they save. It takes only a few minutes to steam or boil a fresh vegetable. Frozen vegetables are the next best thing to fresh and several types, such as chopped spinach and broccoli, can be tremendous time-savers.

Ask the produce person at your market to advise you on the freshness of specific vegetables. Be wary of chemicals, waxes, food colors, and sprays. Scrub vegetables with a brush before using and try to steam or bake in the natural skin to preserve nutrients.

Sautéing the cut-up vegetables for a few minutes in butter or oil is another easy method of preparation. Add water or broth plus a few spices and seasonings, cover, and continue to cook until crunchy. Serve with the liquid to retain important nutrients.

Stir-frying is yet another easy and quick way to cook vegetables. The shape and roominess of a wok make it a perfect vehicle. You brown the vegetables quickly in hot oil, turning them around and around over very high heat and, in so doing, preserve their crunchy texture, vibrant colors, natural flavors, and nutrients. The hot oil seals in the vegetables' juices, while at the same time extracting their flavors. All ingredients should be readied in advance and placed in the area near the wok so that the final cooking is truly Make-It-Easy.

Baked vegetables—cooked alone or combined with noodles, rice, cheese, or other staple ingredients—share a similar Make-It-Easy advantage. They can be prepared well in advance, cooked, and reheated at serving time.

Stuffed vegetables are an especially attractive side dish but often appear too complicated to prepare. The stuffed vegetable recipes in this chapter show how, with a few hints, tips, and shortcuts, it is easy to cook *Tomatoes Filled with Peas,* or prepare stuffed artichoke bottoms, or patty pan squash. In addition, stuffed vegetables can be assembled in advance and reheated just before serving, while maintaining optimum flavor and texture.

You may also find some close encounters with vegetables of an unfamiliar kind. Spaghetti squash, chayote, and daikon are the kinds of exotic arrivals you're bound to find in your supermarket produce section or at the green grocer's. So some Make-It-Easy recipes are included to bring them down to earth.

In general, cut vegetables right before cooking to avoid vitamin loss and, whenever possible, cook them at the last minute to preserve crispness, bright color, and great flavor.

Crisp Fresh Asparagus

SERVES: 4
Preparation time: 10 minutes
Cooking time: 8–10 minutes

I find boiling asparagus in an uncovered skillet (yes, a large frying pan) is the easiest way to prepare them. It ensures a bright green color and even cooking. Peeling the base of the asparagus is optional, but it makes them very attractive and the stalks tender and totally edible. The hollandaise can be prepared in advance and kept warm in a Thermos jar that has been rinsed with hot water.

The Ingredients:

2 pounds fresh spring asparagus
Water
Salt
Garnish: Hollandaise Sauce (*see* Hollandaise with Ease, Chapter 2), or 3–4 tablespoons unsalted butter, melted

The Steps:

1. Wash asparagus in cold water and break off tough ends. If desired, peel asparagus 2–3 inches up the stalk. (An asparagus peeler or vegetable peeler can be used.)
2. Bring large skillet of salted water to a boil and drop in asparagus. Cook uncovered 8–10 minutes depending on thickness of the vegetable. Do not overcook! The tips and stalks should be *al dente*, crunchy but tender.
3. Drain at once and serve immediately with Hollandaise with Ease or melted butter.

Variations:

Serve asparagus with a light sprinkling of fresh lemon juice instead of hollandaise or butter to reduce calories.

Buttered bread crumbs can be used as an alternate topping for asparagus. Place 4 tablespoons (½ stick) unsalted butter in a small saucepan with ¼ cup dry bread crumbs and toss until lightly brown. Sprinkle over hot asparagus.

Leftover asparagus, although a rare occurrence at today's prices, make a wonderful cold salad tossed with *Laurie's Basic Vinaigrette* dressing.

Make-It-Easy Tips:

√ An asparagus steamer can be used instead of a skillet. Asparagus should be tied together, placed upright in enough boiling water to cover stalks but not tips, covered, and steamed until just tender. The timing of steamed asparagus should be about 15 minutes but color will not be as green since they are cooked covered.

Baked Asparagus

SERVES: 4
Preparation time: 15 minutes
Cooking time: 13 minutes

Here's a great, easy way to prepare fresh asparagus in advance while still preserving the texture and flavor of steamed or boiled asparagus.

Thin asparagus work best in this dish. Prepare in the spring when they are in season.

The Ingredients:

1½ pounds very thin, fresh asparagus
3 tablespoons unsalted butter, melted
1 tablespoon lemon juice
¼ teaspoon freshly ground white pepper
½ cup freshly grated Parmesan cheese

The Steps:

1. Wash asparagus and break off tough ends.
2. Place asparagus in large skillet; add lightly salted, boiling water to cover, bring to a boil again, and cook uncovered for 3 minutes or until almost crisp. Drain asparagus and run under cold water to refresh. Drain again on paper towels.
3. Brush an oven-proof dish with 1 tablespoon melted butter and lay asparagus in dish.
4. Top asparagus with remaining 2 tablespoons melted butter, lemon juice, pepper, and, finally, Parmesan cheese. (The saltiness of the cheese precludes the need for any added salt.) At this point, the dish can be covered with plastic wrap and refrigerated until ready to use.
5. At serving time, bring casserole to room temperature, if possible. Preheat oven to 400° and bake asparagus, uncovered, for 5–10 minutes until hot and bubbling.

Variation:

Buttered bread crumbs can be baked atop asparagus.

Carrots and Parsnips Combined

SERVES: 4
Preparation time: 15 minutes
Cooking time: 6 minutes

This vegetable combination is quick to prepare with a food processor or blender, and makes an especially colorful side dish.

The Ingredients:

4 medium carrots, peeled
4 medium parsnips, peeled
2–3 tablespoons unsalted butter
½ teaspoon salt
¼ teaspoon freshly ground white pepper
½ teaspoon dried tarragon, crumbled (optional)

The Steps:

1. Shred or grate carrots and parsnips in food processor, blender, or by hand.
2. Drop into a large pot of salted water and allow to cook for 2 minutes or until barely tender. Drain and run under cold water. Drain again. (Can be prepared up to this point and refrigerated until ready to use.)
3. At serving time, heat butter in a large skillet. Quickly sauté vegetables in hot butter and season to taste with salt and pepper, and tarragon, if desired.

Variations:

Other shredded vegetables can be substituted for carrots and parsnips according to taste preference, color appeal, and accompanying main dish: For example, zucchini and carrots with veal, or turnips and carrots with turkey.

Make-It-Easy Tips:

√ When selecting parsnips, choose small- to medium-size ones that are solid and have an even surface.

√ To prepare vegetables in blender, cut them coarsely and fill jar half full; cover with water, replace top of jar, and place hand lightly on cover top. Blend on "high" until just chopped. (Watch carefully!) Drain thoroughly in a colander.

Carrot Purée in Artichoke Bottoms

SERVES: 8
Preparation time: 1 minute
Cooking time: 20 minutes

A simple Carrot Purée can be served plain in a bowl garnished with parsley or piled into artichoke bottoms, patty pan squash, or small zucchini boats for an especially attractive presentation. The Carrot Purée is so sweet and creamy tasting, guests often mistake it for mashed sweet potatoes—yet the calorie count is low since only a tablespoon of butter is used in the preparation.

The Ingredients:

2 cans artichoke bottoms, drained
1 pound carrots, peeled and thickly sliced
½ teaspoon salt, or to taste
¼ teaspoon freshly ground white pepper
1 tablespoon unsalted butter

The Steps:

1. Bring large pot of salted water to boil. Drop carrots into water and boil, covered, for 15–20 minutes or until tender.
2. Drain carrots and purée in food processor or blender.
3. Season with salt and pepper; add butter and continue to purée until very smooth.
4. Taste, adjust seasoning if necessary, and pile into artichoke bottoms.
5. Serve immediately, or reheat in a 325° oven for 10 minutes.

Variations:

For a lower calorie vegetable dish, omit the butter.

For an extra-fancy presentation, pipe carrot purée through a cake decorating bag.

Make-It-Easy Tip:

√ Do not store carrots with apples. Apples release a gas that gives carrots a bitter taste.

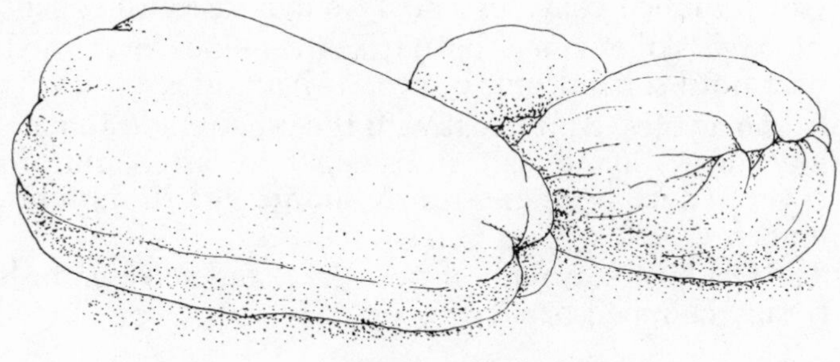

Chayote squash

Sautéed Chayote with Tomatoes

SERVES: 4–6
Preparation time: 15 minutes
Cooking time: 25 minutes

Chayote, also called Mango Squash and Vegetable Pear, is a squash cultivated in tropical regions. Originally from Mexico and South America, it is now grown in Florida and some other regions of the United States. It can be used interchangeably with zucchini in recipes. To prepare to serve alone, cut in half; remove the pulp and mash it; season well and add butter to taste. Pile into scooped-out shells, and bake.

The Ingredients:

2 chayotes, scrubbed clean with a brush
2 tablespoons unsalted butter
1 medium onion, minced
1 16-ounce can tomatoes, drained and roughly chopped
1 tablespoon freshly chopped parsley
Pinch of sugar
Pinch of thyme
1 tablespoon freshly chopped parsley
½ teaspoon salt, or to taste
¼ teaspoon freshly ground pepper, or to taste

The Steps:

1. Cut scrubbed chayotes into 1″ cubes, discarding center seed.
2. In large skillet, melt butter; sauté onions over medium-low heat until soft but not brown, 5–7 minutes.
3. Add chayotes, stir to coat with the onions; add tomatoes, parsley, sugar, thyme, salt and pepper to taste; bring to a boil, cover, reduce heat, and slowly simmer for 20 minutes or until tender.
4. Taste, adjust seasoning if necessary, and serve garnished with freshly chopped parsley.

Variation:

For a spicier version, add chopped green chilies in Step 3, according to taste.

Make-It-Easy Tip:

√ Select hard, firm, smooth chayotes, without blemishes.

Braised Daikon

SERVES: 4
Preparation time: 10 minutes
Cooking time: 10 minutes

Long, white, tapered, and hotter in taste than a regular radish, daikon is often used as decoration since it's easily carved. This Japanese radish can also be shredded for salad, or thinly sliced and braised like a turnip.

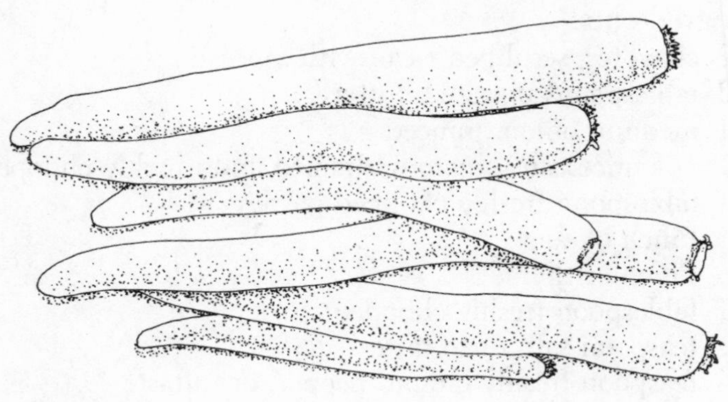

The Ingredients:

1½ pounds daikon, peeled
Chicken broth
2 tablespoons unsalted butter
¼ teaspoon salt, or to taste
Freshly ground white pepper

The Steps:

1. Thinly slice daikon by hand or in food processor.
2. Place in saucepan, cover with chicken broth, bring to boil. Cover, reduce heat, and simmer slowly for 8–10 minutes or until vegetable softens.
3. Drain off all broth, place in bowl, top with butter, salt and pepper, and serve immediately.

Variations:

For a lower calorie version, use only 1 teaspoon butter for flavoring.

For an Oriental Salad, slice daikon and marinate overnight in a dressing of 1 cup water, ¾ cup Japanese or white vinegar, ⅓ cup brown sugar, and 2 teaspoons salt or to taste, stirred together.

Make-It-Easy Tips:

√ Peel daikon with a vegetable peeler as if peeling a carrot.
√ Store daikon in the refrigerator as you would store a red radish.

Eggplant Szechwan-Style

SERVES: 4–6
Preparation time: 15 minutes
Cooking time: 8–10 minutes

Eggplant Szechwan-Style can be served hot as a side vegetable, or cold as a salad or hors d'oeuvre.

The Ingredients:

1 medium eggplant (about 1 pound), unpeeled and cut into 1½″ cubes

- 1 large clove garlic, finely minced
- 1 slice ginger, finely minced
- ¼ cup chicken broth
- 1 tablespoon soy sauce
- 1 teaspoon sugar
- 1 teaspoon chili paste with garlic, or more to taste (available at oriental groceries or by mail order, *see* Appendix A)
- 2 teaspoons Japanese vinegar or white wine vinegar
- 1 tablespoon oriental sesame oil
- 4–5 tablespoons peanut oil

The Steps:

1. Place eggplant and garlic and ginger near cooking area; combine broth, soy sauce, sugar, and chili paste in small bowl and place near cooking area; place vinegar and sesame oil within reach.
2. Heat wok or large skillet, add oil, and stir-fry eggplant over medium heat until softened, 4–5 minutes; remove with slotted spoon.
3. Turn heat to high, add additional tablespoon oil if necessary, and stir-fry garlic and ginger for 30 seconds.
4. Add broth mixture, bring to boil, return eggplant to wok and cook, stirring, for 2 minutes.
5. Add vinegar and sesame oil, stir to combine, and serve hot as a vegetable side dish, or cold as a salad or hors d'oeuvre.

Variation:

If a spicier flavor is desired, increase the amount of chili paste, at your own risk!

Make-It-Easy Tips:

√ Both garlic and ginger can be smashed together with the side of a cleaver and then peeled and chopped easily.

√ Four to five tablespoons of oil are needed because eggplant tends to absorb oil readily and will begin sticking to wok or skillet if there is not enough oil.

√ When selecting an eggplant, check bottom end (without the stem). The shape of the greyish "scar" or indentation on this end is an indicator of the number of seeds. If the scar is oval or oblong, there will be many seeds and the eggplant will be bitter. Select the one with the round scar, about the size of a dime, which will have fewer seeds and thus be less bitter.

Baby Lima Beans and Prosciutto

SERVES: 6
Preparation time: 10 minutes
Cooking time: 15 minutes

The Ingredients:

3 slices prosciutto, diced
1 tablespoon unsalted butter
¼ cup finely minced onion
2 10-ounce packages frozen baby lima beans, thawed and drained
½ cup chicken broth
¼ teaspoon salt, or to taste
¼ teaspoon freshly ground pepper

The Steps:

1. In a small skillet, sauté prosciutto over medium heat until it releases its fat.
2. Add butter to pan and sauté onions until soft but not brown, about 5 minutes.
3. Add lima beans, broth, salt, and pepper; cover, and simmer for 8–10 minutes or until beans are tender.
4. Taste, adjust seasoning if necessary, and serve hot.

Variations:

If baby lima beans are unavailable, substitute regular lima beans and cook until tender.

If prosciutto is unavailable, substitute Westphalian ham or use 2 slices diced bacon. (If using bacon, omit butter.)

Make-It-Easy Tip:

√ Dice prosciutto easily with kitchen shears.

Petit Pois Française

SERVES: 4
Preparation time: 10 minutes
Cooking time: 4–5 minutes

This dish utilizes the traditional French approach to cooking peas with lettuce. The lettuce releases its moisture to braise the peas.

The Ingredients:

1½ cups shredded lettuce
2 10-ounce packages frozen tiny peas, thawed
¼ cup minced scallions (green and white included)
1 teaspoon sugar
¼ teaspoon salt, or to taste
⅛ teaspoon freshly ground white pepper
2 tablespoons unsalted butter, cut into bits

The Steps:

1. In a small saucepan, place ¾ cup shredded lettuce.
2. Top with peas and scallions, sprinkle with sugar, salt, and pepper; dot with butter.
3. Top with remaining lettuce, cover tightly, and cook over medium low heat for 3–4 minutes or until peas are tender.
4. Adjust seasoning to taste, and serve hot.

Variations:

Chopped shallots can be substituted for scallions.

Substitute regular green peas and cook for 5–10 minutes or until tender.

Garnish peas with freshly chopped mint for a refreshing taste.

Potatoes Boiled in Jackets

SERVES: 4
Preparation time: 5 minutes
Cooking time: 15–20 minutes

This recipe is for the small, round, red potatoes that look more attractive and are better nutritionally when cooked in their vitamin-rich jackets. New potatoes in thin skins can also be used and cooked until tender.

The Ingredients:

8 small, round, red or other boiling potatoes
1 teaspoon salt
½ teaspoon salt, or to taste
¼ teaspoon freshly ground pepper, or to taste
2–3 tablespoons unsalted butter, melted
1 tablespoon freshly chopped parsley

The Steps:

1. Scrub potatoes clean with a stiff brush.
2. In large pot, put enough water to cover the potatoes, plus 1 teaspoon salt, and bring to a boil.
3. Add potatoes and cook covered in boiling water until just tender, 15–20 minutes. (Do not allow to overcook or they will be mushy.)
4. Drain potatoes and toss in bowl with ½ teaspoon salt, pepper, melted butter, and parsley.
5. Serve immediately, piping hot.

Variations:

For a low-calorie version, potatoes can be served plain without butter or seasonings. They are delicious as is.

Leftover cooked potatoes can be chopped and sautéed in butter with onions the next day as hash browns. They can also be used in roast beef salad, potato salad, corned beef hash, or sautéed in omelets.

Make-It-Easy Tips:

√ A clean, stiff toothbrush makes a great vegetable brush.

√ Do not store potatoes in the refrigerator. The starch will convert to sugar and an unpleasant sweetish taste will result. If you have already done this, simply remove from refrigerator, store at room temperature, and the starch will be converted back. Also, do not store potatoes with onions. Onions release a gas that hastens the spoilage of potatoes.

Perfect Baked Potatoes

Preparation time: 5 minutes
Cooking time: 1 hour

The Ingredients:

Baking potatoes, 1 per person (Idaho potatoes, also called Russets, are best for baking)
Garnishes: Butter, sour cream, grated cheese, chives, bacon

The Steps:

1. Preheat oven to 400°.
2. Scrub potatoes well, prick with a fork to allow steam to escape, and bake on center rack for 1–1¼ hours, depending on size.
3. Remove from oven; hold each potato with pot holder and gently squeeze to test for doneness, and also to make them fluffy.
4. Cut a cross in top to allow steam to escape and to avoid soggy potatoes.
5. Serve hot with butter or sour cream and assorted garnishes, such as chopped chives, bacon bits, or grated cheese.

Variation:

For a low-calorie potato, top with pepper, yogurt, and fresh herbs such as chives, parsley, or dill.

Make-It-Easy Tips:

√ On hot nights when you don't want to heat the oven, bake potatoes in the toaster-oven at 375° for 1½–2 hours. The outside will be crispy and the inside powdery soft.

√ A Potato Party can be an inexpensive way to entertain. Just bake lots of potatoes and have an assortment of condiments on hand, like chili, guacamole, cheese, chopped onions, shredded lettuce, chilies, bacon, salsa, etc.

√ For a softer skin, rub with oil prior to baking.

√ A metal prong or baking nail speeds up cooking time 10–15 minutes by acting as a heat conductor on the inside of the potato.

√ Do not use foil to wrap potatoes. The results will be soggy skins and lumpy, hard interiors.

Baked Potato Skins

SERVES: 6–8
Preparation time: 10 minutes
Cooking time: 5 minutes

The Ingredients:

6 Idaho potatoes, baked
⅓ cup unsalted butter, melted
½ teaspoon salt, or to taste
¼ teaspoon freshly ground white pepper
Garnish: Sour cream and chives (optional)

The Steps:

1. Preheat broiler.
2. Cut potatoes in half and scoop out all the potato inside (reserve for mashed potatoes or other recipe).
3. Cut skins in half again, generously paint with melted butter, and sprinkle to taste with salt and pepper.
4. Brown under the broiler, 5–6 inches from heat, until crisp, about 3 minutes, watching carefully.
5. Serve skins hot, garnished with sour cream and chives if desired.

Accompaniments:

A variety of fillings and toppings can be used on potato skins, such as bacon, chives, grated Cheddar or Swiss cheese, Guacamole, or even sour cream and caviar.

Variations:

Cut the skins in strips and serve as a cocktail party canapé, plain or filled with sour cream and caviar.

Make-It-Easy Tips:

√ Prepare the potatoes early in the day, cut skins, and then butter, season, and broil at the last minute.

√ Potato skins can also be baked in a 475°–500° oven for 8–10 minutes or until crisp.

Stir-Fried Spinach

SERVES: 3–4
Preparation time: 5 minutes
Cooking time: 3 minutes

The Ingredients:

1 pound fresh spinach leaves, washed, with tough stems removed
2 tablespoons peanut oil
½ teaspoon salt, or to taste
Pinch sugar

The Steps:

1. Heat wok or large, heavy skillet, add oil and, when hot, stir-fry spinach for 1 minute.
2. Add salt and sugar and continue to stir-fry for 1 minute.
3. Taste, adjust seasoning if necessary, and serve immediately.

Make-It-Easy Tips:

√ Select fresh bunches of spinach with dark green leaves without blemishes. If fresh bunches are unavailable, the cellophane-wrapped packages are the next best choice.

√ One pound of fresh spinach equals approximately 1 cup of cooked spinach.

Baked Spinach with Cheese

SERVES: 4
Preparation time: 15 minutes
Cooking time: 30 minutes

The Ingredients:

2 10-ounce packages frozen chopped spinach, thawed and thoroughly squeezed dry
2 eggs, lightly beaten
⅓ cup grated Monterey Jack or Muenster cheese
1 tablespoon grated onion
½ teaspoon salt, or to taste
¼ teaspoon freshly ground pepper
¼ teaspoon nutmeg
1½ tablespoons unsalted butter, diced
2 tablespoons freshly grated Parmesan cheese

The Steps:

1. Preheat oven to 325°. Generously butter small casserole or au gratin dish.
2. In bowl, combine spinach, eggs, cheese, onion, salt, pepper, and nutmeg and spoon into casserole.
3. Bake for 15 minutes; dot with butter and Parmesan cheese and bake for an additional 15 minutes. Serve hot and bubbly.

Make-It-Easy Tips:

√ Baked Spinach with Cheese can be assembled through Step 2 and refrigerated until ready to bake. Bring to room temperature before baking.

Stir-Fried Straw and Hay Summer Squash

SERVES: 6
Preparation time: 10 minutes
Cooking time: 3–4 minutes

Although this dish does not have oriental ingredients, it benefits from the stir-frying technique. The zucchini and yellow squash maintain their crunchy textures, vibrant colors and juicy flavors. The dish gets its name from the pasta dish called Straw and Hay or *Paglia e Fieno*, referring to its green and white colors.

The Ingredients:

- 2 tablespoons olive oil
- 3 scallions, finely chopped (green and white parts included)
- 3 medium crookneck squash (yellow summer squash), cut into ½″ slices
- 3 medium zucchini, cut into ½″ slices
- ¼ cup chicken broth
- Pinch of salt
- ¼ teaspoon freshly ground white pepper
- Garnish: Freshly chopped parsley

The Steps:

1. Heat wok or large heavy skillet until very hot; add oil and heat 30 seconds.
2. Add scallions and stir-fry 1 minute, stirring constantly.
3. Add crookneck and zucchini and continue to stir-fry until squash begins to turn lightly golden.
4. Add broth, cover, and cook over low heat for 2 minutes, until just tender.
5. Season to taste with salt and pepper and serve immediately, sprinkled with freshly chopped parsley.

Variations:

If vegetable is to accompany beef dish, substitute beef broth.

The new hybrid, yellow "gold rush" squash, can be substituted for the crookneck.

Make-It-Easy Tip:

√ When selecting summer squash, choose small- to medium-size ones with a rind tender enough to be punctured by a fingernail.

Baked Acorn Squash

SERVES: 4
Preparation time: 15 minutes
Cooking time: 1 hour

Acorn squash has a variety of names including Table Queen, Danish, or Des Moines.

The Ingredients:

- 2 acorn squash, cut in half lengthwise
- ¼ cup dark brown sugar
- ¼ cup (½ stick) unsalted butter, melted
- ¼ cup unsweetened applesauce
- 4 teaspoons grated onion
- ½ teaspoon cinnamon
- ¼ teaspoon nutmeg
- ⅛ teaspoon ground ginger
- 1 tablespoon dark rum
- ½ teaspoon salt, or to taste
- ¼ teaspoon freshly ground white pepper, or to taste

The Steps:

1. Preheat oven to 350°.
2. Remove seeds and fibers from cut squash and place cut side down in a shallow baking pan. Pour ½″ of hot water in bottom of pan and bake for 25 minutes; drain off water and turn squash upright.
3. In small bowl, combine brown sugar, butter, applesauce, onion, cinnamon, nutmeg, ginger, rum, salt, and pepper and stir well.
4. Spoon mixture into squash shells, dividing it evenly among the 4 halves.

5. Return to oven and bake an additional 35–40 minutes or until golden brown, basting once or twice.
6. Serve squash hot, or reheat for 2–3 minutes under a broiler until golden, watching carefully.

Make-It-Easy Tips:

√ Squash can be assembled through Step 2 and refrigerated until ready to use.

√ Acorn squash can be found in either a dark-green color, meaning it was recently picked, or an orangy color, indicating longer storage. Both are good to use.

√ Place aluminum foil in pan before proceeding with Step 4 to avoid messy clean-ups.

Banana Squash Purée

SERVES: 4
Preparation time: 10 minutes
Cooking time: 10 minutes

The oversize banana squash is generally cut up into usable sections in the grocery store since it runs a staggering, tapering 18″ to 24″ long and 5″ to 6″ wide. A pale olive gray at first, it becomes creamy pink upon storage, with bright orange flesh. Since it is often sold cut, it will not keep more than a week under refrigeration, but if purchased whole it will last about four weeks in a dry place.

The Ingredients:

1 1-pound section banana squash
3 tablespoons unsalted butter
2 tablespoons light brown sugar
1 tablespoon Curaçao or other orange-flavored liqueur
½ teaspoon cinnamon
½ teaspoon salt
¼ teaspoon nutmeg
Pinch mace
Garnish: Grated lemon rind or grated orange rind

The Steps:

1. Peel hard outer shell from squash and cut flesh into 2″ squares.
2. Drop the squash into pot of boiling salted water and, when water returns to a boil, cook covered over medium heat for 8–10 minutes, or until tender; drain.
3. Purée in food processor, blender, or through a food mill until just smooth. (Do not over-process or it will become too pasty in texture.)
4. Remove to a mixing bowl, add the butter, brown sugar, liqueur, cinnamon, salt, nutmeg, and mace; stir until smooth.
5. Taste, adjust seasoning if necessary, and serve hot, garnished with grated lemon or orange rind.

Make-It-Easy Tips:

√ The squash purée can be reheated in a double boiler.

√ When selecting pre-cut banana squash, choose crisp, clean flesh. Avoid discolored, blemished, or bruised pieces, which indicate age.

Baked Spaghetti Squash

SERVES: 4–6
Preparation time: 10 minutes
Cooking time: 1½ hours

Spaghetti Squash, also called Vegetable Spaghetti, Diet Spaghetti, Manchurian Squash (owing to its oriental origin), Cucuzzi or Suzza Melon, is actually an edible gourd. A large oval-shaped yellow vegetable, it owes its name to the stringy texture of its flesh which, when cooked, turns into spaghetti-like strands ready for anything from meat sauce to an Alfredo treatment.

The Ingredients:

2 pounds spaghetti squash
3–4 tablespoons unsalted butter
3–4 tablespoons freshly grated Parmesan cheese
½ teaspoon salt, or to taste

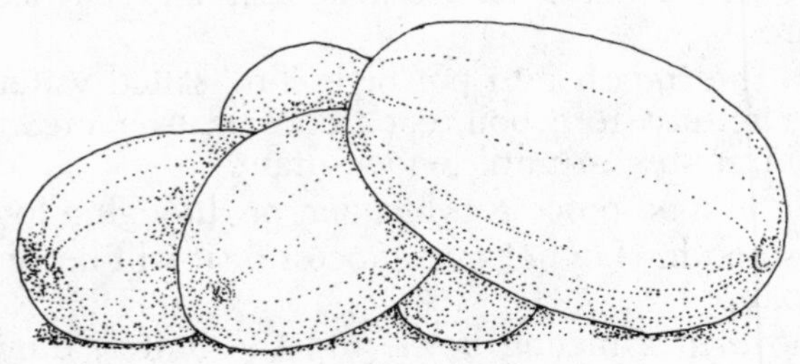

Spaghetti squash

½ teaspoon freshly ground white pepper, or to taste
Garnish: Freshly grated Parmesan cheese

The Steps:

1. Preheat oven to 350°.
2. Prick squash all over with a fork; place on rack in oven and bake for 1½ hours, turning once during cooking.
3. Split in half horizontally, scoop out seeds and discard.
4. With a fork, string fibers out of each half into a large serving bowl and toss with butter, cheese, salt, and pepper.
5. Serve in bowl, or return to shell halves to serve with additional cheese on the side.

Variation:

Use limited amounts of butter and cheese for a low-calorie "spaghetti" dish.

Make-It-Easy Tips:

√ Store unblemished squash in a cool, dry place for up to 4 weeks.

√ Spaghetti squash often contains a sticker explaining how to cut and steam it. I have yet to find anyone who can cut through this gourd with anything less than a hacksaw. Baking or boiling whole softens the skin and makes cutting easy.

Sweet Potato Soufflé

SERVES: 8
Preparation time: 15 minutes
Cooking time: Potatoes–40 minutes
Casserole–45 minutes

Sweet Potato Soufflé is the perfect Thanksgiving accompaniment but can be used year 'round with any poultry or baked ham dish. It is called a soufflé but that doesn't mean it has to be watched carefully. It can be assembled a day in advance and refrigerated until ready to use. The easiest way to prepare the dish is in an electric mixer. A food processor or blender will overmix the potatoes, causing them to become gluey and pasty.

The Ingredients:

6 large sweet potatoes
5 tablespoons unsalted butter
1 cup heavy cream
⅓ cup granulated sugar
⅓ cup dark brown sugar
3 large eggs, lightly beaten
1 teaspoon grated orange rind
½ teaspoon nutmeg
½ teaspoon salt, or to taste

The Steps:

1. Bring large pot of salted water to a boil; add potatoes, bring to boil and cook, covered, about 40 minutes or until very tender. Drain and allow to cool slightly. Peel.
2. Preheat oven to 350°. Generously butter a large, round 2-quart casserole or rectangular baking dish.
3. Place hot potatoes in bowl of electric mixer (or use hand mixer) and beat in butter; add cream, white and brown sugars, eggs, orange rind, nutmeg, and salt and continue to beat until smooth.
4. Pour mixture into prepared casserole and bake for 40 minutes.
5. Serve immediately.

Variations:

Yams can be substituted for sweet potatoes.

And . . . for those who nostalgically connect sweet potatoes with a marshmallow topping—place 2 cups of tiny marshmallows on top of the baked casserole and return to the oven for just 3–4 minutes or until melted, watching very carefully.

Cherry Tomatoes Flavored with Dill

SERVES: 6
Preparation time: 10 minutes
Cooking time: 4–5 minutes

The Ingredients:

3 tablespoons unsalted butter
2 pints cherry tomatoes, washed and stems removed
¼ cup freshly snipped dill or 2 teaspoons dried dill
½ teaspoon salt, or to taste
½ teaspoon freshly ground pepper, or to taste

The Steps:

1. In large saucepan, melt butter; when hot and foamy add cherry tomatoes, dill, salt, and pepper.
2. Cover, reduce heat, and cook slowly for 4–5 minutes until the tomatoes are just cooked but not bursting open.
3. Taste, adjust seasoning if necessary, and serve immediately.

Variations:

Heavy cream can be added with the seasonings for a rich vegetable dish.

Freshly chopped chives or freshly chopped basil, when in season, can be substituted for the dill.

Make-It-Easy Tip:

√ Wash tomatoes first and then remove stem ends to prevent loss of juice.

Tomatoes Filled with Peas

SERVES: 4
Preparation time: 10–15 minutes
Cooking time: 10–15 minutes

The Ingredients:

4 medium-size tomatoes
1 tablespoon unsalted butter
2 tablespoons finely minced onion
1 10-ounce package frozen tiny peas, thawed
½ teaspoon salt, or to taste
¼ teaspoon freshly ground pepper, or to taste

The Steps:

1. Preheat oven to 325°.
2. Cut tops off tomatoes, scoop out centers with a grapefruit spoon or similar tool; discard the seeds and pulp and allow to drain upside down for 5 minutes on paper towels.
3. Place tomatoes in a baking pan and bake for 10 minutes, until just softened.
4. While tomatoes are baking, heat butter in small saucepan; sauté onion over medium heat until soft but not brown, about 5 minutes. Add peas and stir to coat with onion-butter mixture; cover, and cook for 2 minutes or until just warmed through.
5. Season to taste with salt and pepper, fill baked tomatoes with peas, and serve hot.

Variations:

Tomatoes can also be filled with chopped spinach, which has been sautéed with onion and butter and enriched with sour cream; or filled with chopped broccoli, sautéed with butter and garlic and enriched with Parmesan cheese.

Make-It-Easy Tips:

√ Place tomatoes in a muffin tin to keep them from falling over.
√ To prepare in advance, cook the shells only 7 minutes, fill with peas and, when ready, reheat in a moderate 350° oven for 3–4

minutes. Do not overcook or tomatoes will become too soft and may fall apart.

√ Select tomatoes by color, lack of blemishes, and especially odor. Local, vine-ripened tomatoes have a distinct, flavorful aroma as opposed to the ones that are ripened during shipping, which have little or no aroma. And vine-ripened tomatoes contain almost twice the amount of vitamin C.

Tomato Pie

SERVES: 6
Preparation time: 15 minutes
Cooking time: 40 minutes

This Tomato Pie makes an attractive side dish, but can also be served as a lunch or brunch dish.

The Ingredients:

1 frozen pastry shell (9″)
4 medium, ripe tomatoes, sliced, and slices cut in half
¼ cup chopped chives or scallion stalks
¾ teaspoon freshly chopped basil or ¼ teaspoon dried basil, crumbled
¼ teaspoon dried oregano, crumbled
¼ teaspoon salt, or to taste
¼ teaspoon freshly ground pepper, or to taste
1 cup grated Swiss Gruyère cheese
¼ cup mayonnaise

The Steps:

1. Preheat oven to 425°.
2. Bake pie crust for 5 minutes. Remove from oven. Reduce heat to 400°.
3. Place tomato pieces on bottom of pie shell.
4. Sprinkle tomatoes with chives or scallions, basil, oregano, salt, and pepper.
5. Combine cheese and mayonnaise and carefully spread mixture

evenly over tomatoes, making sure it reaches edges of pie crust and seals in tomatoes completely.

6. Bake for 35 minutes or until hot and bubbly.
7. Allow to sit for 5–10 minutes, cut in wedges, and serve hot.

Variations:

Grated Cheddar or Monterey Jack can be substituted for Swiss cheese.

Make-It-Easy Tips:

√ Pie can be frozen successfully for future use. Double the recipe to save extra work.

√ The pie crust is pre-baked for 5 minutes to prevent it from becoming soggy.

√ Ripen tomatoes to full maturity in a brown paper bag that has been pierced with a few holes, or in one of the new Lucite fruit ripeners, checking daily. Do *not* ripen in direct sunlight. Warmth, not light, ripens tomatoes.

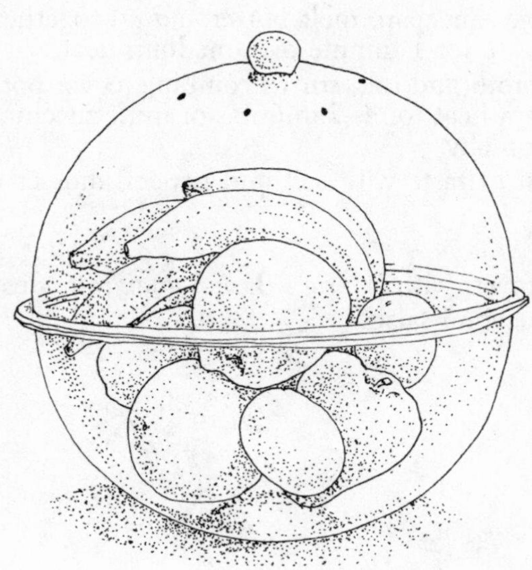

Fruit ripener

Dilled Zucchini

SERVES: 4
Preparation time: 10 minutes
Cooking time: 7–8 minutes

Dilled Zucchini is low in calories.

The Ingredients:

- 1 tablespoon unsalted butter
- 1 teaspoon olive oil
- 1 pound zucchini, cut in ¼″ slices (thick julienne strips)
- ¼ cup chicken broth
- 1–2 tablespoons freshly snipped dill, or 1 teaspoon dried dill, to taste
- ½ teaspoon salt, or to taste
- ¼ teaspoon freshly ground pepper, or to taste

The Steps:

1. In large saucepan, melt butter and oil together; add zucchini and sauté for 1 minute over medium heat.
2. Add broth and dill, stir to combine; cover pot and cook over medium heat for 4–5 minutes or until zucchini is cooked but still crunchy.
3. Season to taste with salt and pepper and serve immediately.

Variation:

Serve leftovers with *Laurie's Basic Vinaigrette* dressing to make a cold zucchini salad.

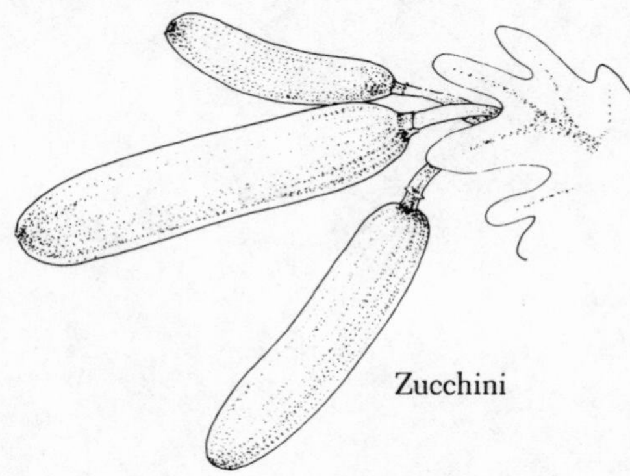

Zucchini

Italian Zucchini Bake

SERVES: 8
Preparation time: 15 minutes
Cooking time: 30–35 minutes

The Ingredients:

3–4 tablespoons unsalted butter
2 large onions, sliced
3 pounds zucchini, washed and cut into ¼″ slices
3 tablespoons tomato paste
2 tablespoons freshly grated Parmesan cheese
½ teaspoon salt, or to taste
¼ teaspoon freshly ground pepper
¼ teaspoon freshly minced garlic
3 tablespoons freshly grated Parmesan cheese

The Steps:

1. Preheat oven to 350°. Generously butter a 9″ x 12″ x 2″ baking dish.
2. Melt butter in large skillet; add onions and zucchini; sauté over medium heat until golden brown, 5–7 minutes.
3. Remove from heat and add tomato paste, 2 tablespoons cheese, salt, pepper, and garlic and toss well.
4. Pour into baking dish, sprinkle 3 tablespoons remaining cheese on top, and bake for 25–30 minutes or until golden brown on top; serve hot.

Make-It-Easy Tips:

√ A wok is a handy pot to use when sautéing zucchini. This large amount of vegetables can be tossed around in a wok without falling out.

√ Zucchini Bake can be assembled through Step 3, poured into baking dish, and refrigerated until ready to bake. Bring to room temperature and proceed with recipe.

CHAPTER EIGHT

SALADS

Flavored Vinegar
Raspberry Vinegar
Raspberry Vinaigrette Dressing
French Dressing
Laurie's Basic Vinaigrette and Variations
Basic Blender Mayonnaise
Mustard Mayonnaise
Thousand Island Dressing
Curry Mayonnaise
Dill Mayonnaise
Lemon-Caper Mayonnaise
Spinach Mayonnaise
Green Goddess Salad Dressing
Low-Calorie Buttermilk Dill Dressing
Yogurt Dressing
Spicy Tomato Dressing with No Oil
Low-Calorie Buttermilk Thousand Island Dressing
Greek Salad
Romaine Salad with Litchi Nuts
Caesar Salad
Spinach Salad
Spinach Salad with Creamy Dressing
Tossed Salad with Red Onions
Cabbage Salad with Caraway Seeds
Chinese Asparagus Salad with Spicy Dressing
Bean Sprout Salad
Broccoli Florets Vinaigrette
Dilled Cucumber Salad
Middle Eastern Salad
Raw Mushroom Salad
Snow Pea Salad
String Bean Salad
Tomato and Onion Salad
Oriental Zucchini Salad
Pasta Salad with Chicken and Vegetables
Oriental Noodle Salad
Rice Salad Niçoise
Curried Brown Rice Salad with Fruit
Tabbouleh
Roast Beef Salad
Marinated Oriental Beef and Pepper Salad
Oriental Roast Pork and Snow Pea Salad
Chinese Seafood Salad
Madame Chu's Szechwan Peppercorn Chicken Salad
Curried Chicken Salad
Chinese Chicken and Cucumber Salad

Salads have been around since ancient times. As early as 1390, a recipe for "sallet" from *The Forme of Cury,* a cookbook compiled by the cooks of Richard II, listed lettuce and vegetables prescribing they be washed, torn with the hands, and well dressed with oil, vinegar, and salt.

The first published literary work on Salads was *Acetaria, a Discourse of Sallets,* written by John Evelyn in 1699, who states that "we are by Sallets to understand a particular Composition of certain Crude and Fresh Herbs, such as usually are, or may safely be eaten with some Acetous Juice, Oyl, Salt, etc. to give them a grateful Gust and Vehicle."

Today's salads are no longer lost as a side dish. They are used as first courses, either hot or cold, and flavored with exotic ingredients such as *Raspberry Vinegar* or even sea urchins. Salads can be used as main courses, composed of meat, lettuce, vegetables, and even fruits. Main-course salads are often Make-It-Easy summer dinners.

The important points to remember in salad preparation are:

1. Purchase first-quality ingredients. A salad is only as good as the sum of its parts. Buy *green* lettuce, no brown or yellow or wilted leaves. Buy good-quality oils and vinegars—the taste will tell the difference.
2. Make the salad attractive. Presentation is important no matter how simple the recipe. Place the ingredients in an attractive manner in the bowl, selecting them on the basis of color, eye appeal, and taste.
3. Be imaginative, be creative and, above all—have fun! This is the time to be inventive and also the time to use up some precious leftovers. Why not try *Romaine Salad with Litchi Nuts,* or how about *Oriental Roast Pork and Snow Pea Salad*?

PROCEDURE FOR MAKING SALADS

1. Wash, and then dry the salad greens in a colander, salad spinner, salad basket or between paper towels. Salad greens must be thoroughly dried or the dressing won't cling to the leaves and it will be diluted.
2. Wrap dried lettuce in absorbent towels and place in a plastic bag in the refrigerator to chill for about an hour before serving. This chore can be done in the morning and the greens will remain crisp for dinner.

3. Additional salad vegetables should be shredded, chopped, or sliced and placed, covered, in the refrigerator until ready to use.
4. When ready to serve the salad, break the larger lettuce leaves into the bowl. Do *not* use a knife—it may bruise the greens. The smaller leaves can remain whole.
5. Once the greens are prepared in the bowl, pour on the dressing, toss, and serve immediately with lots of freshly ground pepper.

SALAD DRESSINGS

Most of the prepared, bottled salad dressings on the market, besides tasting awful, are full of chemicals, salt, and preservatives. It's easy to prepare fresh salad dressings that are flavorful.

The following dressings offer a wide range of choice to enhance any type of greens. Beginning with a basic vinaigrette and a quick blender mayonnaise, and concluding with several unusual low-calorie dressings, there is something for everyone—and every green.

OIL

A good-quality oil is essential to a great salad. Olive oil is the traditional salad oil but its prohibitive cost makes it a luxury. Olive oil in combination with a lighter vegetable oil such as corn, peanut, soy, sunflower, or safflower saves on cost and gives a lighter more delicate flavor than the heavier olive oil alone. Exotic oils such as walnut or hazelnut are interesting taste additions to salads but are extremely costly.

Flavored oils are easy to prepare and add an extra zing to the salad. Oil can be flavored with fresh herbs, such as basil, dill, or rosemary. A peeled clove of garlic or a peeled shallot impaled on a bamboo skewer inserted in a bottle of olive oil will add something extra to the salad. These flavored oils and the flavored vinegars make excellent gifts year 'round.

VINEGAR

A good French wine vinegar is important to a great salad. Either red or white, it adds a subtle flavoring to the salad dressing.

Spanish sherry vinegar imparts a slightly sweet taste, which complements fruit or cheese salads. Cider vinegar is best used in limited amounts in sweet fruit salads, for pickling, or as a basis for mayonnaise.

Japanese rice vinegar is so delicate in flavor that it can be used in larger quantities than most other vinegars.

The newest vinegar on the market is called Balsamico which, loosely translated, means "that which is good for the health." Balsimic vinegar is prepared from special sweet grapes and aged for many years, resulting in a dark brown vinegar that is intensely aromatic and so flavorful that it can stand on its own as a salad dressing, especially on slices of ripe tomatoes.

The flavored vinegars are my favorites. They are simple to prepare, make excellent gifts, and the subtle flavors contribute to the success of a salad.

Flavored Vinegar

YIELD: As desired
Preparation time: 5 minutes
Marinating time: 2 weeks

The Ingredients:

Old bottle (the cruets with stoppers make the herb-vinegar a beautiful gift)
Few sprigs fresh herbs (dill, basil, rosemary, tarragon, oregano, etc.)
Red or white wine vinegar

The Steps:

1. Wash bottle.
2. Place fresh herbs in bottle and fill with wine vinegar. Cover and allow to steep for two weeks before using.
3. Herbs can remain in jar or they can be removed, if desired, after the two weeks of steeping time.

Herb-Flavored Vinegar will keep for at least 1 year, tightly sealed.

Raspberry Vinegar

YIELD: 3 quarts
Preparation time: 5–10 minutes
Marinating time: 12 hours
Cooking time: 2–3 minutes

Raspberry vinegar has been made popular by the school of *Nouvelle Cuisine* where the French chefs use this sweet vinegar in warm, first-course salads. They also use Raspberry Vinegar like a wine to deglaze a pan after sautéing poultry or fish, resulting in an amazing sauce.

The Ingredients:

1 10-ounce package frozen, unsweetened raspberries, thawed
3 quarts red wine vinegar
Glass jars

The Steps:

1. Place raspberries in colander and wash under cold running water. Drain, and place in large enamel or stainless steel pot covered with the vinegar for 12 hours or overnight.
2. The next day, heat raspberries and vinegar and bring to a boil; then turn off heat and allow to cool.
3. Strain vinegar into bottles, cover tightly, and label.

Raspberry Vinaigrette Dressing

YIELD: ¾ cup
Preparation time: 5 minutes

This dressing is especially delicious on a salad of crisp greens topped with toasted walnut halves.

The Ingredients:

8 tablespoons olive oil (or 2 tablespoons walnut oil and 6 tablespoons olive oil)

1½–2 tablespoons raspberry vinegar
1 teaspoon Dijon mustard
½ teaspoon salt
¼ teaspoon freshly ground pepper
1 teaspoon freshly snipped chives (optional)

The Steps:

1. Combine oil, vinegar, mustard, salt, and pepper in a screw-top jar, cover, and shake well.
2. Add chives, if desired, and toss with crisp greens.

Variations:

Add minced garlic, minced dill, or minced parsley, and a few tablespoons of sour cream or *Crème Fraîche* (*see* Chapter 2).

FRENCH DRESSING

"French" dressing is a misnomer, like "Danish" pastry, "Russian" dressing or "English" muffins. The classic French salad dressing is the versatile vinaigrette, basically composed of oil, vinegar, salt, and pepper. Variations come in the proportions, the methods of mixing, and the additional ingredients added to it.

My general preference is 3 parts oil to 1 part vinegar, but this pattern varies slightly, depending on the heaviness of the oil and the acidity of the vinegar. I also add a small amount of lemon juice to certain vinaigrettes for added flavor.

I try to make the preparation as easy as possible, so I shake the dressing in a jar or I use the food processor to do the mixing for me, especially when minced garlic is included.

My basic recipe (*Laurie's Basic Vinaigrette*) makes about 1½ cups of dressing. I make it a practice to add only a few tablespoons at a time to the salad bowl. A little vinaigrette travels far. As a rule, I use only ¼–⅓ cup of dressing for four people but I always perform the taste test on a few greens before serving.

The cardinal rule in serving green salads that are not marinated is to toss at the very last minute. I keep my greens chilled and my dressing at room temperature (unless it contains egg or cream) and toss just before serving.

Laurie's Basic Vinaigrette (and Variations)

YIELD: 1½ cups
Preparation time: 5 minutes

The Ingredients:

- ¾ cup olive oil (or ¼ cup olive oil, ½ cup corn, safflower, or soy oil)
- ¼ cup wine vinegar
- 1 teaspoon Dijon mustard
- ½ teaspoon dry mustard
- ¼ teaspoon granulated sugar
- ½ teaspoon salt, or to taste
- ½ teaspoon freshly ground white or black pepper, or to taste

The Step:

1. Combine oil, vinegar, Dijon mustard, dry mustard, sugar, salt, and pepper in a screw-top jar and shake to combine.

Variations:

Add 1 tablespoon lemon juice, especially if mushrooms are used. I toss the mushrooms in the lemon juice to marinate them and then add both to the salad.

Add 1 teaspoon crushed garlic or shallots: a more subtle way of adding garlic is to crush a clove and allow it to sit, whole, in the oil for several days to release the garlic flavor.

Fresh herbs: 2 tablespoons minced chives, parsley, tarragon, basil, dill (one, or all).

Worcestershire sauce: ½ teaspoon for spiciness.

Capers: 1 teaspoon chopped capers.

Curry powder: ½ teaspoon curry powder.

Egg yolk: 1 egg yolk adds body and lemony color.

Chopped, hard-cooked egg: 1 chopped, hard-cooked egg adds texture.

Cheese: 2 tablespoons freshly grated Parmesan cheese or 2 tablespoons crumbled Roquefort or Bleu cheese.

Make-It-Easy Tip:

√ Any unused Vinaigrette dressing can be refrigerated until ready to use. If possible, bring to room temperature before serving.

Basic Blender Mayonnaise

YIELD: 1¾ cups
Preparation time: 10 minutes

Preparing your own mayonnaise may not appear to be a Make-It-Easy recipe, but the blender or food processor really does make it a simple chore. The taste is wonderful, the cost is less, and it can be prepared without salt and sugar for those on restricted diets.

The Ingredients:

1 whole egg
1 tablespoon fresh lemon juice or 1 tablespoon cider vinegar
½ teaspoon dry mustard
½ teaspoon salt, or to taste
¼ teaspoon freshly ground white pepper
Pinch of cayenne pepper
¼ cup olive oil
1 cup corn, safflower, or soy oil, or any other vegetable oil desired

The Steps:

1. Place egg, lemon juice, mustard, salt, white pepper, and cayenne in blender or food processor and process quickly for 5 seconds, just to blend.
2. Start machine again and, while machine is running, gradually pour olive and vegetable oils into container until the mixture becomes thickened. (Do not overprocess.)
3. With a rubber spatula, remove mayonnaise from work bowl, place in a jar or plastic container, and refrigerate until ready to use.

Variation:

Two egg yolks can be substituted for 1 egg.

Make-It-Easy Tips:

√ Because there are no preservatives, the mayonnaise will keep for only 8–10 days in the refrigerator.

√ To avoid splatters, loosely cover top of blender container with a towel when adding oil in Step 2.

√ If mayonnaise does not thicken as it should, do not despair. Pour mixture into another bowl and rinse out blender jar or work bowl. Place another egg in cleaned bowl, start machine, gradually pour mixture back into bowl, and process until the mayonnaise thickens.

MAYONNAISE VARIATIONS

Mustard Mayonnaise

YIELD: 1½ cups
Preparation time: 5 minutes

The Ingredients:

1 cup mayonnaise
4 teaspoons Dijon mustard
1 teaspoon lemon juice
½ teaspoon freshly ground white pepper
2 tablespoons minced *cornichons* (sour pickles), optional
2 tablespoons minced fresh parsley (optional)

The Steps:

1. Combine mayonnaise, mustard, lemon juice, and pepper in a bowl and mix until smooth.
2. Add *cornichons* and parsley, if desired, and serve immediately, or chill until ready to use.

Thousand Island Dressing (for Cold Seafood or Salads)

YIELD: 2 cups
Preparation time: 5 minutes

The Ingredients:

1 cup mayonnaise
½ cup chili sauce
2 tablespoons India Relish
1 hard-cooked egg, chopped
1 tablespoon minced onion or scallion
Pinch of paprika

The Steps:

1. Combine all ingredients in a bowl and mix until smooth.
2. Serve immediately, or chill until ready to use.

Curry Mayonnaise (for Dips)

YIELD: 1 cup
Preparation time: 2 minutes

The Ingredients:

1 cup mayonnaise
1½–2 teaspoons curry powder, dissolved in
2 teaspoons lemon juice

The Steps:

1. Combine in a bowl and mix until smooth.
2. Serve immediately, or chill until ready to use.

Dill Mayonnaise (for Seafood or Salads)

YIELD: 1 cup
Preparation time: 5 minutes

The Ingredients:

1 cup mayonnaise
1–2 tablespoons snipped fresh dill or 1 teaspoon dried dill

The Steps:

1. Combine in a bowl and mix until smooth.
2. Serve immediately, or chill until ready to use.

Make-It-Easy Tip:

√ Dill is easily snipped with kitchen shears.

Lemon–Caper Mayonnaise (for Dips or Seafood)

YIELD: 1½ cups
Preparation time: 5 minutes

The Ingredients:

1 cup mayonnaise
3 tablespoons lemon juice
2 tablespoons capers, drained and minced
2 tablespoons freshly minced parsley

The Steps:

1. Combine all ingredients in a bowl and mix until smooth.
2. Serve immediately, or chill until ready to use.

Spinach Mayonnaise

YIELD: 3 cups
Preparation time: 15 minutes
Chilling time: 4–6 hours or overnight

Spinach Mayonnaise accompanies poached fish dishes and steamed vegetables, or can be used by itself as a dip for crudités.

The Ingredients:

- 2 10-ounce packages frozen chopped spinach, thawed and squeezed dry
- 4 scallions, finely minced (green and white included)
- ½ cup chopped parsley
- 1 tablespoon freshly snipped dill or 1 teaspoon dried dill
- 2 cups mayonnaise
- 1 tablespoon lemon juice
- ½ teaspoon salt, or to taste
- ¼ teaspoon freshly ground pepper

The Steps:

1. In food processor or blender, chop spinach with scallions, parsley, and dill, pulsating until finely chopped.
2. Add the mayonnaise and lemon juice and continue to process until smooth.
3. Season to taste with salt and pepper; mix again, and chill for 4–6 hours or overnight.
4. Serve sauce chilled with cold fish, vegetables, or as a dip.

Make-It-Easy Tips:

√ Sauce can be kept for several weeks in a jar in refrigerator.

√ Squeeze spinach dry by placing in a sieve and pressing down on it. Place ball of spinach in your fist and squeeze out any remaining liquid.

Green Goddess Salad Dressing

YIELD: 2 cups
Preparation time: 10–15 minutes

This dressing was created in California by a chef honoring George Arliss, the actor, who was opening in William Archer's play, *The Green Goddess.* It is best served over very crisp romaine lettuce with watercress and sliced endive added. The dressing can be prepared easily in a food processor or blender and used for a salad, or refrigerated and used as a dip with crudités.

The Ingredients:

4 anchovy fillets, drained
¼ cup parsley, coarsely chopped
¼ cup snipped chives
3 tablespoons tarragon vinegar
1 scallion, diced (green and white included)
1 clove garlic, smashed and peeled
½ teaspoon dry mustard
½ teaspoon Worcestershire sauce
½ teaspoon dried tarragon, crumbled, or ½ tablespoon freshly chopped tarragon
½ teaspoon chili powder
½ teaspoon salt, or to taste
¼ teaspoon freshly ground pepper
1 cup mayonnaise
1 cup dairy sour cream

The Steps:

1. Place all ingredients, except mayonnaise and sour cream, in food processor or blender. Process until smooth.
2. Add mayonnaise and sour cream and process just until blended.
3. Taste, adjust seasoning if necessary with salt and pepper, and chill in tightly covered jar in refrigerator until ready to use.
4. Serve over crisp romaine, leaf lettuce, or spinach leaves.

Variation:

If chives are unavailable, increase the amount of scallions to 2.

Make-It-Easy Tip:

√ The dressing should keep for a week to 10 days in the refrigerator.

Low-Calorie Buttermilk Dill Dressing

SERVES: 4
Preparation time: 10 minutes

The Ingredients:

2 teaspoons finely minced parsley
2 scallions, finely minced (green and white included)
½ cup low-fat buttermilk
1½ tablespoons mayonnaise
½ teaspoon freshly snipped dill or ¼ teaspoon dried dill
¼ teaspoon freshly ground white pepper
Pinch of salt

The Steps:

1. Mince parsley and scallions together in food processor or blender, add remaining ingredients, and process until smooth dressing is formed.
2. Serve immediately, or chill until ready to use.
3. Serve over crisp greens with cherry tomatoes.

Variation:

Leftover dressing can be used as a low-calorie dip for vegetable crudités.

Make-It-Easy Tips:

√ It is difficult to prepare any less than the dressing amount indicated, so refrigerate any leftover for future salads.

√ This dressing has only about 12 calories per tablespoon. To further reduce, check the calorie listings on several buttermilks and choose the lowest.

Yogurt Dressing

SERVES: 4
Preparation time: 15 minutes
Chilling time: 2 hours

The spicy seasonings in this low-calorie salad dressing make a delicious addition to green or leafless salads. I use it as a dressing when I combine bean sprouts, radishes, mushrooms, cucumbers, and scallions. It's a refreshing accompaniment for spicy lamb or Szechwan stir-fried dishes, and is only about 20 calories per serving.

The Ingredients:

6 ounces plain yogurt, low-fat or whole milk
1 tablespoon soy sauce
1 teaspoon lemon juice
¼ teaspoon ground coriander
¼ teaspoon ground cumin
½ teaspoon salt, or to taste
¼ teaspoon freshly ground white pepper

The Steps:

1. Combine all ingredients in a bowl and whisk or stir until smooth.
2. Serve immediately, or chill until ready to use.

Variation:

For a low-salt version, substitute the new, milder, salt-restricted soy sauce, and eliminate the ½ teaspoon salt.

Spicy Tomato Dressing with No Oil

YIELD: 1½ cups
Preparation time: 10 minutes
Chilling time: 2–3 hours

This dressing has only five calories per tablespoon!

The Ingredients:

1 cup tomato juice or vegetable juice
¼ cup chopped green pepper
¼ cup chopped scallions (green and white included)
3 tablespoons red wine vinegar
2 teaspoons Worcestershire sauce
1 teaspoon Dijon mustard
½ teaspoon freshly minced garlic
½ teaspoon salt, or to taste
½ teaspoon freshly ground black pepper
Pinch of sugar or a few drops of honey

The Steps:

1. In a food processor or blender, combine all ingredients and process until smooth.
2. Chill for 2–3 hours or until ready to use.
3. Serve dressing over tossed greens, sprouts, sliced radishes, and sliced carrots.

Variation:

For a creamier-style dressing, ½ cup low-fat cottage cheese can be pureed with the dressing until smooth.

Low-Calorie Buttermilk Thousand Island Dressing

YIELD: 1½ cups
Preparation time: 10 minutes
Chilling time: 2–3 hours

This dressing has only 13 calories per tablespoon.

The Ingredients:

- ⅓ cucumber, peeled, seeded, cut into chunks
- 1 scallion, cut into 2″ sections (green and white included)
- ⅓ cup buttermilk
- ¼ cup tomato sauce
- 3 tablespoons cider vinegar
- 2 tablespoons vegetable oil
- ½ teaspoon Dijon mustard
- ½ teaspoon salt, or to taste
- ¼ teaspoon freshly ground pepper

The Steps:

1. Place cucumber and onion in food processor or blender and chop fine.
2. Add remaining ingredients, process until smooth, and chill for 2–3 hours or until ready to use.
3. Serve over tossed greens and tomatoes.

Make-It-Easy Tip:

√ The dressing can be prepared by hand and whisked until smooth, but vegetables must then be finely chopped.

SALADS WITH GREENS AND LEAFLESS SALADS

Choosing from the variety of greens available, we can create quick and easy salads that can no longer be labeled "plain green salad."

As a change from the usual tossed green salads, leafless salads add variety and creativity to the meal. By using vegetables in the salad, you've combined two courses in one, saving on kitchen chores. Vegetable haters may actually be inspired to like vegetables when they're combined in international salads such as *Chinese Asparagus Salad with Spicy Dressing* or *Middle-Eastern Salad.* Remember to taste marinated salads just before serving. Chilling diminishes flavors and an adjustment of seasoning is often necessary.

Greek Salad

SERVES: 4
Preparation time: 15 minutes

The Ingredients:

1 large head Boston lettuce, torn in pieces
1 cucumber, peeled and cut into ¼″ slices
3 ripe tomatoes, cut into small chunks
12 Greek olives, or black olives
1 small red onion, thinly sliced into rings
¼ pound Feta cheese (¾ cup), crumbled

Dressing:

½ cup olive oil (Greek or Italian)
2 tablespoons red wine vinegar
½ teaspoon minced garlic
½ teaspoon salt, or to taste
¼ teaspoon freshly ground black pepper
¼ teaspoon dried oregano, crumbled
¼ teaspoon dried basil, crumbled

Garnish: Freshly chopped parsley, capers, chopped pimientos

Optional Additional Ingredients: Drained marinated mushrooms, drained marinated artichoke hearts, red or green pepper strips, pimiento-stuffed olives, drained marinated stuffed eggplants.

The Steps:

1. Place lettuce, cucumbers, tomatoes, olives, and onions in a bowl and chill (covered with paper towel and plastic wrap until ready to use).
2. When ready to serve, crumble Feta cheese over greens.
3. Combine dressing ingredients in a screw-top jar and shake to combine well.

4. Pour dressing over salad, toss well, and serve immediately, garnished with chopped parsley, capers, and chopped pimientos (optional). Additional vegetables can be added if desired.

Variations:

Greek Salad can be transformed into a main course by adding one 7-ounce can tuna, drained and chunked. It can be served as a supper or lunch dish with buttered, toasted pita bread.

To transform the Greek Salad into an Italian Salad, omit the Feta cheese and Greek olives and add Parmesan cheese and pimiento-stuffed olives, pimientos, cubes of Mozzarella cheese and, for a main course, add chopped salami and ham.

Romaine Salad with Litchi Nuts

SERVES: 4–6
Preparation time: 10 minutes

This is an unusual combination of crisp greens and sweet litchi nuts. It can be especially effective as a side dish to accompany curries or oriental dishes.

The Ingredients:

1 large head romaine lettuce, washed and dried
1 11-ounce can litchi nuts, thoroughly drained
½ cup chopped walnuts

Dressing:

½ cup olive oil or vegetable oil
2 tablespoons white wine vinegar
2 tablespoons chili sauce
1 tablespoon lemon juice
½ teaspoon sugar
½ teaspoon salt, or to taste
¼ teaspoon freshly ground black pepper, or to taste
¼ teaspoon dry mustard
Pinch of paprika

The Steps:

1. Break up pieces of lettuce into salad bowl.
2. Add litchi nuts and sprinkle with walnuts.
3. Combine dressing ingredients in a screw-top jar and shake to combine; pour over salad, toss, and serve immediately.

Caesar Salad

SERVES: 4
Preparation time: 10 minutes

A traditional Caesar Salad should be prepared in a wooden bowl at the last minute at the table. Romaine lettuce, garlic, Parmesan cheese, lemon juice, anchovies, and an egg are all essential to a Caesar Salad.

The Ingredients:

1 head romaine lettuce, washed and dried
1 clove garlic, pressed or finely chopped
1 2-ounce can anchovy fillets, drained and mashed
¼ teaspoon salt, or to taste
½ teaspoon freshly ground black pepper, or to taste
½ cup olive oil
1 teaspoon Dijon mustard
3 tablespoons lemon juice
1 egg
¼ cup freshly grated Parmesan cheese
1 cup toasted croutons
Garnish: Freshly cracked black pepper

The Steps:

1. Wash and dry lettuce, break into small pieces, and set aside or chill until ready to use.
2. In wooden salad bowl, place garlic and anchovies. Add salt and pepper and mash together.
3. Add oil, mustard, and lemon juice and stir to combine.
4. Add crisp romaine lettuce pieces and toss with dressing.
5. Carefully lower an egg (in shell) into boiling water, allow to sit

for 1 minute, and crack over salad; toss until lettuce is well-coated.
6. Sprinkle with Parmesan cheese and croutons, toss again, and serve immediately with additional freshly cracked pepper.

Variation:

If you're not fond of anchovies, by all means omit them, but increase the salt to ½ teaspoon, or to taste.

Make-It-Easy Tip:

√ Croutons without preservatives are now available at the market. If you prefer to make them yourself, you can bake them easily in the oven without the messy job of frying. Brush both sides of bread with melted butter (or garlic-flavored butter, if desired), cut into cubes, spread on an ungreased baking sheet and bake, uncovered, for 15–20 minutes, turning occasionally.

Spinach Salad

SERVES: 6
Preparation time: 10 minutes

The Ingredients:

1½ pounds fresh spinach leaves, washed and dried
4 scallions, sliced into ¼″ pieces (green and white included)

Dressing:

½ cup corn oil
3 tablespoons white wine vinegar
2 teaspoons Dijon mustard
1 teaspoon soy sauce
½ teaspoon curry powder
½ teaspoon sugar
½ teaspoon salt, or to taste
¼ teaspoon freshly ground white pepper, or to taste
Garnish: One tablespoon toasted sesame seeds

The Steps:

1. Remove tough stems from spinach; tear leaves into small pieces and place in a salad bowl along with scallions.

2. Combine all dressing ingredients in a screw-top jar and shake until smooth.
3. Pour dressing over spinach leaves, toss well, and serve immediately, garnished with toasted sesame seeds.

Variations:

Peanut, safflower, soy or any other light oil can be substituted for corn oil.

One peeled, chopped Pippin, Granny Smith or other tart apple can be added together with ⅓ cup roasted Spanish peanuts.

Make-It-Easy Tips:

√ An easy way to dry spinach is to wrap up leaves in layers of paper towels or tea towels, place in plastic bag, tie up, and refrigerate for several hours. The spinach will be dry and crisp.

√ To prepare ahead of time, prepare greens as above, make salad dressing, chop scallions, and refrigerate all until ready to use. (If time permits, allow dressing to come to room temperature before using.)

Spinach Salad with Creamy Dressing

SERVES: 4
Preparation time: 10 minutes

The Ingredients:

1 pound fresh spinach, stems removed
2 hard-cooked eggs, finely chopped
2 scallions (green and white included), minced

Dressing:

¼ cup dairy sour cream
2 tablespoons mayonnaise
1 tablespoon lemon juice
Pinch of sugar
¼ teaspoon minced garlic
½ teaspoon salt, or to taste
¼ teaspoon freshly ground pepper, or to taste
Garnish: Freshly chopped parsley

The Steps:

1. Place spinach in salad bowl, grate egg over top, sprinkle on scallions.
2. In small bowl, combine remaining ingredients and whisk until smooth.
3. Toss dressing with spinach/egg/scallion combination and serve immediately, garnished with freshly chopped parsley.

Variation:

Crisp bacon bits can be added for extra flavor and texture.

Make-It-Easy Tip:

√ Dressing can be prepared in advance, in a food processor to save time, and chilled for up to a week. Dressing can also be used as a dip for fresh vegetables.

Tossed Salad with Red Onions

SERVES: 4
Preparation time: 10 minutes

The Ingredients:

1 head Boston lettuce, broken into pieces
1 bunch watercress
3 slices red onions, broken into rings

Dressing:

6 tablespoons olive oil
2 tablespoons red wine vinegar
½ teaspoon Dijon mustard
¼ teaspoon dried oregano, crumbled
½ teaspoon salt, or to taste
¼ teaspoon freshly ground white pepper

The Steps:

1. Place lettuce, watercress, and onion rings in a salad bowl and chill, covered with paper towels and plastic wrap, in the refrigerator.

2. Combine dressing ingredients in screw-top jar and shake to combine.
3. When ready to serve, toss greens with dressing and serve immediately.

Variations:

Corn, peanut, safflower or soy oil can be substituted for olive oil.

Cabbage Salad with Caraway Seeds

SERVES: 4
Preparation time: 15 minutes
Chilling time: 2–4 hours or overnight

The Ingredients:

1 large head cabbage, shredded
1 small onion, finely minced by hand or in food processor
2 tablespoons lemon juice
½ teaspoon salt, or to taste
½ teaspoon freshly ground white pepper, or to taste
⅔ cup mayonnaise
1 tablespoon caraway seeds
Garnish: Tomatoes, parsley sprigs

The Steps:

1. Place cabbage in bowl; add onion, lemon juice, salt, and pepper.
2. Add mayonnaise and caraway seeds, toss well, and chill for 2–4 hours or overnight.
3. Serve in bowl garnished with cherry tomatoes, or with tomato wedge in center and parsley sprigs around the edges.

Make-It-Easy Tip:

√ The easiest way to shred cabbage in a food processor is with the *slicing* blade, not the shredding blade.

Chinese Asparagus Salad with Spicy Dressing

SERVES: 4–6
Preparation time: 15 minutes

Prepare this salad during the spring when asparagus is in season, or year 'round using frozen asparagus.

The Ingredients:

1 pound fresh asparagus or two 10-ounce packages frozen asparagus spears

Dressing:

3 tablespoons soy sauce
3 tablespoons oriental sesame oil
1 teaspoon sugar
2–3 shakes Tabasco, or to taste

The Steps:

1. Break off tough, rubbery stalk ends of asparagus and discard. Cut asparagus on the diagonal into 1″ pieces. (If using frozen asparagus, thaw slightly and cut as above.)
2. Drop fresh asparagus pieces into pot of boiling salted water and cook for 2–3 minutes or until barely tender. Drain, run under cold water, and drain again. (If using frozen asparagus, place in a strainer or colander and rinse with boiling water to cook slightly without actually parboiling; drain.)
3. Combine dressing ingredients in small bowl, whisk to combine, and toss over asparagus spears.
4. Serve at room temperature or chilled.

Variations:

The Chinese serve this salad garnished with red preserved ginger cut into strips. Pimientos, cut into strips, can be substituted as a colorful garnish.

Make-It-Easy Tips:

√ When selecting asparagus, choose firm, bright green spears with tips that are compact.

√ Break off tough stem ends easily by allowing them to snap off where they will.

Bean Sprout Salad

SERVES: 4–6
Preparation time: 10 minutes

Sprouts can be grown indoors in a jar in no time, which makes this salad possible to prepare at any time of the year.

The Ingredients:

4 cups fresh bean sprouts (the popular mung or soy bean sprouts are best to use)
¾ cup shredded green pepper (can be done in food processor)

Dressing:

¼ cup soy sauce
3 tablespoons wine vinegar (Chinese or Japanese are preferable, if available)
4 teaspoons peanut oil
4 teaspoons oriental sesame oil
½ teaspoon salt, or to taste
¼ teaspoon freshly ground pepper, or to taste
Garnish: Red preserved ginger, optional (available at oriental grocery stores or by mail order, *see* Appendix A), 3 tablespoons sesame seeds (toasted in toaster-oven or in a hot skillet)

The Steps:

1. Place bean sprouts and green pepper in salad bowl.
2. Combine dressing ingredients in screw-top jar and shake until smooth.
3. Toss sprouts and green pepper with dressing, garnish with optional red preserved ginger and toasted sesame seeds, and serve immediately.

Variations:

Other vegetables can be used as alternatives or with the sprouts: Snow peas; broccoli, partially cooked; asparagus, partially cooked; sliced water chestnuts; zucchini slices, partially cooked.

Sliced pimiento strips can be substituted for the red preserved ginger.

Make-It-Easy Tip:

√ If fresh sprouts are unavailable, substitute canned sprouts that have been drained and soaked overnight in cold water. The next day, drain them, place in boiling water, drain again, and use for salad.

Broccoli Florets Vinaigrette

SERVES: 6
Preparation time: 15 minutes
Chilling time: 2–3 hours or overnight

Parboiled vegetables marinated in a zesty vinaigrette dressing can be a great change of pace from the typical tossed green salad. Broccoli, with its bright green color, can be used, or try cauliflower, zucchini, string beans, or whatever seasonal vegetable you prefer.

The Ingredients:

4 cups broccoli florets, about 2 pounds (reserve the stems for another use)

Vinaigrette Dressing:

6 tablespoons olive oil
2 tablespoons red wine vinegar
¼ teaspoon salt, or to taste
¼ teaspoon freshly ground white pepper
⅛ teaspoon dried oregano, crumbled
⅛ teaspoon dried basil, crumbled
Pinch of dry mustard
Pinch of sugar

Mimosa Topping:

1 teaspoon freshly chopped parsley
2 hard-cooked egg yolks, grated

The Steps:

1. Drop broccoli florets into large pot of boiling salted water and, when water returns to boil, cook, uncovered, for 2–3 minutes, or until just tender but still crunchy. Drain in colander and rinse under cold running water.
2. Combine vinaigrette ingredients in screw-top jar and shake until smooth.
3. Toss florets with vinaigrette dressing and chill for 2–3 hours or overnight.
4. When ready to serve, prepare Mimosa Topping: Combine chopped parsley and grated egg and sprinkle over salad. Serve chilled or at room temperature.

Variation:

The amount of olive oil can be reduced to save on calories; use 3 tablespoons oil and 1½ tablespoons vinegar.

Make-It-Easy Tip:

√ The florets are immediately rinsed with cold water after parboiling to stop the cooking process at once and to preserve the intense green color.

Dilled Cucumber Salad

SERVES: 4
Preparation time: 15 minutes
Chilling time: 30 minutes plus 2 hours or overnight

The Ingredients:

4 medium cucumbers
½ teaspoon salt
1 cup dairy sour cream
2 tablespoons lemon juice
2 tablespoons freshly snipped dill or 2 teaspoons dried dill

1 tablespoon minced chives or scallion stalks
¼ teaspoon paprika
½ teaspoon salt, or to taste
¼ teaspoon freshly ground white pepper, or to taste
Garnish: Sprigs of dill or watercress

The Steps:

1. Peel cucumbers and thinly slice into bowl of ice water. Add ½ teaspoon salt and allow cucumbers to sit for ½ hour, covered, in refrigerator.
2. In the meantime, combine sour cream, lemon juice, dill, chives or scallions, paprika, salt, and pepper.
3. Drain cucumbers and blot dry on paper towels. Pour dressing over cucumbers and mix well. Chill again for 2 hours or overnight.
4. Taste, and adjust seasoning if necessary. Serve the cucumbers chilled, garnished with sprigs of dill or watercress.

Variations:

Two European hothouse hydroponic cucumbers can be substituted. They are especially easy to use since they need no salting.

Make-It-Easy Tip:

√ The cucumbers are salted to extract the excess water.

Middle-Eastern Salad

SERVES: 4
Preparation time: 15 minutes
Chilling time: 30 minutes

The combined flavors of cracked wheat, mint, tomatoes, and onions create a Middle-Eastern treat that can be served as a salad, side dish, or appetizer.

The Ingredients:

1 large ripe tomato, cubed
1 small white onion, coarsely chopped

1 slice cracked-wheat toast, cut into small cubes
1 cup freshly chopped parsley

Dressing:

3 tablespoons olive oil
2 tablespoons red wine vinegar
1 tablespoon chopped fresh mint leaves or 1 teaspoon dried mint leaves, crumbled
½ teaspoon ground allspice
½ teaspoon salt, or to taste
¼ teaspoon freshly ground pepper, or to taste
Garnish: Coriander or parsley

The Steps:

1. Combine tomato, onion, toast cubes, and parsley in bowl and gently toss to combine.
2. Combine dressing ingredients in screw-top jar and shake until smooth.
3. Half an hour before serving, gently toss salad ingredients with dressing, chill for ½ hour, and serve garnished with sprigs of coriander or parsley.

Variation:

If cracked-wheat bread is unavailable, use any other whole grain bread, toasted.

Make-It-Easy Tip:

√ Store extra chopped parsley in a sealed jar in the refrigerator. Store fresh parsley sprigs wrapped in a towel and placed in a large jar or plastic bag, tightly closed.

Raw Mushroom Salad

SERVES: 4
Preparation time: 10 minutes
Chilling time: 1 hour

Mushroom Salad is a light and refreshing salad served with the meal or as a first course, California-style. The mushrooms should be tossed with dressing immediately after they are sliced, so prepare the dressing first.

The Ingredients:

1 pound fresh mushrooms, sliced

Dressing:

5 tablespoons olive oil
2 tablespoons lemon juice
½ teaspoon salt, or to taste
¼ teaspoon freshly ground black pepper
2 tablespoons capers, drained
Garnish: Freshly chopped parsley, freshly ground black pepper

The Steps:

1. Combine dressing ingredients in screw-top jar and shake to combine.
2. Immediately toss sliced mushrooms with dressing to keep from discoloring.
3. Add capers, and chill for 1 hour or until ready to serve.
4. Serve on chilled salad plates topped with freshly chopped parsley and freshly ground black pepper.

Make-It-Easy Tips:

√ A mushroom brush, or similar style soft brush, dipped in lemon juice is a handy tool for cleaning mushrooms without soaking them.

√ The mushrooms should not be sliced until the dressing is ready or they may discolor on standing.

√ Store mushrooms most successfully in a brown paper bag, which absorbs excess moisture.

Snow Pea Salad

SERVES: 4
Preparation time: 15 minutes

Crisp Chinese snow peas are becoming more and more popular as a stir-fried vegetable or as a salad ingredient, either with a Chinese flavor or as here with a French vinaigrette dressing.

The Ingredients:

1 pound fresh Chinese snow peas, stringed

Vinaigrette Dressing:

½ cup olive oil (or vegetable oil)
2 shallots or scallions (white part only), finely chopped
2 tablespoons lemon juice
1 tablespoon white wine vinegar
½ teaspoon Dijon mustard
½ teaspoon salt, or to taste
¼ teaspoon freshly ground white pepper, or to taste
Pinch of sugar

The Steps:

1. Drop peas into pot of boiling salted water and, when water returns to boil, drain peas into colander. Place colander under cold running water.
2. Combine dressing ingredients in a food processor, blender, or screw-top jar.
3. Toss dressing with snow peas in salad bowl and serve at room temperature or chilled.

Variation:

Substitute sugar snap peas, the new vegetable on the market that is an ingenious cross between the Chinese snow pea and the standard pea. They are prepared and eaten shell and all. Cook sugar snap peas 1 minute longer than snow peas.

Make-It-Easy Tips:

√ The snow peas are immediately rinsed with cold water after the parboiling to stop the cooking at once and to preserve the intense green color.

√ Frozen snow peas cannot be substituted in a salad because they turn soggy immediately after thawing. If stringing and parboiling the snow peas requires too much work, try using bean sprouts in combination with thinly sliced zucchini or cucumber.

String Bean Salad

SERVES: 4
Preparation time: 15 minutes

The Ingredients:

1 pound fresh string beans, washed

Vinaigrette Dressing:

6 tablespoons olive oil
2 tablespoons red wine vinegar
¼ teaspoon freshly minced garlic or ⅛ teaspoon garlic powder
¼ teaspoon salt, or to taste
¼ teaspoon freshly ground pepper, or to taste
⅛ teaspoon dried oregano, crumbled
⅛ teaspoon dried basil, crumbled
⅛ teaspoon paprika
Pinch of sugar

The Steps:

1. Break tip ends off string beans, drop into pot of salted boiling water; bring to boil again and cook until just tender but still crunchy, 7–9 minutes. Drain in colander, rinse under cold running water, and drain again.
2. Combine the vinaigrette ingredients in screw-top jar and shake to combine.
3. Combine drained string beans with vinaigrette dressing, toss well to combine, and serve at room temperature or chilled.

Variations:

Haricots Verts, the new, delicate, tiny French green beans, can be substituted for large green beans but should be cooked only 5–6 minutes, or until tender.

Raspberry vinegar can be substituted for the red wine vinegar. In this case, omit the sugar.

If beans are very large, cut on diagonal into 1½″ pieces and parboil only 5–6 minutes, or until tender.

Frozen whole green beans, thawed, can be substituted if time is limited but they will not be as crisp in texture.

Make-It-Easy Tip:

√ Green beans are immediately rinsed with cold water to stop cooking process at once and preserve intense green color.

Tomato and Onion Salad

SERVES: 4
Preparation time: 10 minutes

Serve this salad during the summer months when tomatoes and Spanish onions are in season. It makes a wonderful side dish or even a first course for an outdoor barbecue.

The Ingredients:

3 large beefsteak tomatoes
1 large white Spanish onion (or red onion), cut into ½″ cubes
½ cup olive oil (Italian is preferable)
2 tablespoons red wine vinegar
½ teaspoon salt, or to taste
¼ teaspoon freshly ground black pepper, or to taste
Pinch of sugar
Garnish: Freshly chopped parsley

The Steps:

1. Cut tomatoes in half horizontally and remove excess water and seeds by gently squeezing. Then cut tomatoes into ½″ cubes and place in bowl.
2. Add onions to tomatoes.
3. Combine oil, vinegar, salt, pepper, and sugar in screw-top jar and shake together until smooth.
4. Pour dressing over salad and chill for 1 hour or serve immediately, garnished with freshly chopped parsley.

Variations:

For an Italian flavor, dried, crumbled oregano and basil can be added to the dressing and allowed to marinate for 10 minutes to soften.

To reduce calories, prepare the dressing with a substitution of 3 tablespoons oil and 3 tablespoons vinegar.

Make-It-Easy Tip:

√ A serrated tomato or bread knife is an invaluable tool to use when cutting tomatoes.

Oriental Zucchini Salad

SERVES: 6
Preparation time: 10 minutes
Cooking time: 3 minutes

Oriental Zucchini Salad is a spicy, refreshing, crisp salad that is low in calories.

The Ingredients:

6 medium zucchini, cut into 2″ julienne strips

Dressing:

2 tablespoons soy sauce
2 tablespoons oriental sesame oil
2 tablespoons Japanese rice vinegar or white vinegar
1 tablespoon sugar
2 teaspoons sake (Japanese wine) or dry sherry
½ teaspoon salt, or to taste
Garnish: Chopped scallion stalks

The Steps:

1. Bring pot of salted water to boil, add zucchini and, when water returns to boil, cook for 2–3 minutes or until just fork tender. Drain, rinse under cold running water, and drain again. Place zucchini in salad bowl.
2. Combine dressing ingredients in a screw-top jar and shake until smooth.
3. Pour dressing over zucchini and toss.
4. Serve at room temperature or slightly chilled, garnished with chopped scallion stalks.

Variation:

For a low-salt version, substitute the new milder salt-restricted soy sauce and eliminate the ½ teaspoon salt.

Make-It-Easy Tip:

√ Drained zucchini are placed under cold running water to stop the cooking process immediately and to preserve the bright green color.

PASTA AND RICE SALADS

Spaghetti was not made just for a tumble with tomato sauce; fettuccine was meant for more than a treatment Alfredo; rice needn't be served only alongside chicken—any one of these staple starches can also be used as a salad. And, I'm not just talking about mundane macaroni salad. The following recipes are designed to show the adaptability of pasta and rice to the salad course.

Pasta Salad with Chicken and Vegetables

SERVES: 6–8
Preparation time: 15 minutes
Cooking time: 12 minutes

This Pasta Salad can be served chilled or at room temperature.

The Ingredients:

1 pound linguini, perciatelli, or spaghetti
2 teaspoons vegetable oil
½ cup *Laurie's Basic Vinaigrette* dressing (*see* page 246) including 1 teaspoon capers and 1 tablespoon chopped parsley
½ cup mayonnaise
1 teaspoon paprika, or to taste
1 large, whole chicken-breast, poached and shredded
1 7-ounce jar roasted Italian peppers cut into strips (if unavailable, use pimientos)
1 medium zucchini, cut into thin julienne strips
½ teaspoon salt, or to taste

½ teaspoon freshly ground pepper to taste
Garnish: Freshly chopped parsley and chopped chives or scallion stalks

The Steps:

1. Cook linguini in boiling salted water until just tender, *al dente,* and drain in colander. Run under cold water and drain again. Toss with vegetable oil and set aside.
2. In the meantime, mix vinaigrette dressing with mayonnaise and paprika and whisk until smooth.
3. Toss pasta with vinaigrette mixture, coating thoroughly.
4. Add chicken, roasted peppers, and zucchini; toss again until well mixed.
5. Cool, and then chill in refrigerator.
6. Taste, and adjust seasoning with salt and freshly ground pepper. Serve cold or at room temperature, garnished with freshly chopped parsley and chopped chives.

Accompaniment:

Crunchy French bread.

Variations:

White meat turkey breast can be substituted for chicken.

Additional vegetables can be added for color or texture, as desired.

Make-It-Easy Tips:

√ Place zucchini in boiling water for 2 minutes, run under cold water to give it an *al dente* texture like the pasta, and drain thoroughly.

√ For an easy method to poach chicken, *see Madame Chu's Szechwan Peppercorn Chicken Salad.*

√ If possible, use imported Italian pasta which is easier to cook to *al dente* perfection than the American varieties.

Oriental Noodle Salad

SERVES: 4–6
Preparation time: 20 minutes
Cooking time: 8–10 minutes
Chilling time: 2 hours

Cold Oriental Noodle Salad can be used as a side dish or as an appetizer for an oriental or American dinner.

The Ingredients:

½ pound thin egg noodles or linguini
2 tablespoons peanut oil
1 cup fresh bean sprouts
¼ cup chopped radishes
2 cups shredded lettuce (Iceberg is preferable)

Dressing:

2 tablespoons peanut butter
2 tablespoons water
2 tablespoons soy sauce
2 tablespoons rice vinegar, or white wine vinegar
2 tablespoons peanut oil
2 tablespoons oriental sesame oil
2 tablespoons minced scallion stalks
2 teaspoons sugar
½ teaspoon minced garlic
½ teaspoon minced fresh ginger
½ teaspoon salt, or to taste
Dash hot chili oil, optional (available at oriental groceries or by mail order, *see* Appendix A)
Garnish: Toasted sesame seeds

The Steps:

1. Cook noodles in boiling salted water until *al dente,* just tender; drain, and toss with 2 tablespoons peanut oil to keep from sticking.
2. Place bean sprouts, radishes, and lettuce in a large bowl and chill until ready to use.

3. Combine dressing ingredients in food processor, blender, or bowl and process or whisk until smooth.
4. Toss dressing with the cooked noodles and chill until ready to use.
5. When ready to serve, toss the dressed noodles with the vegetables, garnish with toasted sesame seeds, and serve.

Variation:

Serve the Oriental Noodle Salad as an appetizer.

Make-It-Easy Tips:

√ Toast sesame seeds easily in a toaster-oven, on top brown, tossing lightly once and watch carefully.

√ Fresh sprouts can be grown in only a few days indoors in a sprouting jar available at oriental groceries or health food stores.

Rice Salad Niçoise

SERVES: 8
Preparation time: 15–20 minutes
Chilling time: 2 hours or overnight

Any leftover rice, either brown or white, can be put to good use in this salad.

The Ingredients:

1 3-ounce can solid packed tuna, drained (water- or oil-packed)
½ small red onion, chopped
8 small pitted ripe olives
2 teaspoons capers, drained
4½ cups cooked rice (1½ cups raw rice)

Vinaigrette:

½ cup olive oil
2 tablespoons red wine vinegar
1 tablespoon lemon juice
2 teaspoons freshly chopped parsley

½ teaspoon Dijon mustard
½ teaspoon salt, or to taste
¼ teaspoon freshly ground black pepper, or to taste
Garnish: Two hard-cooked eggs, cut in wedges; four anchovy fillets, drained; 4 thin strips pimiento

The Steps:

1. Crumble the tuna in a large bowl; add the red onion, olives, and capers.
2. Combine vinaigrette ingredients in screw-top jar and shake until smooth.
3. Pour dressing over the tuna and vegetables; toss to combine.
4. Add rice, continue to toss, coating all grains well. Cover, and chill for 2 hours or overnight.
5. When ready to serve, adjust seasonings to taste with salt and pepper; serve garnished with hard-cooked egg wedges, drained anchovy fillets, and strips of pimiento attractively laid on top.

Variations:

Thawed frozen peas or string beans, or additional cooked vegetables can be added to taste.

Make-It-Easy Tips:

√ Rice Salad will keep for several days, covered, in the refrigerator.
√ Pimientos can be frozen individually. Shave into thin pieces easily while semi-frozen.
√ For the best way to cook rice for salads, *see Plain White Rice, the Chinese Way.*

Curried Brown Rice Salad with Fruit

SERVES: 6–8
Preparation time: 20 minutes
Chilling time: 2 hours or overnight

Add cut-up chicken or roast pork to this salad and it can be served as a main course.

The Ingredients:

½ cup mayonnaise
½ cup heavy cream
1 tablespoon curry powder
1 tablespoon lemon juice
4½ cups cold cooked brown rice (about 1½ cups raw brown rice)
1 cup finely chopped carrots
1 11-ounce can Mandarin-orange segments, drained
1 8-ounce can juice-packed crushed pineapple, drained
½ cup seedless golden raisins
2 ounces chopped walnuts
¼ cup toasted pine nuts (*pignoli*) or toasted almonds
2 tablespoons chopped chutney
¼ teaspoon salt, or to taste
¼ teaspoon freshly ground white pepper, or to taste
Garnish: Toasted pine nuts or slivered almonds

The Steps:

1. In large bowl, prepare dressing by whisking mayonnaise with cream until smooth.
2. Make a paste of the curry powder and lemon juice and add to mayonnaise mixture.
3. Add rice to dressing, and stir to coat all the grains.
4. Add carrots, oranges, pineapple, raisins, walnuts, pine nuts, chutney, salt and pepper to taste; cover, and chill for 2 hours or overnight.
5. Taste, adjust seasoning with salt and pepper to taste, and serve garnished with toasted pine nuts.

Variations:

Additional chopped fresh fruits and nuts can be added or substituted to taste.

The salad can be prepared with white rice but is more flavorful and healthier with brown rice.

For the best way to cook brown rice, *see Plain Brown Rice.*

Curry powder is actually a blend of many spices. Taste varies with different brands so try out several to find the one you like best. Curry powder should be dissolved in liquid before adding to recipes.

Tabbouleh, or Tabbouli (Wheat Pilaf Salad)

SERVES: 4–6
Preparation time: 15–20 minutes
Marinating time: 1–2 hours
Chilling time: 2 hours or overnight

Tabbouleh is a salad made with the Middle-Eastern grain called bulgur, a cracked wheat, which is marinated in olive oil with lemon juice, scallions, and fresh mint. Tabbouleh is low in calories, high in fiber, and is a refreshing complement to spicy dishes. Fresh mint is essential to the preparation of Tabbouleh. For best results, use a fine-grained bulgur.

The Ingredients:

1 cup fine-grain bulgur (cracked wheat)
2 cups boiling water
1 cup seeded and coarsely chopped tomato
1 small onion, minced
2 scallions (green and white included), finely chopped
¾ cup freshly chopped parsley
¼ cup lemon juice
¼ cup olive oil
3 tablespoons chopped fresh mint
½ teaspoon salt, or to taste
¼ teaspoon freshly ground black pepper, or to taste
Garnish: Halved cherry tomatoes, fresh mint sprigs

The Steps:

1. Pour boiling water over bulgur to cover, and allow to stand 1–2 hours or until wheat is light and fluffy. Drain through a fine mesh strainer, pushing out excess water.
2. Combine remaining ingredients, toss with bulgur, and mix well; chill, covered, in refrigerator for 2 hours or overnight.
3. Taste, adjust seasoning with salt and pepper to taste, and serve Tabbouleh chilled, garnished with halved cherry tomatoes and fresh mint sprigs.

Variations:

Lime juice can be substituted for the lemon juice.

Chopped pecans can be added, to taste.

Make-It-Easy Tips:

√ To seed a tomato quickly, slice in half and, using your hand, gently squeeze until seeds have fallen out. Remove any remaining seeds with a spoon.

MAIN-COURSE SALADS

A hot summer night is not the only time when a soothingly cool, main-course salad is appealing. There are plenty of long, hectic days when a light, cold supper can actually help you to unwind. These salads are easy to prepare and can often serve as one-dish suppers, with bread and wine.

No more banal chef's salads; no more marshmallows, Miracle Whip, or maraschinos, either. Main-Course Salads have progressed beyond this familiar territory to include wild game, pâté, and exotic seafood. Even an old standby like seafood salad takes on new life with the addition of curry and water chestnuts.

Roast Beef Salad

SERVES: 4
Preparation time: 15 minutes
Chilling time: 2–3 hours

The Ingredients:

½ pound rare roast beef, cut into julienne strips (matchstick)
1 large or 2 small cooked potatoes, peeled and diced
½ cup thinly sliced red or white onion
1 hard-cooked egg, chopped

Vinaigrette:

½ cup olive oil
3 tablespoons red wine vinegar
2 tablespoons freshly chopped parsley

1 tablespoon chopped sour pickles (*cornichons*)
1 tablespoon finely chopped chives or scallion stalks
1 teaspoon lemon juice
1 teaspoon Dijon mustard
½ teaspoon salt, or to taste
¼ teaspoon freshly ground pepper
¼ teaspoon Worcestershire sauce
Garnish: Freshly chopped parsley

The Steps:

1. Place beef, potato, and onion in bowl; top with chopped egg.
2. Combine vinaigrette ingredients in screw-top jar and shake until smooth (for an extra-smooth dressing, prepare in food processor or blender).
3. Toss dressing with beef and potatoes and allow to marinate, covered, in refrigerator for 2–3 hours.
4. Adjust seasonings to taste and serve salad chilled or at room temperature, garnished with chopped parsley.

Accompaniment:

Mustard Herb Toast.

Variations:

Any kind of cooked beef will work in this salad—pot roast, steak, London broil, or whatever is available. Rare roast beef is often available at a delicatessen. Ask for the very rare, unsliced portion.

Make-It-Easy Tips:

√ A leftover baked potato can be used, or 2 small new potatoes, boiled for 20–40 minutes, depending on size. *See* page 221, *Potatoes Boiled in Jackets.*

√ An easy way to hard-cook eggs is to pierce them with a thumbtack or egg piercer and place in cold salted water; bring to a boil, cover, turn off heat entirely, and allow to sit undisturbed for 20 minutes.

√ An easy way to chop a hard-cooked egg fine is to grate it on the medium side of a kitchen grater.

Marinated Oriental Beef and Pepper Salad

SERVES: 6
Preparation time: 20 minutes
Marinating time: 3 hours

This salad is a great way to use up leftover meat—roast beef, steak, or even pot roast.

The Ingredients:

3 cups rare roast beef, steak, or other cooked beef, cut into 2″ x 1″ strips
1 green pepper, cut into thin strips (julienned)
2 tomatoes, cut into small wedges
3 scallions, minced (green and white parts included)
½ cup mushrooms, sliced (optional)
½ cup jicama (a Mexican vegetable) cut in julienne strips, or substitute
½ cup sliced water chestnuts (optional)
4 cups mixed greens: leaf lettuce, red lettuce, or romaine

Marinade:

½ cup teriyaki sauce
⅓ cup dry sherry
3 tablespoons peanut oil
3 tablespoons Japanese rice vinegar or white wine vinegar
2 tablespoons oriental sesame oil
1½ teaspoons freshly grated ginger (or 1 teaspoon ground ginger)

The Steps:

1. In large bowl, place beef, green pepper, tomatoes, scallions, mushrooms, and jicama.
2. Combine marinade ingredients in screw-top jar and shake until smooth.
3. Pour marinade over meat and vegetables and toss well.
4. Cover, and refrigerate for 3 hours.
5. At serving time, drain off excess marinade; line a large salad bowl with the lettuce, place marinated meat and vegetables on top, and serve immediately.

Accompaniment:
Pita Toast.

Make-It-Easy Tips:
√ Rare roast beef is generally available at delicatessens. Ask for about a pound of the rarest meat and slice into strips at home.
√ A serrated tomato or bread knife is an invaluable tool to use for cutting tomatoes.

Oriental Roast Pork and Snow Pea Salad

SERVES: 4–6
Preparation time: 15–20 minutes
Cooking time: 2 minutes

This dish requires Chinese roast pork, which can be purchased at a Chinese restaurant the day before or the day on which the dish is to be served. Leftover glazed pork loin can be substituted, sliced into strips, and tossed in this unusual and fabulous salad.

The Ingredients:
1 pound Chinese roast pork, thinly sliced
½ pound snow peas, stringed
2 large carrots, shaved with a vegetable peeler into curls
2 scallions, finely minced (green and white parts included)
Dressing:
2 tablespoons soy sauce
2 tablespoons oriental sesame oil
2 tablespoons Japanese rice vinegar or white wine vinegar
1 tablespoon dry sherry or sake (Japanese wine)
1 tablespoon sugar
½ teaspoon salt
Garnish: Coriander, parsley, or watercress

The Steps:
1. Slice pork and place in bowl.
2. Drop snow peas into pot of boiling salted water, stir once and,

when water returns to boil, drain peas into colander. Run under cold water and, when drained, place atop pork.

3. Shave carrots with a vegetable peeler to form curls. (Curls can be made in advance and placed in bowl of water in refrigerator to chill.) Place curls in salad bowl.
4. Top pork and vegetables with minced scallions.
5. Combine dressing ingredients in screw-top jar and shake to combine.
6. Pour dressing over salad, toss, and serve at room temperature, garnished with coriander, parsley, or watercress.

Accompaniments:

Stir-Fried Shrimp, and white rice for a complete oriental dinner.

Variations:

Oriental (dried) mushrooms, soaked in water and then cut into strips, are another good addition to this salad.

Sliced, drained water chestnuts can be added for color and texture.

Make-It-Easy Tip:

√ Carrot curls don't take as long to make, but carrots julienned into matchstick strips and boiled with the snow peas are a wonderful addition.

Chinese Seafood Salad

SERVES: 4
Preparation time: 15 minutes
Chilling time: 2–3 hours

Chinese Seafood Salad should be eaten the same day it is prepared (the next day at the latest). Any combination of cooked seafood can be used.

The Ingredients:

1 pound cooked medium or large shrimp
½ pound cooked crab, flaked

½ pound cooked sea scallops, cut in half (or bay scallops whole)
1 8-ounce can water chestnuts, drained and cut in half (or use can of pre-sliced water chestnuts)
4 scallion stalks, cut in ½″ slices

Oriental Dressing:

3 tablespoons peanut oil
3 tablespoons soy sauce
1 tablespoon oriental sesame oil
2 teaspoons sugar
1 teaspoon grated fresh ginger
½ teaspoon salt, or to taste
¼ teaspoon freshly ground white pepper
Garnish: Coriander or parsley sprigs

The Steps:

1. Mix seafood together in a bowl, add water chestnuts and scallions; toss.
2. Combine oriental dressing ingredients in screw-top jar and shake until smooth.
3. Toss seafood with dressing and allow to marinate for 2–3 hours, covered, in refrigerator.
4. Serve salad chilled, garnished with sprigs of coriander or parsley.

Accompaniment:

Pita Toast.

Variation:

Cold poached fish can be substituted for some of the seafood for a less expensive version of the salad.

Make-It-Easy Tip:

√ Store peeled ginger, covered with sherry, in a jar in the refrigerator.

Madame Chu's Szechwan Peppercorn Chicken Salad

SERVES: 6
Preparation time: 20 minutes
Cooking time: 35 minutes

This recipe was taught to me many years ago by Madame Grace Zia Chu, who helped introduce Chinese cooking to Americans with her participatory classes in New York City. This dish is amazingly easy to prepare and most unusual. The chicken is cooked "white-cut" style, which is a perfect way to poach chicken to a velvety texture.

The Ingredients:

2 whole chicken breasts
2 slices fresh ginger root
1 scallion stalk
3 cups shredded Iceberg lettuce

Sauce One:

3 tablespoons peanut oil
3 tablespoons chopped scallion stalks
1 tablespoon minced ginger root
1 teaspoon Szechwan peppercorns, crushed (available in oriental groceries or by mail order, *see* Appendix A)
¼ teaspoon crushed chili pepper

Sauce Two:

2 tablespoons soy sauce
2 cloves garlic, minced
1 tablespoon dark Karo syrup
1 tablespoon Hoisin sauce (available in oriental groceries or by mail order, *see* Appendix A)
Garnish: Sprigs of coriander or parsley

The Steps:

1. Bring 2 quarts of water or chicken broth to a boil in a pot large enough to hold the chicken breasts comfortably; add chicken breasts, ginger slices, and scallion stalk; bring to boil again, cover tightly, reduce heat to medium, and cook without peeking for 15 minutes.

2. Turn flame off entirely and allow to cool in cooking liquid in covered pot for 20 minutes.
3. Skin and bone the chicken and pull the meat apart into shreds.
4. Place lettuce in a bowl and top with chicken.
5. Place ingredients for Sauce One in small pot and heat until boiling.
6. Combine ingredients for Sauce Two in small bowl and mix until smooth.
7. Combine the two sauces and mix well. Toss well with chicken and lettuce.
8. Serve immediately, garnished with sprigs of coriander or parsley.

Accompaniments:

Oriental rice crackers or sesame crackers.

Make-It-Easy Tips:

√ Crush the peppercorns between sheets of waxed paper with the side of a cleaver.

√ If poaching a whole chicken "white-cut" style, follow directions for chicken breasts but simmer for 30 minutes. Allow chicken to cool in cooking liquid in covered pot.

Curried Chicken Salad

SERVES: 6
Preparation time: 15 minutes

The Ingredients:

4 cups cooked chicken, cubed or shredded
½ cup drained, chopped water chestnuts
2 tablespoons chopped scallions, white part only (save the greens for garnish)

Dressing:

¾ cup dairy sour cream
¼ cup mayonnaise
1 tablespoon chopped chives or scallion stalks

1 teaspoon Dijon mustard
½ teaspoon salt, or to taste
½–1 teaspoon curry powder, or more to taste
¼ teaspoon freshly ground white pepper
Pinch of paprika
Garnish: Toasted slivered almonds
Additional Garniture: Chopped scallion stalks, cold asparagus, sliced black olives, capers, or sliced tomatoes

The Steps:

1. Place the chicken in large bowl. Top with water chestnuts and scallions; chill until ready to serve.
2. In separate bowl, combine dressing ingredients until smooth, and chill until ready to serve.
3. When ready to serve, combine chicken with dressing and toss to combine. Serve garnished with toasted slivered almonds and additional garniture of scallion stalks, cold asparagus, sliced black olives, capers, or tomato slices.

Accompaniment:

Sliced rye bread.

Variations:

Leftovers can be blended into a smooth paste in a food processor. Serve the paste with sesame crackers as an hors d'oeuvre.

Turkey breast meat can be substituted for chicken, but it will be slightly drier.

A few teaspoons of mango chutney can be added, to taste.

Make-It-Easy Tips:

√ Prepare chicken "white-cut" method. *See Madame Chu's Szechwan Peppercorn Chicken Salad.*

√ The salad can be assembled earlier in the day or even the night before and refrigerated until ready to serve. Garnish at the last minute.

Chinese Chicken and Cucumber Salad

SERVES: 4–6
Preparation time: 15 minutes

Chinese Chicken and Cucumber Salad can be served as a main course for lunch or dinner, as a brunch dish, or as an appetizer.

The Ingredients:

2 cups cooked chicken, cut into julienne strips
1 large European hothouse hydroponic cucumber or 2 regular cucumbers, peeled and cut into julienne strips
¼ cup chopped scallion greens

Dressing:

2 tablespoons soy sauce
2 tablespoons Japanese rice vinegar or white wine vinegar
2 tablespoons oriental sesame oil
1 tablespoon sugar
2 teaspoons sake (Japanese wine) or dry sherry
½ teaspoon salt, or to taste
2 shakes Tabasco, or to taste
Garnishes: Four tablespoons toasted sesame seeds and coriander or parsley sprigs. (Pre-roasted sesame seeds are available at oriental groceries or by mail order, *see* Appendix A)

The Steps:

1. Put chicken, cucumber, and scallions in salad bowl and toss.
2. Combine all ingredients for dressing in a screw-top jar and shake until smooth.
3. Pour dressing over salad, toss, and serve immediately on a platter garnished with toasted sesame seeds and coriander or parsley sprigs.

Accompaniment:

Sesame seed or oriental rice crackers.

Variation:

Shredded turkey breast meat can be substituted for the chicken.

Make-It-Easy Tips:

√ The chicken, cucumber, and scallions can be prepared in advance and refrigerated. The dressing can be combined and set aside, and all that is left to do is a quick tossing.

√ Prepare chicken "white-cut" method. *See Madame Chu's Szechwan Peppercorn Chicken Salad.*

CHAPTER NINE

BREADS

Pita Toast
Mustard Herb Toast
Pumpernickel Cheese Crisps
Garlic Bread and Variations
Quick Popovers
Light Beer Bread
Custardy Corn Bread
Banana Nut Bread
Blueberry-Orange Bread
Spicy Pumpkin Bread

Long-rising yeast breads cannot be considered Make-It-Easy, so in this chapter I have included only "quick" breads that all take 20 minutes or less to prepare. There are also some clever ways of improving bread that you buy, such as pita, so that it has an herb-toasted homemade quality.

Quick breads and muffins depend on the leavening power of baking powder, baking soda, or a combination of both rather than long-rising yeast. Quick breads require no extensive kneading. Simply combine the dry and wet ingredients, pour into pans, and bake. Quick breads should be made in advance and allowed to cool before cutting. They are easier to cut and taste better if allowed to cool thoroughly.

The following hints and tips will help in the preparation of quick breads or muffins.

Bake in mini-loaf pans for shorter baking time.

For dusting flour on buttered pans, use a powdered-sugar shaker or even a powder puff to sprinkle evenly.

For the height of luxury, indulge in one of those battery-operated, cordless sifters, especially when doubling recipes that require much sifting.

If you've forgotten to soften the butter, don't fret; just grate it and it will soften quickly.

Do not overbake breads. They will be moist and flavorful if slightly underbaked.

Mix dry ingredients together first, to distribute evenly throughout the batter.

Fill pans only two-thirds full to avoid overflows and oven mess.

To prevent sogginess, allow bread to cool in pans for five minutes and then remove and place on a rack to cool thoroughly.

Quick bread recipes can be baked in muffin pans as cupcakes. Bake them for approximately one-third the amount of the cooking time.

Double recipes for quick breads, bake them in mini-loaf pans, wrap tightly in plastic wrap or foil, and freeze for future use. It's nice to have them available if company arrives, and they make excellent house gifts.

Pita Toast

SERVES: 8–10
Preparation time: 10 minutes
Cooking time: 2–3 minutes

Pita Toast accompanies soups or stews and can also be served as a canapé.

The Ingredients:

8 large Pita breads (plain, whole-wheat, or sesame)
6 ounces (1½ sticks) unsalted butter, softened to room temperature
2 tablespoons freshly chopped parsley
1 tablespoon freshly chopped chives
1 tablespoon lemon juice
1 clove garlic, minced
½ teaspoon salt, or to taste
¼ teaspoon freshly ground pepper

The Steps:

1. Preheat broiler.
2. Cut Pita bread in half so there are four wedges from each Pita bread.
3. In food processor, blender, or by hand, blend butter with herbs, lemon juice, garlic, and seasonings until smooth.
4. Arrange Pita pieces on cookie sheet; generously spread interiors with herb butter and broil until butter is bubbly and tops begin to brown.
5. Serve toast hot and crisp.

Variations:

Toast can be spread with softened butter, sprinkled with Parmesan cheese and herbs, and broiled until golden.

Toast can be baked in the top third of a 450° oven for 5 minutes instead of broiling.

Make-It-Easy Tip:

√ If made in advance, keep the cooked toast in a tightly sealed jar or plastic bag to keep fresh. Warm again before serving.

Mustard Herb Toast

SERVES: 8–10
Preparation time: 15 minutes
Cooking time: 20 minutes

Crisp Mustard Herb Toast accompanies hot soups or stews.

The Ingredients:

4 ounces (1 stick) unsalted butter, softened
¼ cup freshly chopped parsley
2 tablespoons minced scallions
2 tablespoons Dijon mustard
1 tablespoon toasted sesame seeds
1 teaspoon lemon juice
1 loaf French, Italian, or sourdough bread, cut into 1″ slices

The Steps:

1. Preheat oven to 350°.
2. In a food processor or blender, process butter, parsley, scallions, mustard, sesame seeds, and lemon juice until smooth. (This butter mixture can be prepared in advance, refrigerated for several days, and brought to room temperature before spreading.)
3. Lightly spread the butter on both sides of bread; arrange on a cookie sheet and bake for 10 minutes on each side or until crisp.
4. Serve toast hot with soups or stews.

Variations:

Slice bread almost all the way through; spread each cut surface with butter mixture, wrap in foil, and bake in a 400° oven for 15–20 minutes. Serve in a long breadbasket.

Make-It-Easy Tip:

√ Toasted sesame seeds are available in supermarkets and at oriental grocery stores, or by mail order, *see* Appendix A.

Pumpernickel Cheese Crisps

SERVES: 4
Preparation time: 10 minutes
Cooking time: 5 minutes

Pumpernickel Cheese Crisps can be served as an appetizer, or with soups or salads.

The Ingredients:

8 slices hors d'oeuvre bread, such as Westphalian Pumpernickel
½ stick unsalted butter, softened
¼ cup freshly grated Parmesan cheese

The Steps:

1. Preheat broiler.
2. Lay slices of bread on cookie sheet and broil on one side for 1–2 minutes to lightly toast.
3. Remove from broiler; turn bread, spread with butter and sprinkle with cheese, and return to broiler to cook for a minute or two until the cheese is hot and bubbly.
4. Serve warm, or keep in airtight container until ready to use. Heat again before serving, if desired.

Variation:

Melba toast crackers can be substituted for pumpernickel.

Garlic Bread (and Variations)

SERVES: 8–10
Preparation time: 5 minutes
Cooking time: 15–20 minutes

The Ingredients:

¼ pound (1 stick) unsalted butter, softened

1 clove garlic, peeled and minced
1 loaf French, Italian, or sourdough bread, about 18″ long

The Steps:

1. Preheat oven to 400°.
2. Blend butter and garlic until smooth.
3. Slice bread 1″ thick, cutting almost through to bottom crust but leaving it attached.
4. Spread both sides of each slice with garlic butter; wrap in aluminum foil leaving a small portion unwrapped at the top.
5. Bake in preheated oven for 15–20 minutes or until golden brown.

Variations:

Herb-Garlic Bread: Add 2 tablespoons freshly chopped parsley, ¼ teaspoon dried crumbled oregano, and ¼ teaspoon dried crumbled basil to the softened butter.

Cheese-Garlic Bread: Add 2–3 tablespoons freshly grated Parmesan cheese to the butter. The bread will be extra-golden brown.

Herbed Italian Bread: Mix basil, oregano, and a pinch of thyme to taste with softened butter and Parmesan cheese.

Bread can be split horizontally, spread on both cut sides with butter and broiled open-faced until golden. Slice and serve hot.

Make-It-Easy Tip:

√ Bread can be assembled through Step 4, wrapped well in foil, and refrigerated. When ready to serve, leave a small portion unwrapped at the top and proceed with the recipe.

Quick Popovers

SERVES: 6–8
Preparation time: 10 minutes
Cooking time: 30–35 minutes

The Ingredients:

1 cup sifted flour
1 cup whole milk

2 eggs
½ teaspoon salt

The Steps:

1. Preheat oven to 425°. Lightly butter 6 large metal, or 8 small metal or glass, muffin molds.
2. Combine flour, milk, eggs, and salt in blender, food processor, electric mixer, or by hand, mixing until smooth.
3. Place greased pans on a cookie sheet in the oven to preheat for 2 minutes.
4. Pour batter into preheated cups, filling two-thirds full; return to oven and bake in top third of oven for 30–35 minutes or until puffy and golden brown.
5. Serve immediately with whipped sweet butter.

Make-It-Easy Tips:

√ The large metal popover tins, which are deeper and fuller than regular muffin tins, are best to use since they can be preheated and turn out larger, lighter, and airier popovers.

√ The best volume is achieved if ingredients are at room temperature when combined.

Light Beer Bread

YIELD: One 9″ x 5″ x 3″ loaf
Preparation time: 10 minutes
Rising time: 1–1½ hours
Cooking time: 1 hour

This recipe was passed on to me by the actor Pat Rooney, who promised it would work, and it certainly did! The beer and the self-rising flour act to make the bread rise in only 1 hour. Serve this bread warm or toasted, with whipped sweet butter.

The Ingredients:

3¼ cups self-rising flour
3 tablespoons granulated sugar
1 12-ounce bottle of light beer, at room temperature

The Steps:

1. Lightly butter a large loaf pan or spray it with nonaerosol vegetable shortening.
2. Mix flour and sugar together in large bowl; pour in beer and stir together until sticky dough is formed.
3. Place dough in prepared pan, shape into a loaf and allow dough to rise covered with a dampened dish towel for 1–1½ hours.
4. Preheat oven to 350°.
5. Bake for 1 hour or until lightly browned on top.
6. Serve bread warm with whipped sweet butter.

Variations:

Sesame seeds can be sprinkled on top before baking.
Herbs can be added to the dough for a flavorful herb bread.
Regular beer may be substituted for light beer.

Make-It-Easy Tips:

√ It's easiest to mix the dough with your hands and much more fun!
√ One of the new, superstrength paper towels can be dampened and used to cover the rising bread dough.
√ If dough is too sticky to the touch, add a few tablespoons of flour.

Custardy Corn Bread

SERVES: 6–8
Preparation time: 15 minutes
Cooking time: 30 minutes

I use this corn bread in place of rice or potatoes as a side dish since it is so creamy and rich.

The Ingredients:

1 cup stone-ground yellow cornmeal
¼ cup all-purpose flour
2 teaspoons sugar
1 teaspoon baking powder

½ teaspoon salt
1½ cups whole milk
1 egg, lightly beaten
2 tablespoons unsalted butter
Garnish: Whipped sweet butter

The Steps:

1. Preheat oven to 400°.
2. In mixing bowl, combine cornmeal, flour, sugar, baking powder, and salt.
3. Add 1 cup of the milk and stir to combine; then add egg and stir until well mixed.
4. Melt butter in 8″ square baking pan in oven.
5. When butter is melted and hot, pour prepared batter in pan.
6. Pour remaining ½ cup milk over the top but do *not* stir.
7. Bake for 30 minutes or until golden on top but still custardy on the inside.
8. Serve hot, with whipped sweet butter.

Variations:

White cornmeal can be substituted for yellow.

Chopped pimientos or diced green chilies can be added for a spicy variation.

Banana-Nut Bread

YIELD: Three 8″ x 4″ x 2″ loaves or eight 6″ x 3½″ x 2″ mini-loaves
Preparation time: 20 minutes
Cooking time: 45 minutes–1 hour

This bread can be served as a bread with lunch or dinner, as a sweet for dessert, certainly as a tea bread, and even as a sweet bread for breakfast!

The Ingredients:

2½ cups all-purpose flour
2 teaspoons cornstarch
2 teaspoons baking soda

1 teaspoon salt
1 cup (2 sticks) unsalted butter, softened
2 cups granulated sugar
5 medium ripe bananas, mashed (about 3 cups)
4 eggs, lightly beaten
½ cup sour cream
1¼ cups chopped walnuts

The Steps:

1. Preheat oven to 350°. Lightly butter 3 large loaf pans or 8 mini-loaf pans and dust with flour.
2. Sift flour, cornstarch, baking soda, and salt together.
3. Cream butter and sugar together with electric beater until light and lemon-colored, about 3 minutes.
4. Add bananas, eggs, and sour cream and continue to beat until smooth.
5. Combine flour mixture with banana mixture but do not overbeat. Stir in walnuts.
6. Pour into prepared pans and bake for 45 minutes for mini-loaves, 55 minutes for larger loaves, or until firm in the center and the edges begin to separate from the pan.
7. Let rest on rack for 10 minutes; remove from pans, allow to cool slightly, and serve.

Variations:

Omit nuts and replace with raisins or chopped dates.

Make-It-Easy Tips:

√ Quick breads are easier to slice, and the flavors will mellow, if given 2–3 hours to sit after removing from pans.

√ Cornstarch is added to the flour to make it more crumbly in texture, reminiscent of cake flour.

√ Soften butter in its paper wrapper, place butter in mixing bowl, and use wrapper to butter the pans without getting fingers greasy.

Blueberry-Orange Bread

YIELD: One 9″ x 5″ x 3″ loaf or four 6″ x 3½″ x 2″ mini-loaves
Preparation time: 15–20 minutes
Cooking time: 40–60 minutes

The Ingredients:

- ½ cup orange juice
- ¼ cup hot water
- 2 tablespoons unsalted butter, melted
- 1½ teaspoons grated orange rind
- 1 egg, lightly beaten
- ⅓ cup dairy sour cream
- 2 cups all-purpose flour
- 1 cup granulated sugar
- 1 teaspoon baking powder
- ½ teaspoon salt
- ¼ teaspoon baking soda
- 1 cup fresh blueberries (or frozen, thawed; or canned, well drained)
- 2 tablespoons all-purpose flour

The Steps:

1. Preheat oven to 350°. Grease and dust with flour 1 large or 4 mini-loaf pans.
2. Combine orange juice, water, butter, and orange rind in a bowl; add egg and sour cream and mix well.
3. Combine 2 cups flour, sugar, baking powder, salt, and baking soda in a bowl; add these dry ingredients to juice mixture and mix until smooth.
4. Sprinkle blueberries with 2 tablespoons flour, toss lightly, and gently fold into batter.
5. Pour in pans and bake large loaf for 55–60 minutes; mini-loaves for 40–45 minutes or until an inserted knife comes out clean.
6. Let rest in pan for 10 minutes; remove from pan and allow to cool for 10–15 minutes before slicing.

Variations:

Chopped walnuts or pecans can be added in Step 4; stir them in before adding blueberries.

Make-It-Easy Tips:

√ The blueberries are dusted with flour to keep them from sinking in the batter.

√ The egg should be at room temperature to avoid curdling when adding to the warm liquid.

√ When grating orange rind, grate extra and freeze in small containers for future use.

Spicy Pumpkin Bread

YIELD: Three 8″ x 4″ x 2″ loaves or seven 6″ x 3½″ x 2″ mini-loaves
Preparation time: 20 minutes
Cooking time: 45–60 minutes

Spicy Pumpkin Bread can be eaten as a breakfast or lunch bread with sweet butter, or as a dessert, or as a snack by itself.

The Ingredients:

3½ cups all-purpose flour
2 teaspoons baking soda
1 teaspoon baking powder
1 teaspoon salt
1 teaspoon ground cinnamon
1 teaspoon ground nutmeg
1 teaspoon ground allspice
½ teaspoon ground cloves
2½ cups granulated white sugar
1 cup light brown sugar
1 cup corn oil
3 eggs
1 16-ounce can cooked pumpkin
1 cup buttermilk
1 cup diced pecans (two 2¼-ounce packages)
Garnish: Sweet butter

The Steps:

1. Preheat oven to 350°. Generously butter 3 large loaf pans or 7 mini-loaf pans and lightly dust with flour.

2. Sift flour, baking soda, baking powder, salt, cinnamon, nutmeg, allspice, and cloves and set aside.
3. In a large bowl with an electric beater, beat sugars and oil until smooth.
4. Add eggs and beat well; add pumpkin, continuing to beat until smooth.
5. Add dry ingredients, alternating with the buttermilk, beating until batter is smooth.
6. Fold in pecans; pour into prepared loaf pans and bake for 45 minutes for mini-loaf pans and 55 minutes–1 hour for larger loaves or until a knife inserted comes out clean.
7. Let rest for 10 minutes in pans, then turn out onto a wire rack to cool. Serve warm or at room temperature with sweet butter or by itself.

Variation:

Half whole-wheat flour and half white flour can be substituted for white.

Make-It-Easy Tips:

√ If diced nuts are not available, chop whole shelled nuts in blender or food processor.

√ If buttermilk is unavailable, add 1 tablespoon vinegar or 1 tablespoon lemon juice to 1 cup whole milk and allow to stand and thicken for 5 minutes.

CHAPTER TEN

DESSERTS

Ice Cream Cookie Freakout
Cassis Froth
Instant Ice Cream
Instant Sorbet
Hazelnut Topped Ice Cream plus Variations
Zabaglione
Crème aux Fruits
Apple Crumble
Blueberry Pudding
Blackberry Cobbler
Strawberries with Almond Cream
Poached Pears
Apricot Apples
Quick Chocolate Mousse
Bar Cookies
Pecan-Butterscotch Squares
Lemon Squares
Raspberry Tea Squares
World's Tastiest Brownies
Double Fudge Chip Cake
Short Shortbread
Chocolate Meringue Pie
Mud Pie
Frozen Lime Pie
Raisin Pie

Unless sweets are your "thing," you probably want dessert to be the simplest part of the meal to prepare. At least, that's how I feel about it. So I have selected recipes, many of which appear to be very elegant, but are a snap.

You will find a number that involve ice cream—just about everybody's favorite. It can be used in cakes, pie fillings, or whips and is always a major hit. Try the *Ice Cream Cookie Freakout,* which is simply crushed Oreos mixed with vanilla ice cream to form a "cookie ice cream," or combine chocolate wafers with coffee ice cream to form a "mocha freakout."

The ultimate Make-It-Easy dessert is a bowl of fresh fruits accompanied by assorted cheeses. In the summer, berries, especially, provide a base for whipped cream, ice cream, sour cream, or crème fraîche. In the winter months, pears and apples can be baked or served fresh with cheese for quick, easy, and refreshing finishes to dinner. If fresh fruit is unavailable, substitute frozen, unsweetened fruits—they work well in baked dishes, sauces, or puddings.

Baking cakes, pies, cookies, on the other hand, requires care, patience, and an exactness that only time will allow. The measuring, sifting, mixing, greasing, flouring, creaming, whipping, preheating, first rising, second rising, cooling, and frosting are time-consuming activities befitting the Sunday afternoon pastry chef who loves to concoct extravaganzas.

There's definitely nothing wrong with the activity. It can be totally relaxing and, best of all, can satisfy a craving for that picture on the front of the current *Bon Appétit* magazine, the one with the dripping chocolate sauce over the coffee mousse with the whipped cream and shaved chocolate curls and. . . .

I'm talking fun! But when there's no time for such fun, and a dessert is called for, I have a few hints that will make baking quicker and easier. For example, cakes can be assembled by using crumbled cookies and layering them with ice cream or whipped cream and garnishing with chips, chocolate, or even crushed candy bars (I have a "thing" for crushed Heath Bars!)

Bar cookies are the easiest form of cookie to bake. They can be blended together, poured into a large pan, baked, cooled, and cut into dozens of cookies.

Pies are made Make-It-Easy with crumb crusts. Although prepared crusts are available, whipping up a cookie crust in the blender or food processor requires no more than five minutes. Besides, you can vary the taste by using graham crackers, gingersnaps, chocolate wafers, vanilla wafers, macaroons, or Amaretti cookies.

Pies can be prepared in Pyrex or metal pie pans, or in springform pans with a sprinkling of crumbs on the edges to save preparing a crust. The usual procedure for a crumb crust is to mix 1–1⅓ cups crumbs with 2 tablespoons sugar (or less, according to the sweetness of the crumbs). Add ½ stick of softened or melted butter, and combine in blender or food processor until crumbly. Variations can be made by adding grated lemon or orange rind, cinnamon, shredded coconut, cereal crumbs, or chopped nuts.

Whether it's ice cream, fruit, cakes, or cookies for dessert, remember to serve it attractively. It takes no time to pour an ice cream dessert into long-stemmed glasses, or arrange cookies on a paper-lace doily on a pretty plate. This extra special touch will make even the simplest dessert look elegant.

What's best about the desserts in this section, besides the taste, is that you can make most of them in 15 minutes or less.

Ice Cream Cookie Freakout!

SERVES: 3–4
Preparation time: 5 minutes

This is my family's favorite recipe to test. We must test it two or three times a week just to make sure we get it right! The best part about it is that an Ice Cream Cookie Freakout can be made on the spur of the moment. Just keep gobs of vanilla ice cream and Oreo cookies around—just in case. . . .

The Ingredients:

5 Oreo cookies
1 pint vanilla ice cream, softened for 3–4 minutes at room temperature

The Steps:

1. In food processor or blender, crush cookies slightly.
2. Add ice cream in scoops and process until smooth.
3. Pour into goblets or sherbet glasses and serve immediately.

Variations:

Variations on the Freakout are innumerable. Try gingersnaps and vanilla ice cream, Oreos and coffee ice cream for a Mocha Freakout, oatmeal cookies and chocolate ice cream, peanut butter cookies and vanilla ice cream, or the totally sinful Oreos and chocolate fudge ice cream for a Double Fudge Freakout! By all means, improvise and come up with your own Freakout!

Make-It-Easy Tips:

√ Use regular Oreo cookies, *not* the "double" ones, which will be too sweet. Hydrox cookies are also good. Test the Oreos versus the Hydrox to determine your personal preference.

√ Ice Cream Cookie Freakout can be frozen for future use but the best part of it is the soft texture reminiscent of those times as a child when you mashed your cookies and ice cream together.

√ If using a blender, it may be necessary to prepare the Freakout in 2 batches.

Cassis Froth

SERVES: 6–8
Preparation time: 5 minutes

Any flavor liqueur or ice cream can be used to make a Froth. Try Crème de Cacao or Kahlua with coffee ice cream, Crème de Menthe with chocolate ice cream, apricot brandy with peach ice cream or Cherry Herring with cherry-vanilla ice cream. Improvise and come up with your own Froth.

The Ingredients:

2 pints vanilla ice cream, softened 3–4 minutes at room temperature
6–8 tablespoons Crème de Cassis
Garnish: Fresh berries (optional)

The Steps:

1. Just before serving, place ice cream in food processor or blender container.

2. Add liqueur and blend until smooth. The consistency should be thick, like a double-thick milk shake.
3. Pour into stemmed goblets or sherbet glasses and serve immediately, garnished with fresh berries if desired.

Make-It-Easy Tips:

√ If using a blender, do in 2 or 3 batches.

√ The Cassis Froth can be frozen again for future use, but it is best served immediately, when it has a soft, creamy texture.

Instant Ice Cream

SERVES: 3–4
Preparation time: 5 minutes

A food processor or very strong blender is necessary to prepare this dish. Just drop the frozen fruit into the cream, and presto! Instant Ice Cream! I find it the perfect dessert to serve to unexpected guests, or to my family, who likes to watch it being prepared.

The Ingredients:

1 cup heavy cream
⅓ cup granulated sugar
1 20-ounce package (loosely packed) unsweetened frozen fruit (strawberries, raspberries, blueberries, cherries, or peaches)

The Steps:

1. Place cream and sugar in food processor bowl (fitted with steel knife) and blend for 1 minute.
2. Through the feed tube, add frozen fruit, a few pieces at a time, and process until smooth (an ice cream will form).
3. Serve immediately, garnished with cookies or fresh fruit.

Make-It-Easy Tip:

√ The dessert can be frozen, but it's best when served immediately.

Instant Sorbet

SERVES: 4
Preparation time: 5 minutes
Freezing time: 4–6 hours

The food processor transforms fresh frozen fruit into Sorbet (French sherbet) in a matter of minutes. Freeze any fruit desired, mix with sugar to taste, and brandy or liqueur, process, and *voilà!* Sorbet!

The Ingredients:

3–4 large ripe bananas
1 teaspoon lemon juice
4–6 tablespoons apricot brandy (or Crème de Banana)
1 tablespoon confectioners' sugar or to taste (optional)
Garnish: Sprigs of fresh mint (optional)

The Steps:

1. Peel bananas, wrap tightly in plastic wrap and freeze for 4–6 hours or overnight.
2. Unwrap bananas, cut into 1″ slices, place in food processor with lemon juice; pulsate on and off to combine.
3. Add liqueur and continue to process until smooth.
4. Add confectioners' sugar, if desired, and serve in a goblet or attractive dish garnished with mint sprigs, if desired. (The Sorbet can be placed in small freezer-proof dishes, covered, and frozen for future use.)

Variations:

Be creative and make up your own variations. The fruit selected should be fleshy without a lot of peel. Grapes and blueberries should be avoided. Remember to peel the fruit and seal it in plastic wrap before freezing to keep from browning. Don't forget to cut it in small pieces before processing. Here are a few variations on which to start: Melon with Grand Marnier; peaches with peach brandy; pear with apple brandy; kiwi with apple brandy.

Make-It-Easy Tips:

√ Frozen, unsweetened fruit such as peaches can be used and placed right in food processor, bypassing Step 1.

√ The lemon juice is added to fruit to prevent it from turning brown.

Hazelnut-Topped Ice Cream (plus Variations)

SERVES: 6
Preparation time: 5 minutes

The easiest dessert to whip up at the last minute is ice cream with a special topping or liqueur. Select a favorite ice cream or sherbet, some unusual toppings or liqueurs, and an instant and always pleasing dessert is created.

The Ingredients:

1 5-ounce hazelnut chocolate bar (Cadbury or other good brand)
2 pints coffee ice cream or "rainbow" sherbet (or use whatever flavor desired)

The Steps:

1. Break chocolate bar into small pieces and crumble in food processor or blender. (Chocolate bar can be frozen, placed in a strong plastic bag, and pounded with a hammer until crumbly.)
2. Place scoops of ice cream or sherbet in tall goblets or sherbet glasses, top with chocolate crumbs, and serve immediately.

Variations:

Chocolate ice cream topped with crushed peppermint candies.

Butter-pecan ice cream topped with crushed Amaretti or macaroon cookies.

Mocha ice cream topped with Amaretto liqueur and toasted slivered almonds.

Coffee ice cream topped with coffee liqueur, whipped cream, and crushed toffee candy.

Vanilla ice cream topped with sliced, ripe pears and Crème de Menthe liqueur.

Vanilla ice cream topped with a mixture of 1 thawed, 12-ounce package frozen raspberries pureed, and berry-flavored liqueur.

Vanilla ice cream topped with candied chestnuts (*marrons glacés*).

Vanilla ice cream topped with warmed apricot jam thinned with Kirsch.

Orange sherbet and vanilla ice cream topped with Grand Marnier and mandarin orange segments.

Orange sherbet topped with warmed ginger marmalade thinned with brandy.

Pineapple sherbet topped with crushed pineapple and chopped fresh mint.

Raspberry sherbet topped with Crème de Cassis.

Zabaglione

SERVES: 6–8
Preparation time: 10 minutes
Cooking time: 5–10 minutes

A small double boiler is essential to the successful preparation of Zabaglione.

The Ingredients:

- 4 egg yolks, at room temperature
- ¼ cup granulated sugar
- 2½ tablespoons dry Marsala
- 1 tablespoon grated lemon rind
- 2 pints fresh strawberries, blueberries, raspberries, or other fruit

The Steps:

1. In top of double boiler, combine egg yolks, sugar, Marsala, and lemon rind; whip with a whisk until smooth.

2. Place the double boiler top over simmering water on high heat and whisk vigorously until the mixture becomes foamy and begins to thicken.
3. Spoon immediately over fresh berries or fruit, or cake.

Variation:

Zabaglione can also be served chilled.

Make-It-Easy Tips:

√ If not using the Zabaglione immediately, it can be kept warm in the top of the double boiler with the heat turned off for 10 minutes.

√ Freeze egg whites individually in ice-cube trays. Once frozen, remove from tray and store in a sealed plastic bag to be used as needed.

√ If using a large double boiler, double the recipe so that you can whisk the ingredients easily.

Crème aux Fruits

SERVES: 6
Preparation time: 20 minutes
Cooking time: 50–60 minutes
Chilling time: 4–6 hours or overnight

The custard of this dessert is the traditional base for crème brulée, the sinfully rich French concoction. Instead of the time-consuming caramelizing procedure, I've substituted berries as the topping. Serve it on the Fourth of July for a red, white, and blue dessert.

The Ingredients:

2 cups heavy cream
4 egg yolks, at room temperature
¼ cup granulated sugar
Pinch of salt
1 teaspoon vanilla extract
1½ pints washed blueberries or halved strawberries (or a combination of both)

The Steps:

1. Preheat oven to 350°.
2. In a small saucepan, scald cream by heating until bubbles just begin to appear around the edges; allow to cool for 5 minutes.
3. In the meantime, beat yolks until thickened and a light lemon color; gradually beat in sugar and salt until smooth.
4. Slowly pour cream into egg-yolk mixture, whisking constantly; flavor with vanilla and pour into a shallow, one-quart baking dish.
5. Place dish in a larger pan. Add hot water to larger pan until it reaches 1″ up the sides of the baking dish. Bake for 50–60 minutes or until a knife inserted comes out clean; cool for 30 minutes.
6. Chill in refrigerator for 4–6 hours or overnight.
7. Just before serving, garnish with berries.

Variations:

Dessert can be baked in 6 individual ramekins or Pyrex cups.

Other varieties of fruit can be used as a garnish, such as sliced kiwi, sliced grapes, or poached peaches or apricots.

For a more authentic variation, slice a vanilla bean and add to the cream while scalding (discard bean). Omit vanilla extract from recipe.

Make-It-Easy Tips:

√ The scalded cream must be cooled slightly before adding to egg yolks to prevent curdling.

√ Hot water bath in Step 5 prevents the custard from curdling or overcooking.

√ The dessert is best when prepared a day in advance and allowed to chill thoroughly overnight.

√ For a glazed effect, dip the blueberries and halved strawberries into ¼ cup currant jelly that has been melted and glaze each before garnishing in Step 7.

Apple Crumble

SERVES: 4–6
Preparation time: 15 minutes
Cooking time: 45–50 minutes

Apple Crumble is a combination of apple pie and apple brown betty, but can be prepared in only 15 minutes. It can be made in a 9″ pie plate, in 4 small, individual quiche pans, or in flat oven-proof dishes.

The Ingredients:

4 tart apples
2 tablespoons lemon juice

Streusel Topping:

⅓ cup all-purpose flour
½ cup brown sugar
½ teaspoon ground cinnamon
¼ teaspoon freshly grated nutmeg
4 tablespoons unsalted butter, softened
Garnish: Vanilla ice cream or whipped cream

The Steps:

1. Preheat oven to 375°. Generously butter a 9″ pie plate or 4 individual dishes.
2. Peel and core apples and cut each into 8 wedges.
3. Place sliced apples in prepared dish and sprinkle with lemon juice.
4. Prepare streusel topping in food processor or blender or by hand by blending flour, brown sugar, cinnamon, nutmeg, and butter together until just crumbly but not overprocessed.
5. Sprinkle streusel topping atop apples and bake in preheated 375° oven for 45–50 minutes or until tip is golden and apples are tender (smaller dishes should be done in 45 minutes).
6. Serve Apple Crumble warm, garnished with vanilla ice cream or whipped cream.

Variations:

Sliced peaches or berries can be substituted for the apples.

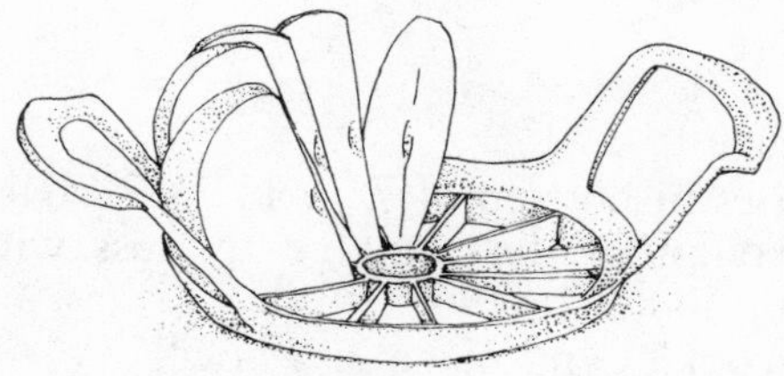

Apple corer

Make-It-Easy Tips:

√ A gadget called an apple slicer cores and slices apples in one swift motion.

√ Crumble may be prepared earlier in the day and reheated before serving.

√ The lemon juice is sprinkled on the apples to keep them from discoloring.

√ Streusel topping can also be used on coffee cakes or similar fruit bakes.

Blueberry Pudding

SERVES: 6–8
Preparation time: 15 minutes
Cooking time: 30–35 minutes

The Ingredients:

1 quart fresh blueberries, washed, or two 12-ounce boxes frozen blueberries, thawed
2 tablespoons granulated sugar
1 tablespoon flour
1 teaspoon grated orange rind
24 coconut or almond macaroon cookies (one 13-ounce package)
2 eggs, lightly beaten
¼ cup light brown sugar
1 teaspoon grated lemon or orange rind
2 tablespoons unsalted butter, diced
Garnish: Vanilla or lemon ice cream, or *Crème Fraîche* (*see* Chapter 2)

The Steps:

1. Preheat oven to 350°.
2. Place berries in bottom of 7″ x 11″ x 2″ baking dish or similar-size oven-proof dish and gently toss with 2 tablespoons sugar, flour, and 1 teaspoon rind.
3. Crumble cookies and place in a bowl.
4. Add eggs, brown sugar, 1 teaspoon rind and stir well.
5. Spread mixture evenly over blueberries, dot with butter bits, and bake for 30–35 minutes or until top is lightly golden.
6. Serve warm with vanilla or lemon ice cream, or *Crème Frâche*.

Variations:

Other berries, such as raspberries, blackberries, boysenberries, or strawberries, can be similarly baked, varying the sweetener to taste and substituting lemon for the orange rind if desired.

Make-It-Easy Tips:

√ Cookies can be crumbled easily in a food processor or blender.
√ Blueberry pudding can be cooked and frozen for future use.
√ Orange and lemon rind can be grated in large quantities and kept frozen for future use.
√ When buying fresh berries, look on the underside of the container to be sure there are no decaying berries. If you find some after you get home, remove them before the mold spreads.

Blackberry Cobbler

SERVES: 6–8
Preparation time: 15 minutes
Cooking time: 45 minutes–1 hour

A cobbler is a deep-dish pie with no bottom crust and a top crust of streusel or biscuit dough. It is derived from the early American expression "to cobble up," meaning to put together quickly. This dish is put together in even less time with the help of a food processor.

The Ingredients:

4 cups fresh blackberries, or frozen unsweetened blackberries, thawed
½ cup granulated sugar
¼ pound (1 stick) unsalted butter, broken into bits, at room temperature
1 cup all-purpose flour
½ cup granulated sugar
Pinch of cinnamon
Pinch of nutmeg
Garnish: Vanilla ice cream, or whipped cream or *Crème Fraîche* (*see* Chapter 2).

The Steps:

1. Preheat oven to 350°.
2. Place the blackberries in bottom of a deep-dish pie plate or a rectangular oven-proof baking dish.
3. Sprinkle with ½ cup granulated sugar and gently toss.
4. In bowl of food processor (or in a mixing bowl) combine butter, flour, ½ cup granulated sugar, cinnamon, and nutmeg; pulsate with several on-off turns of the processor until butter/sugar mixture is crumbly. Or use fork, or your fingers, and crumble by hand.
5. Sprinkle topping over sweetened berries and bake until lightly browned, 45 minutes–1 hour.
6. Serve hot, with vanilla ice cream, whipped cream, or *Crème Fraîche.*

Variations:

Blueberries, raspberries, or peaches can be used in a cobbler.

Make-It-Easy Tips:

√ The cobbler can be cooked and frozen for future use.
√ Cinnamon and nutmeg, as well as many other spices, are now available in disposable grinders at supermarkets. The grinders produce a fresh-ground taste and aroma, and extend the shelf-life of the spices, which remain constantly sealed.

Strawberries with Almond Cream

SERVES: 4–6
Preparation time: 10 minutes
Chilling time: 1 hour

The Ingredients:

Sauce:

1 cup (8 ounces) dairy sour cream
3 tablespoons confectioners' sugar
1½ tablespoons almond liqueur (I use Amaretto)
1 teaspoon almond extract
2 pints fresh strawberries, washed, hulled and split in half

The Steps:

1. In small bowl combine sour cream, sugar, liqueur, and almond extract; stir until smooth. Cover, and chill for 1 hour or until ready to use.
2. Serve almond cream over hulled and split berries.

Variations:

A combination of berries (strawberries, raspberries, and blueberries) can be used.

Crème Fraîche (*see* Chapter 2) can be substituted for sour cream.

Make-It-Easy Tips:

√ Cream can be prepared a day or two in advance and chilled until ready to use.

√ Wash strawberries before hulling to prevent loss of juice.

√ A strawberry huller, an inexpensive gadget shaped like a fat tweezer, is a wonderful tool for hulling strawberries. It is available at gourmet specialty shops. If unavailable, use a beer can opener to pick out the hull.

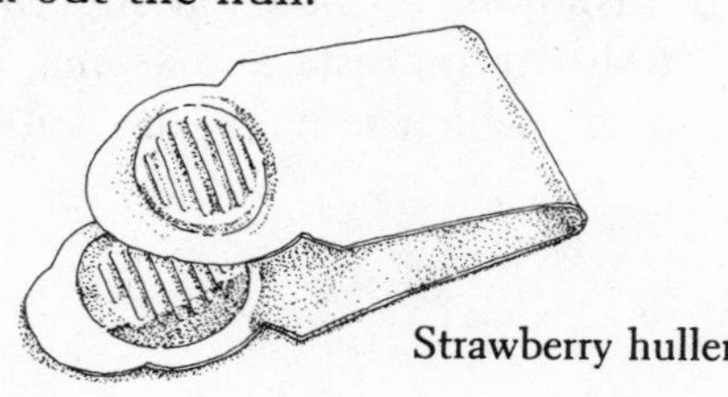

Strawberry huller

Poached Pears

SERVES: 3–4
Preparation time: 10 minutes
Cooking time: 20 minutes

This is a light, low-calorie dessert.

The Ingredients:

2 pears, medium ripe
1 cup unsweetened apple juice
1 teaspoon lemon juice
1 stick cinnamon
1 whole clove
Pinch of nutmeg
Garnish: *Reduced-Calorie Sour Cream*

The Steps:

1. Preheat oven to 350°.
2. Peel pears, slice in half lengthwise, and remove the cores and seeds.
3. Place pears, cut side down, in a small casserole.
4. In small bowl, combine apple juice, lemon juice, cinnamon stick, clove, and nutmeg. Stir and pour over the pears.
5. Cover pan and bake for about 20 minutes or until tender. (Do not overcook or they will be mushy.)
6. Remove pan from oven and allow to cool in liquid for 10 minutes.
7. Discard cinnamon stick and serve warm with *Reduced-Calorie Sour Cream*, if desired.

Variations:

For a higher calorie version, top pears with vanilla ice cream or sweetened whipped cream.

Poached Pears can also be served cold.

Make-It-Easy Tips:

√ Pears can be cooked earlier in the day for 5 minutes. When ready to serve, heat for an additional 15 minutes and serve.

√ Anjou or Bosc pears are excellent for baking.

Apricot Apples

SERVES: 4
Preparation time: 10 minutes
Cooking time: 40–50 minutes

Baked apples do not need gobs of syrup and sugar to taste good. Try these apples covered with juice and reduced-sugar preserves.

The Ingredients:

4 baking apples (Rome Beauty, Pippin, or Granny Smiths can be used)
4 teaspoons lemon juice
½–¾ cup low-calorie (reduced sugar) apricot jam
1 cup unsweetened apple juice
1 teaspoon cinnamon
½ teaspoon grated nutmeg

The Steps:

1. Preheat oven to 350°.
2. Wash apples, remove cores with an apple corer or knife, and immediately sprinkle open cores with lemon juice.
3. Arrange apples in baking dish and fill cavities with apricot jam.
4. Pour juice into pan, sprinkle cavities with cinnamon and nutmeg, and bake for 40–50 minutes or until apples are tender, basting occasionally with pan juices.
5. Serve apples hot, at room temperature, or chilled.

Variations:

Other low-calorie preserves, such as strawberry or grape, can be substituted for apricot.

Make-It-Easy Tip:

√ Lemon juice is sprinkled over openings in apples to prevent discoloration.

Quick Chocolate Mousse

SERVES: 6–8
Preparation time: 10 minutes
Chilling time: 6 hours or overnight

This is a super-fast mousse to prepare on a moment's notice. Keep the chips and liqueur on hand and you're ready to go.

The Ingredients:

1 6-ounce package semisweet chocolate chips
2 eggs
3 tablespoons very strong, hot coffee
2 tablespoons coffee liqueur (I use Kahlua)
¾ cup scalded milk
Garnish: Sweetened whipped cream or *Crème Fraîche* (*see* Chapter 2)

The Steps:

1. In container of food processor or blender, place chocolate chips, eggs, hot coffee, Kahlua, and scalded milk and process until very smooth.
2. Pour into 6 ramekins, or 8 *pots de crème* dishes, or 1 large, 1½-quart dish, and chill 6 hours or overnight.
3. Serve chilled with sweetened whipped cream or *Crème Fraîche.*

Make-It-Easy Tips:

√ Instant coffee can be used, with or without caffeine, for the strong, hot coffee.

√ To scald milk, heat until milk just begins to bubble around the edge of the pan.

BAR COOKIES

No, bar cookies are not the sweet-tooth equivalent of pretzels and peanuts, something to be wedged between the mixed drinks and the bartender at holiday get-togethers. They are, in fact, a cross between a traditional cookie and a cake and are baked in sheets, cooled, and then cut into squares, triangles, or whatever shape you prefer. They can be frozen in small batches and defrosted whenever the spirit moves you—a totally Make-It-Easy cookie!

Before you begin baking your bar cookies, here are a few tips to keep in mind:

1. Always use real (as opposed to artificial) ingredients. Even though they're more expensive, you'll taste the difference.
2. Soften the butter or cream cheese ahead of time.
3. Use a large (9″ x 13″) baking pan; for thicker cookies, use a 7″ x 11″ or an 8″ or 9″ square pan. Adjust cooking time accordingly.
4. Generously grease baking pans before pouring in the batter. Dusting with flour after greasing often makes removing the bars easier.
5. Use an electric mixer or hand beater to make the batter. Do not use a food processor or blender (unless specified), which can overprocess the dough and hence toughen the cookies.
6. Bake the bars on the middle rack of the oven.
7. If you like chewy, fudgy squares, underbake them slightly. The top should be dull, not shiny, and, when you press your finger on the top, a slight imprint should remain. If you prefer cakey squares, bake them until the top springs back to the touch or an inserted toothpick comes out clean.
8. And . . . if you've forgotten to soften the butter, grate it and it will soften in minutes.

Pecan-Butterscotch Squares

YIELD: 4 dozen
Preparation time: 15–20 minutes
Cooking time: 40 minutes

These pecan squares are very popular around my house. If coconut is not your favorite, by all means omit it—they will still be a knockout.

The Ingredients:

¼ pound (1 stick) unsalted butter, softened
½ cup dark brown sugar

1 cup all-purpose flour
2 eggs, lightly beaten
1 cup dark brown sugar
1 teaspoon vanilla extract
1 cup pecans, chopped
1 cup (4 ounces) flaked or shredded coconut
1 6-ounce package butterscotch chips
2 tablespoons flour
Pinch of salt

The Steps:

1. Preheat oven to 375°. Generously butter a 7″ x 11″ baking pan and lightly dust with flour.
2. To prepare crust, cream butter and ½ cup brown sugar together until smooth; gradually add flour; mix until crumbly. Press into prepared pan and bake for 15–20 minutes or until golden.
3. In the meantime, combine eggs, 1 cup brown sugar, pecans, coconut, butterscotch chips, 2 tablespoons flour, vanilla, and salt. Spread mixture over baked crust and return to oven for an additional 20 minutes.
4. Let cool thoroughly and cut into squares.

Make-It-Easy Tips:

√ Freeze squares uncut and later slice into squares while semi-frozen for easier cutting.
√ Prepare crust easily with an electric beater.
√ Nut meats keep indefinitely in the freezer.

Lemon Squares

YIELD: 16 cookies
Preparation time: 20 minutes
Cooking time: 45 minutes

The Ingredients:

1 cup all-purpose flour
6 tablespoons (¾ stick) unsalted butter, softened

¼ cup confectioners' sugar
1½ ounces cream cheese, softened
1 cup granulated sugar
2 tablespoons all-purpose flour
2 eggs, lightly beaten
3 tablespoons lemon juice
1 teaspoon finely minced lemon rind
½ teaspoon baking powder
Garnish: Confectioners' sugar

The Steps:

1. Preheat oven to 350°. Generously butter an 8″ square baking pan and lightly dust with flour.
2. In large mixing bowl with an electric mixer, combine 1 cup flour, butter, ¼ cup confectioners' sugar, and cream cheese and beat until crumbly.
3. Press dough into prepared baking pan and bake for 20 minutes.
4. In the meantime, combine granulated sugar, 2 tablespoons flour, eggs, lemon juice, lemon rind, and baking powder; beat until smooth.
5. Spread mixture over baked layer; bake for additional 25 minutes.
6. Remove from oven, cool in pan for 10 minutes; while still warm, run a knife around outer edge, cut into bars, and sprinkle with confectioners' sugar.

Make-It-Easy Tip:

√ Since this recipe requires a longer preparation time, why not double the recipe and bake in two 8″ square pans or one 9″ x 13″ x 2″ pan, baking for the same amount of time. Freeze extra squares without sprinkling with garnish of confectioners' sugar.

Raspberry Tea Squares

YIELD: 20–24 cookies
Preparation time: 15–20 minutes
Cooking time: 35 minutes

The Ingredients:

6 ounces (1½ sticks) unsalted butter, softened
1 cup granulated sugar
1 egg, lightly beaten
1 teaspoon vanilla extract
2 cups all-purpose flour
Pinch of allspice
1 cup chopped almonds
¾ cup raspberry preserves
Garnish: Confectioners' sugar (optional)

The Steps:

1. Preheat oven to 350°. Generously butter a 9″ square baking pan and lightly dust with flour.
2. In large mixing bowl with an electric mixer, cream butter and sugar until light and fluffy; add egg and vanilla and continue to beat until smooth. Add flour, allspice, and nuts, mixing until well combined.
3. Place half the batter in bottom of prepared baking pan; gently and carefully spread preserves over mixture and top with remaining batter.
4. Bake for 30–35 minutes or until lightly golden.
5. Remove from oven and sprinkle with confectioners' sugar, if desired. Allow to cool 15–20 minutes and cut into squares.

Variations:

Both jam and nuts can be varied to suit your taste. Try apricot with pecans; strawberry with filberts; or peach with walnuts.

Make-It-Easy Tip:

√ Freeze squares uncut and later slice into squares while semi-frozen for easier cutting.

World's Tastiest Brownies

YIELD: 32 brownies
Preparation time: 20 minutes
Cooking time: 20–25 minutes

These brownies require a little extra time, but they are worth every minute of it. They are sensational!

The Ingredients:

1 12-ounce package real chocolate bits
½ pound unsalted butter (2 sticks) or margarine
4 eggs
1 cup sugar
1 teaspoon vanilla extract
1 cup all-purpose flour

The Steps:

1. Preheat oven to 350°. Generously butter two 8″ square baking pans or one 9″ x 13″ x 2″ pan.
2. Melt chocolate bits and butter together in the top of a double boiler, or over low heat in a heavy-bottomed saucepan. Stir until smooth. Allow to cool slightly.
3. In large bowl, beat eggs with an electric beater or by hand. Add sugar and vanilla and continue to beat for 2–3 minutes until smooth.
4. Add chocolate mixture to eggs; add flour and stir well.
5. Pour batter into prepared pans and bake for 20–25 minutes, according to whether you prefer them soft or cakey.
6. Allow to cool slightly, cut into squares, and serve.

Variation:

1 cup chopped walnuts can be added.

Make-It-Easy Tips:

√ Baked brownies can be turned out onto a sheet of aluminum foil, wrapped, and chilled or frozen. Brownies can then be easily cut, cold or semi-frozen, and brought to room temperature before serving.

√ Never cover a pot in which chocolate is melting. Any excess moisture or condensation will "stiffen" the chocolate and prevent it from combining easily with the rest of the ingredients.

Double-Fudge Chip Cake

YIELD: Two 8″ x 4″ x 2″ loaf pans or five 6″ x 3½″ x 2″ mini-loaf pans
Preparation time: 10–15 minutes
Cooking time: 40–55 minutes

The shortening and eggs for this cake are in the unusual form of mayonnaise. It is a very rich and fudgy dessert.

The Ingredients:

2 cups all-purpose flour
1⅓ cups granulated sugar
½ cup unsweetened cocoa
1½ teaspoons baking soda
1½ cups buttermilk
1 cup mayonnaise (not salad dressing)
1 teaspoon vanilla extract
1 12-ounce package semisweet chocolate bits

The Steps:

1. Preheat oven to 350°. Generously butter 2 large or 5 or 6 mini-loaf pans and lightly dust with flour.
2. Combine flour, sugar, cocoa, and baking soda in a large bowl and stir well.
3. Add buttermilk, mayonnaise, and vanilla and beat until smooth.
4. Stir in chips; pour batter in prepared pans.
5. Bake for 40–45 minutes for mini-loaves, or 50–55 minutes for larger loaves.

Variation:

Buttered pans can be dusted with cocoa instead of flour.

Make-It-Easy Tips:

√ Prepare cake in a double batch and bake in mini-loaf pans; freeze. Use loaves as desserts for family, company, or as wonderful house gifts.

√ If buttermilk is unavailable, add 1 tablespoon vinegar or lemon juice to 1 cup fresh milk and allow to stand 5 minutes.

Short Shortbread

SERVES: 8–10
Preparation time: 10–15 minutes
Cooking time: 1 hour

Shortbread, a Scottish delicacy also called shortcake, is a very rich dough made of butter, flour, and sugar that, when baked in a 9″ round pan, comes out like an oversize cookie. It is served broken into wedges.

The shortbread can be split horizontally, filled with preserves or fruit, and used as a cake. A clay shortbread mold carved with designs can be used for an attractive presentation, or a 9″ pie plate can be used. The dough can be prepared in 30 seconds in the food processor.

The Ingredients:

2 cups sifted all-purpose flour
¾ cup confectioners' sugar
Pinch of salt
½ pound (2 sticks) unsalted butter, softened

Shortbread mold

The Steps:

1. Preheat oven to 325°. Lightly spray a clay shortbread mold with vegetable shortening or line a 9″ pie plate with parchment paper or waxed paper.
2. In food processor, with electric mixer, or by hand, combine ingredients until a smooth dough is formed.
3. Press dough firmly into mold or pie pan, making sure dough fits into all crevices of mold or lies flat in pan.
4. Bake filled mold or pan for 50 minutes to 1 hour or until pale in color but not brown.
5. Remove from oven, allow to cool 10–15 minutes, break into pieces, and serve.

Make-It-Easy Tip:

√ Do not overprocess in food processor. Just blend until a dough forms. If too sticky, add additional flour.

Chocolate Meringue Pie

SERVES: 8–10
Preparation time: 15 minutes
Cooking time: 35 minutes
Chilling time: 2–3 hours or overnight

The texture of the meringue-cookie base, topped with the sweetened whipped cream, makes this an unusual and terrific dessert. The whipped cream topping is important because the cold meringue needs an attractive topping.

The Ingredients:

20 chocolate wafers
½ cup chopped walnuts
3 egg whites, at room temperature
½ cup granulated sugar
1 teaspoon baking powder
Pinch of salt
1 teaspoon vanilla extract

Topping:

1 cup heavy cream
1 tablespoon confectioners' sugar
1 teaspoon vanilla extract

The Steps:

1. Preheat oven to 325°. Generously butter a 9″ pie plate.
2. In food processor or blender, chop wafers and nuts briefly. (Do not make them too fine.)
3. Beat egg whites until stiff. Gradually add granulated sugar, baking powder, salt, and vanilla; continue to beat until stiff peaks form.
4. Gently fold in wafer/nut mixture; pour mixture into buttered pie plate and bake for 35 minutes. Cool, and then chill in refrigerator for 2–3 hours or overnight.
5. Whip cream until almost stiff, add confectioners' sugar and vanilla, and continue to whip until stiff.
6. Serve chilled pie topped with the sweetened whipped cream.

Variations:

For an unusual variation, substitute 20 Ritz crackers for the chocolate wafers and increase the granulated sugar to 1 cup.

Pecans can be substituted for walnuts.

Make-It-Easy Tips:

√ Egg whites must be at room temperature before beating to achieve proper volume. To warm chilled egg whites quickly, place in a metal bowl. (Do not use aluminum, which will give whites a greyish tint.) Set bowl in a basin of warm water; stir to remove the chill. To increase volume, add ¼ teaspoon cream of tartar after egg whites are foamy and begin to stiffen.

Mud Pie

SERVES: 8
Preparation time: 20 minutes
Freezing time: ½ hour plus 3–4 hours

The Ingredients:

Crust:
18 Oreo cookies, crushed
⅓ cup unsalted butter, melted

Filling:
1 quart coffee ice cream (or desired flavor), slightly softened

Topping:
2 squares unsweetened chocolate
1 small (5⅓-ounce) can evaporated milk
½ cup granulated sugar
1 tablespoon unsalted butter

The Steps:

1. Crush cookies in blender or food processor. Combine with butter and press into buttered 9″ springform pan or 9″ pie plate.
2. Soften ice cream and place in shell. Freeze for ½ hour.
3. In small saucepan, melt chocolate with milk, sugar, and butter. Cook over low heat or in double boiler until syrupy and smooth, 5–10 minutes.
4. While still warm, pour topping over filling; freeze pie for 3–4 hours. Remove from freezer, allow to stand at room temperature for 10 minutes, and serve in slices.

Variation:

Use mint chocolate chip ice cream for filling and top with crushed toffee candy.

Make-It-Easy Tips:

√ If desired, pie can be prepared up through Step 2 and served in slices with hot sauce on top.

√ Mud Pie can be prepared in advance and frozen for several weeks.

Frozen Lime Pie

SERVES: 8
Preparation time: 20 minutes
Freezing time: ½ hour + 3 hours + ½ hour

The chocolate crust makes this Frozen Lime Pie special, but if time is a problem use a prepared graham cracker crust.

The Ingredients:

Crust:

- ⅓ cup unsalted butter, softened
- 1¼ cups chocolate wafer crumbs (20–22 wafers)
- 3 tablespoons granulated sugar

Filling:

- 1 14-ounce can sweetened condensed milk
- 4 eggs
- 1 tablespoon grated lime rind
- ½ cup fresh lime juice

Topping:

- 1 cup vanilla ice cream, slightly softened
- 1–2 tablespoons grated lime rind

The Steps:

1. Generously butter a 9″ pie pan, or spray with non-aerosol vegetable shortening.
2. Blend butter, crumbs, and sugar. Pat mixture firmly into prepared pie pan and freeze for ½ hour.
3. In food processor, blender, or electric mixer, combine condensed milk, eggs, lime rind, and lime juice and process until smooth.
4. Pour mixture into prepared crust and freeze until firm, about 3 hours.
5. When pie is set, spread softened ice cream over top and freeze until firm, about ½ hour.
6. Just before serving, sprinkle top with grated lime rind.

Make-It-Easy Tips:

√ After ice cream is set, you can cover pie with plastic wrap and keep in freezer for up to two weeks.

√ Remember to grate lime rind first for filling and topping, and then juice peeled limes easily. Limes will release more juice if at room temperature.

Raisin Pie

SERVES: 8
Preparation time: 20 minutes
Cooking time: 35 minutes

The Ingredients:

1¼ cups seedless raisins
⅔ cup chopped pecans (or walnuts)
1 teaspoon grated lemon rind
2 tablespoons lemon juice
4 ounces (1 stick) unsalted butter, softened
⅔ cup granulated sugar
⅓ cup dark brown sugar (firmly packed)
1 teaspoon cinnamon
¼ teaspoon salt
3 eggs
1 9″ frozen unbaked pie shell, thawed
Garnish: Whipped cream, or vanilla ice cream, or *Crème Fraîche* (*see* Chapter 2).

The Steps:

1. Preheat oven to 400°.
2. In a mixing bowl, combine raisins, nuts, lemon rind, and lemon juice; set aside.
3. With electric mixer, food processor, or by hand beat butter until light and fluffy.
4. Add granulated sugar, brown sugar, cinnamon, and salt and continue to beat until well mixed.
5. Add eggs, one at a time, beating well after each addition. Stir in raisin mixture, spoon into pie shell, and bake in 400° oven for 15 minutes.

6. Reduce heat to 350° and continue to bake for an additional 20 minutes or until set.
7. Serve warm or at room temperature, garnished with whipped cream, or vanilla ice cream, or *Crème Fraîche.*

Make-It-Easy Tips:

√ If raisins are dry, place in a strainer and steam over simmering water. They can also be plumped and softened by blanching in boiling water and then draining.

√ To prevent a soggy crust, brush unbaked crust with beaten egg white and then lightly dust with a mixture of flour and sugar.

√ To keep pie crusts from browning too fast, cover edges with foil.

APPENDIX A

MAIL ORDER GUIDE

EQUIPMENT AND GADGETS

Williams–Sonoma
P.O. Box 3792
San Francisco, California 94119

Zabar's
2245 Broadway
New York, New York 10024

The Professional Kitchen
18 Cooper Square
New York, New York 10003

Walter Drake & Sons
Drake Building
Colorado Springs, Colorado 80940

Figi's Collection for Cooking
Marshfield, Wisconsin 54449

The Cook's Magazine
1698 Post Road East
Westport, Connecticut 06880

Colonial Garden Kitchens
270 W. Merrick Road
Valley Stream, L.I., New York 11582

Kitchen Bazaar
4455 Connecticut Avenue, S.W.
Washington, D.C. 20008

The Wooden Spoon
Route 6
Mahopac, New York 10541

The Chef's Catalog
Professional Restaurant Equipment for the Home Chef
725 County Line Road
Deerfield, Illinois 60015

Chef's Warehouse
Box M
Montpelier, Vermont 05602

Chinese

The Chinese Grocer
209 Post Street at Grant Avenue
San Francisco, California 94108
Call toll free: 800-227-3320

Hungarian and German

H. Roth and Son
1577 First Avenue
New York, New York 10028

The Bremen House
218 E. 86th Street
New York, New York 10028

Paprikas Weiss
1546 Second Avenue
New York, New York 10021

Schaller & Weber
1654 Second Avenue
New York, New York 10028

Indian and Middle Eastern

Bezjian Groceries
4725 Santa Monica Boulevard
Los Angeles, California 90029

India Gifts and Foods
1031 W. Belmont Avenue
Chicago, Illinois 60650

K. Kalustyan
Orient Export Trading Corporation
123 Lexington Avenue
New York, New York 10016

Italian

Todaro Brothers
555 Second Avenue
New York, New York 10016

Il Conte di Savoia
555 W. Roosevelt Road
Chicago, Illinois 60607

Manganaro Foods
488 Ninth Avenue
New York, New York 10018

Mexican and Latin American

Casa Moneo
210 W. 14 Street
New York, New York 10011

Spices

Aphrodisia
28 Carmine Street
New York, New York 10014

House of Spices
76–17 Broadway
Jackson Heights, New York 11373

General

Balducci's
424 Avenue of the Americas
New York, New York 10011

Gaspar's Sausage Company
(for Portugese sausages)
P.O. Box 436
North Dartmouth, Massachusetts 02747

Ferris Fine Foods (for cheese)
P.O. Box 5412
Madison, Wisconsin 53705

The Country Store
P.O. Box 9983
St. Paul, Minnesota 55199

APPENDIX B

MAXIMUM FREEZER STORAGE TIMES

The chart below answers the question "How long can I freeze . . . ?"

The maximum storage times reflect foods stored at 0°F. or below. If foods are stored in a freezer that is being constantly opened, maximum storage times should be slightly shortened. Remember to wrap tightly, seal closed, and label and date each package clearly. Fruits and vegetables are not included since they require blanching, steaming, and other complex techniques to freeze.

FOOD	MAXIMUM STORAGE PERIOD	TIPS
Breads		
Quick Breads and Rolls	3–4 months	–Rolls freeze well in food-storage bags. –Slice and butter French, Italian, or sourdough bread; wrap in foil, and it can go from freezer to oven to heat.
Cakes and Cookies	4–6 months	–Freeze frosted cakes before wrapping for 1 hour or until cake can be easily wrapped without damaging frosting.

FOOD	MAXIMUM STORAGE PERIOD	TIPS
Cakes and Cookies (*continued*)	4–6 months	–Use pure vanilla extract rather than the artificial, which tends to turn bitter during freezer storage. –Freeze bar cookies uncut; slice easily semi-frozen.
Cooked Casseroles, Soups, or Stews	4–6 months	–Freeze in foil-lined casserole with enough foil to overlap and cover the top; when frozen solid, remove and return to freezer; reheat in same casserole. –To reheat: uncover and heat for 45 minutes to 1 hour or until hot and bubbly.
Dairy Products		
Butter	6–9 months	–Unsalted butter keeps longer.
Cheese (Hard)	4–6 weeks	–Tends to become crumbly after freezing.
Cheese (Soft)	4–6 weeks	–Freeze Brie and other creamy cheese in wedge shapes when just perfectly ripe and runny.
Cream, Heavy	2–4 months	–Freeze in tightly sealed containers not quite full (leave a small amount of air space at the top). Thaw in refrigerator and use for whipping, not at the table, since it tends to separate when frozen.

FOOD	MAXIMUM STORAGE PERIOD	TIPS
Eggs		
–Whole	9–12 months	–Do not freeze whole eggs in shell; beat lightly and freeze in a labeled container.
–Egg Yolks	9–12 months	–For future use in sweet dishes, add 1 tablespoon light corn syrup; for non-sweet dishes, add 1 teaspoon salt.
–Egg Whites	9–12 months	–Freeze egg whites, one in each square of an ice-cube tray; when frozen, remove from tray and store, dated, in plastic food-storage bags.
Ice Cream	1–2 months	–Ice cream with a very high percentage of cream can be stored longer.
Milk	3–4 weeks	–Freeze in its own container or storage container.
Buttermilk	3–4 weeks	–Freeze in container and thaw in refrigerator.
Fish & Seafood (Raw)		
Fatty Fish (mackerel, salmon, striped bass, trout, tuna, etc.)	2–3 months	–Freeze whole fish, which has been gutted and cleaned, tightly sealed in foil.
Lean Fish (flounder, haddock, halibut, sea bass, sole, etc.)	4–6 months	–Fish should be frozen as fresh as possible.
Seafood		
–Clams	2–3 months	–Steamers and quahogs should be steamed opened and frozen in juice; cherrystones

FOOD	MAXIMUM STORAGE PERIOD	TIPS
		should be packed in liquid to avoid toughening.
–Crabs, Lobsters	2–3 months	–Freeze after boiling or steaming. Pick out meat and freeze in small portions.
–Oysters	2–3 months	–Pack in liquid to avoid toughening.
–Scallops	2–3 months	–Most scallops are only available frozen and must be cooked immediately without refreezing.
–Shrimp	4–6 months	–Freeze either raw or cooked.
Herbs	9–12 months	–Wash, dry, and chop herbs; pack into tightly sealed containers or wrap in foil packets. Use directly from freezer, without thawing.
Meats (Raw)		
Beef and Lamb		
–Roast	4–6 months	–Trim excess fat before freezing.
–Steaks and Chops	4–6 months	–Remove supermarket wrap and tightly rewrap each steak or chop individually.
–Ground	2–3 months	–Save preparation time by packing meat in the form in which it is to be cooked, e.g., patties, loaf, or ½- to 1-pound packages for ground beef dishes.
Liver	Not advisable to freeze	–Highly perishable.
Pork		
–Ground	1–2 months	–Freeze in small patties to use for oriental dishes.

FOOD	MAXIMUM STORAGE PERIOD	TIPS
–Roast & Chops	2–3 months	–The storage time for pork is less than for beef and lamb; therefore, freeze in small quantities.
–Sausages	1–2 months	–Freeze wrapped tightly in foil or plastic wrap.
Meats (Processed)		
Bacon	1 month	–Remove from package and freeze in family-size portions.
Frankfurters	1 month	–Remove from package and wrap individually for quick defrosting.
Ham	1–2 months	–Freeze deli slices in small packets; the texture may become mealy.
Nuts		
Salted	Should not be frozen	–Salt may absorb moisture and make nuts sticky.
Unsalted	9–12 months	–Freeze in small plastic bags.
Pies		
Baked Fruit Pies	2–4 months	–Cool thoroughly, cover, and freeze.
Custard Pies	Do not freeze	–Custards will separate.
Ice Cream Pies	*See* Ice Cream	
Poultry (Raw)		
Chicken or Turkey (Parts/Cut-up)	6–9 months	–Always remove supermarket wrap plus excess fat before freezing.
Chicken or Turkey (Whole)	9–12 months	–Remove giblets from poultry and freeze separately.

FOOD	MAXIMUM STORAGE PERIOD	TIPS
Duck and Geese	6 months	–After cleaning the bird inside and out, tie the legs and wings close to the body and wrap tightly (the bird will take up less freezer space).
Giblets	2–3 months	–Remove from bag and wrap in foil or plastic wrap.
Livers	2–4 weeks	–Chicken livers have a short freezer life.
Salads	Do not freeze	–Greens will wilt.
Soups		
Stock	3–4 months	–Freeze in ice-cube trays, remove, and place individual cubes in plastic storage bag. Add stock cubes to soups and stews for heightened flavor.
Cream Soup	Not advisable to freeze	–Cream soups tend to separate after thawing; whisk while reheating to make smooth again.

INDEX